MYANMAR (BURMA)

CHINA

TAIWAN

Sapa

North

Hanoi

Gulf of Tonkin

Hong Kong
Macau

Chiang Mai

LAOS

Hainan

North

PHILIPPINES

Sukhothai

THAILAND

Hue
Da Nang

VIETNAM

Northeast (Issan)

Lam Narai

Chao Phraya

Central

Hoi An

Central

Kanchanaburi
Ayutthaya

Bangkok ★

East
Sriracha

CAMBODIA

Pattaya

Mekong

Nha Trang
Da Lat

Andaman Sea

Gulf of Thailand (Siam)

South

Ho Chi Minh City (Saigon)

Chumpon

Can Tho

Mekong Delta

SOUTH CHINA SEA

Koh Samui

South

Phuket

Penang (George Town)

Ipoh

MALAYSIA

BRUNEI

Sabah

MALAYSIA

Celebes Sea

Strait of Malacca

Kuantan

★ Kuala Lumpur

Sarawak

Malacca

Johor Baharu

SINGAPORE

INDONESIA

INDONESIA

Equator

0   mi   200
0   km   200

Southeast Asian Flavors

ADVENTURES
IN COOKING
THE FOODS OF
THAILAND
VIETNAM
MALAYSIA &
SINGAPORE

Robert Danhi
Author & Photographer

Foreword by Martin Yan

Jay Weinstein, Editor

Southeast Asian Flavors

ADVENTURES IN COOKING THE FOODS OF THAILAND, VIETNAM, MALAYSIA, & SINGAPORE

Published by Mortar & Press

MORTAR
&PRESS

Copyright © 2008 by
Mortar & Press
211 Sheldon Street
El Segundo, California 90245
310-648-7970
www.southeastasianflavors.com

Photographs and text copyright © by Robert Danhi
Photo editing pages 85 and 131 by Matthew Noel
www.mnoelproduction.com

Edited by Jay Weinstein

Library of Congress Control Number: 2008932504
ISBN: 978-0-9816339-0-9

Designed and Produced by
Favorite Recipes® Press
an imprint of

FRP.

a wholly owned subsidiary of Southwestern/Great American Inc.
P.O. Box 305142
Nashville, Tennessee 37230
800-358-0560

Manufactured in the United States of America
First Printing: 2008
10,000 copies

Table of Contents

To Estrellita Leong

Foreword

For more than a decade, I've had the good fortune to call Robert Danhi both a friend and a professional colleague. Like so many others in our profession, I am privileged by his bountiful energy and inspired by his deep passion for the culinary industry. From the very beginning I've recognized that Robert and I share a strong conviction that as educators of the culinary profession, we must connect cultures with cuisines. For my Yan Can Cook show, I travel throughout Asia so that I can give the dishes on my show their proper cultural, historical, and social context. From the conversations that I have had with Robert over the years, I know that he sees his books in the same way.

It was quite some time ago when Robert first engaged me in a conversation about pursuing Southeast Asian cooking. I have always been impressed by his wealth of knowledge on this subject. So much so, in fact, that I have relied on Robert as an authority on this subject for years. Given the rising popularity of Southeast Asian cooking in the U.S., it was not at all uncommon for many American culinary professionals to familiarize themselves with Asian culinary techniques. What struck me as different about Robert's approach was his total dedication. Instead of treating it as a short-term project to further his knowledge, he was planning an all-out effort, devoting all his might and that trademarked Robert Danhi passion, into this venture.

The rest, as they say, is history. And to borrow another cliché, the pudding of proof is in this book, etched among these three hundred-plus beautifully written and illustrated pages. For my show, I have traveled extensively throughout Malaysia, Thailand, and Vietnam. Reading this book has given me an uncanny sense of déjà-vu. True to its title, *Southeast Asian Flavors* brings out the true flavors, culinary as well as cultural, of this fascinating part of the world. As I marveled at the insightful photos and commentaries, I felt that I was on a return visit.

Some time ago someone coined the term "culinarian." I don't know if that's a real title, but it seems to fit Robert perfectly. He is a dedicated professional on all things culinary, especially when it comes to education. *Southeast Asian Flavors* is his latest triumph. It is a gift to every fan of Southeast Asian cuisine.

Martin Yan

Introduction
This book is different. It's not a cookbook. . . . It's a food book.

There's an Asian idiomatic expression: "Same, same… but different." It essentially means that what appears to be similar on the surface, turns out to have subtle but profound differences once you look a little deeper. That applies to the book you are holding right now! It works like a cookbook, but it's much more. It also takes you inside the life and mind of the people of Asia. Yes, there are recipes (more than 100 actually) and lots of photos (more than 700, all of which I snapped myself). Hundreds were captured as I traveled around Southeast Asia, a few are from around the United States, and hundreds of others were taken in my kitchen studio in Los Angeles.

My goal is to give you not just a taste, but a look, smell, and feel for these four countries: Thailand, Vietnam, Malaysia, and Singapore. A true snapshot. Just as with any picture, although it may be an accurate representation, it is not an all-encompassing image. This subject is too big to cram into a library, let alone one book. There are other books that delve deeper into each region (pg. 364), and you should keep an eye out for my next volumes on each country. I share stories of real people, present recipes for authentic flavors, and provide you with the keys to unlock the mysteries of the ingredients of Asia. If you meander through these colorful pages, read some of the stories, and cook some recipes in each country's chapter, you will gain an understanding of what the true Southeast Asian flavors are. The geography, history, ethnic diversity, and culinary etiquette all converge into authentic recipes that represent culture on a plate.

I have been working on this book for decades and thought of publishing it many years ago. But the reality is that no publishing company was willing to create such an intricate book. Frankly, the cost of including all the photos I felt were needed was reason enough to send their financial teams into a tizzy. I wanted to create a book on my terms, similar to the way a chef opens his own restaurant to express his culinary vision—I wanted to serve you recipes and cultures I live, breathe, and love to cook. Similarly to how my colleagues open their first restaurants, I wanted to have the final say of what was included and how it was conveyed. Since my lifelong mission to share the cuisine and culture of my second home had not diminished, I simply had to start my own publishing company, and hence Mortar & Press was born. My objective is to take you on a cooking adventure through the vibrant foods of a culinary paradise.

I have chosen to focus on only four countries for this book. Yes, there are others countries in Southeast Asia with amazing food, interesting people, and fascinating histories, but these four are where I live when not in the USA. These are the people whom I know abroad. And these four countries' similarities and differences can be illustrated within the context of cuisine and culture.

Southeast Asia Captured My Heart: It Was Love at First Sight

It all started nearly twenty years ago when I met a petite, beautiful Malaysian woman, Estrellita Leong. I had just finished high school and was taking some local culinary courses at El Camino Community College when we met. The next year she took me on my first adventure to Southeast Asia, a gift for which I will be forever grateful. This was the beginning of two love affairs. The first was with my adored wife, Estrellita Leong-Danhi, whom I call Esther. The second love is for the land from which she came, Southeast Asia.

That first trip was intense: a marathon of flight, countless new faces and family, and a menu full of smells, sounds, textures, and tastes that I'll never forget. When we arrived in Malaysia's capital, Kuala Lumpur, we were greeted by Esther's brother, Glenn. They conspired to spoil me on local food even before we made it home. These folks were serious about food. Three weeks later, hooked on the food culture there and deeply attached to my new family, I didn't want to leave. I was in food heaven. We'd even driven down to Singapore, the food obsessed city-state at the most southern tip of the Malay Peninsula. I had a career to return to in America, but I knew this would be the first of many trips to this tropical food paradise.

The Lifelong Adventure

The two decades that followed transformed me into a "hard-boiled egg": a white shell on the outside, but Asian in my soul. I've journeyed for weeks and months at a time through the byways and alleys, farms and fields, markets and private homes of Thailand, Vietnam, Malaysia, and Singapore. The loves and losses, superstitions and idiosyncrasies of that region have been burned into my DNA. Esther's mom, Annie, has been my invaluable culinary guide, not only teaching me about Malaysian food, but also rounding up hard-to-find ingredients and smuggling them to me (thank goodness these ingredients are now available in the U.S.!).

Abroad at Home

Ten years in professional kitchens led me into a side activity that came naturally for me: I began to teach the craft and art of cooking. At first it was in local cooking schools, cooking side by side with home cooks. I was sous chef at a Los Angeles neighborhood (Manhattan Beach) restaurant, working mornings and afternoons. I was approached by educators who wanted to tap my experience as a chef to train some cooks. I soon discovered that when you teach, you learn even more than the students. I began to formally document what I was experiencing on my culinary adventures to Asia. Over the next ten years, I spent time studying and traveling to other parts of Asia. Teaching in Korea, being a guest chef in Japan, wandering the rice paddies of Indonesia, and traversing the spice trails of India—these experiences all helped put these cuisines into context.

The comfort I found in teaching gave me the confidence I needed to talk my way into small kitchens in the back alleys of Malaysia and to convince food vendors in Thailand to share their secrets. I decided to take the leap into education full time. I devoted the next few years to developing the curriculum at the California School of Culinary Arts in Pasadena. The accrediting process I went through there taught me how to analyze a subject to discover its intricacies.

Then the Culinary Institute of America (CIA) brought me on to teach fundamental cooking skills. I wanted to teach the Asian cuisines I'd come to love. I immersed myself even further in the world of Asian cookery. I studied everything I could get my hands on, reading, cooking, and traveling there any chance I got. I was fortunate to lead the team of faculty redeveloping the Cuisines of Asia course at the CIA, an intensive part of the curriculum covering Chinese, Korean, Japanese, Vietnamese, Thai, Malaysian,

Indonesian, and Indian cuisines. To hone my skills in Vietnamese cookery, the CIA sent me to Vietnam.

Vietnam was like stepping back in time. Women walked the bustling streets of Saigon with yokes across their backs, dangling burning embers of coal to keep cauldrons of soup simmering. Nothing could prepare me for the time warp of that country. Although I was on a tour with twenty-five other people, I was part of the crew running the trip, so I had a chance to interact closely with the Vietnamese people. We traveled from the southern capital of Saigon to the northernmost areas of Sapa and Bac Ha.

I stayed behind after the rest of the group went home, taking the opportunity to navigate quickly and cover a lot of ground with a private guide. This is when I realized the value of a dedicated guide in a country where you don't speak the language (Malaysia and Singapore are much easier, as a majority of the population speaks English). To be most efficient, I often used guides to find my way into the kitchens and homes of the small towns and villages in Vietnam, where I mastered the techniques I've committed to the pages of this book.

I've left full-time teaching at the CIA, but still stay involved there, leading projects and courses that require my specialized skills in research and development, culinary education training, and of course the cuisines of Southeast Asia. I now run a consulting business, Chef Danhi & Co., based in Los Angeles. I've developed a niche teaching about the cuisines and culture of Asia, working with restaurant chains, schools, food manufacturers, and professional associations. If you are interested, look at **www.chefdanhi.com** for more details.

How the Book Is Organized

Get the big picture first. The "Southeast Asian Culinary Identity" chapter takes you through the stages of development for each country: where they are, what their climate is like, and who lives there. How do they eat? with chopsticks? Sometimes a concurrent use of the fork and spoon prevails. These nuances do impact the cooking and dining experience.

"The Southeast Asian Pantry" chapter was a battle— it kept growing as the book evolved. I have included some

Each adventure, I immerse myself into my work, literally.
Here I was deep within a palm tree harvesting sap for palm sugar.

historical information about the ingredeints when pertinent. I've included the binomial (Latin) names of vegetables and fruits to make sure you and your grocer are talking about the same thing. Language translations (some phonetic) enable you to find some of these ingredients while you're shopping and traveling. There are photos, lots of photos…. but only when it seems especially useful. Photos of unidentifiable piles of starches and flours seemed meaningless, so I have left them out.

The "Techniques for Building Southeast Asian Flavors" chapter covers fundamental techniques used in Asia. This may be as simple as how lime wedges are cut in Southeast Asia (yes, they do it differently there). There's in-depth exploration, for the more serious cook, of things few will take the time to do, like making coconut milk from scratch. Even if you do not make it, this will help you get a better understanding of what's in the can and how different fresh and canned coconut milk are (recipes in the book use only canned). Buy a Thai curry paste (see recommended brands on page 128) or make your own. Use the traditional method, pounding the ingredients in a mortar, or use a

blender to whirl all the aromatics to an equally authentic paste. I show both methods and leave the choice up to you (see step-by-step curry paste instructions on page 104).

Each Culinary Identity™ section begins with an adventure through the land, meeting the people and seeing how they cook, eat, and drink. Malaysia and Singapore are different nations, actually entirely different cultures (and they are addressed as such), but their foods are not that different. Perhaps they're as different as the foods from southern and northern Thailand. I have chosen to group their recipes into one chapter.

There are more than thirty recipes in each chapter. Some can be made for a simple weekday meal. Others are weekend activities, taking hours to prepare. The recipes here are authentic, the way you can find these dishes made in these lands right now. Not everyone makes Singapore Chili Crabs the same (pg. 314), but no one from Singapore would call the one from this book anything but real.

The Asian Resource Guide points you to places where you can get authentic ingredients, absorb the culture, and learn more about Southeast Asian flavors. Fortunately, there are many other excellent books available for learning other, peripheral things about these cuisines. Refer to the Bibliography (pgs. 364–369) for a list of recommended books.

Don't Stop Now— I Am Your Culinary Guide

There are some hard decisions when writing a book. For me, the most difficult was when to stop. There is so much to share about these cuisines and cultures, and some things must be left out. I have mastered volumes of recipes, taken tens of thousands of photographs, and filmed hundreds of hours of video in my travels. I just have to share them with you. Plus, there are dozens of recipes that just couldn't fit on these pages.

That multimedia experience awaits you at **www.southeastasianflavors.com**. Throughout the book look for the web icon. This icon indicates that there is more to be seen and heard on the Web site. Those emblematic Pad Thai noodles I describe being wrapped up in a thin sheet of egg on page 174? Don't imagine it—see it and hear it in the videos on the Web site. In addition to cultural content for vicarious exploration, I've uploaded countless step-by-step videos where I demonstrate techniques and share tips on how to prepare the recipes in the book. If you have more questions, just e-mail me to get more information.

Get in That Kitchen and Cook . . . or Don't

There are coffee-table books, filled with memoirs, strikingly beautiful pictures, and a few recipes that aren't really meant to be cooked, just imagined. Another category (there are lots) is technique books, which take an analytical approach. As an educator, I love all of these books. *Southeast Asian Flavors* was created with the intention of creating a hybrid of them.

One day you may want to take a virtual journey to the backstreets of Vietnam. Flip through the pages and see (pg. 186-196). Perhaps you're curious to learn about how palm sugar is made (pg. 58). There's nothing wrong with a vicarious journey from the comfort of an armchair.

Consider that cooking shows are among the most popular forms of passive entertainment these days. Most devotees of the cooking shows don't cook what they watch. It is a form of entertainment, and that's great.

But on those days when you want to get in the kitchen, fire up those flames, and get cooking, you hold a guide to the Southeast Asian food world. Fundamental ingredients, techniques, and recipes will keep you busy in the kitchen for as long as you want. Buy that Thai curry paste—or make your own. Use the traditional method of pounding in a mortar—or use a blender to whirl all the aromatics to a smooth paste. It's left up to you.

Hopefully, We Will Cook Together Soon!

There is nothing like cooking with a guide. Hands-on instruction enables all forms of communication to happen right there, right then. It is likely that I will be in your area soon—teaching a cooking class, doing a book signing, or in the kitchen of a restaurant that you frequent. Keep in touch. Visit **www.southeastasianflavors.com** to see a schedule of where and when I'm working. Also consider coming with me to Southeast Asia on one of my Culinary Immersion Tours. There's no substitute for actually being there. I look forward to hearing about *your* culinary adventures one day soon!

Culinary regards,

Robert Danhi

Southeast Asian Culinary Identity™

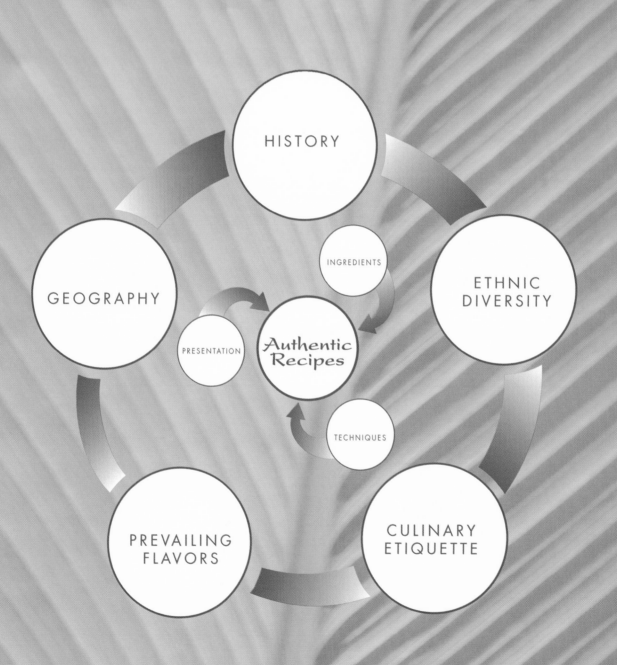

HISTORY

INGREDIENTS

GEOGRAPHY

ETHNIC DIVERSITY

PRESENTATION

Authentic Recipes

TECHNIQUES

PREVAILING FLAVORS

CULINARY ETIQUETTE

To truly understand a region's culinary arts, you must consider all the factors that contribute to its cuisine. Geography, history, ethnic diversity, and culinary etiquette converge to become the building blocks of its food world. Thailand, Vietnam, Malaysia, and Singapore each possesses its own Culinary Identity™—a way of choosing, cooking, and serving food that is immediately identifiable with that nation—yet these selected cuisines have more in common than is apparent to the casual observer. A look into their pantries shows the common threads. A taste of their dishes reveals the different tapestries they weave.

Just as an Italian chef would find many familiar ingredients in a French kitchen, so a Thai home cook would be among many familiar ingredients in a Vietnamese home. It's what they do with their hands and their palates that determines whether the food they produce is Italian or French, Thai or Vietnamese. A cook's influence on raw ingredients as they are combined and transformed into a completed dish is illustrated perfectly by comparing the foods of Southeast Asia and the Caribbean. These two culinary regions are worlds apart both in geography and cuisine. The classic Jamaican curry bears little resemblance to the curries of Northern Thailand in both flavor and appearance; however, if you were to look only at the kitchen pantry they draw from, you would find many commonalities: coriander, cumin, coconut, limes, tamarind, cilantro, and chilies. Good food is far more than the sum total of its ingredients; good food is a result of the synergy produced by combinations of ingredients and culinary techniques applied by the cook. Combining the same or similar ingredients but with different techniques will result in different flavors, textures, and appearances. As the Thais would say, "Same, Same, but different."

CULTURAL VELOCITY
by Ari Slatkin

Culture is dynamic; culture is a living, breathing, ever-changing compilation of all the elements possessed by a people that define and unite them as a distinct group. Culture is the kinetic energy created by the synergy between these defining elements. Far greater than the sum total of its parts, culture is the intangible haze of humanity that encircles and engulfs its people—reverberating and pulsing to the rhythmic heartbeat of an entire culture. Although invisible and intangible, the power and presence of culture is undeniable and blindingly visible from the instant an outsider sets foot in the cultural realm.

A people and its culture share an inherent symbiotic relationship. In this circular relationship, people's actions are influenced, and to a certain extent determined, by the cultural norms of the society; simultaneously, these actions produce the culture itself as it exists at that time. As people and civilizations move forward through time, they are influenced by forces, both internal and external to the respective culture. As people and culture change in reaction to these forces, their actions and habits may diverge from what was traditional. New technological advents, changing social values, and the availability of products and ingredients can all result in the changing of the way things are done; these new ways cannot be considered traditional, as nothing new can be said to possess any tradition. However, they are the very definition of authenticity, as they are the way things are done, here or there and now. An authentic reflection of a culture is the most accurate representation of its people as they exist currently. A traditional reflection of a culture is an accurate portrayal only of a people as they have operated and existed in the past.

Let us approach this scientifically. When attempting to study an object or entity that is perpetually moving and changing, as culture is, the goal is to obtain as much information pertaining to the current state of the object or entity as possible. Things that move can change in two different ways: they can change speed, accelerating or decelerating; or they can change directionally. Exclusive analysis of these elements independently results in knowledge of traditional information—how fast has this object traditionally moved and in what direction has it traditionally traveled? But to acquire an accurate representation of the current state of the object or entity, in this case culture, it is necessary to examine both speed and direction, aka velocity. Thus, an accurate portrayal of a culture at a specific point in time, now in this case, is achieved by examining the "Cultural Velocity" of a people. *Traditional* ways of the past, reacting to changing times, become the *authentic* ways of the present. Cultural Velocity tells the complete story of a culture's past and present and is indicative of its future.

NOTE: The equations below are meant to summarize the preceding paragraphs, not to be taken as functioning mathematical proofs or equations.

TRADITION + CONTEMPORARY INFLUENCES = AUTHENTICITY OF TODAY
TRADITION + AUTHENTICITY = CULTURAL VELOCITY (REALITY OF PAST, PRESENT, AND THE PROBABLE FUTURE)

Geography's Ambivalent Role

Within an ecosystem, topography exerts a powerful influence on climate and dictates the types of crops and livestock that can be grown. The aquatic components of Southeast Asian ecosystems, such as rivers and lakes, abound with wild fish and allow for the grand scale of aquaculture that's arisen in places like Thailand. The climate also helps determine what is grown and creates the seasonality of the cuisine. Vietnam's expansive coastline provides a steady stream of both wild-caught and cultivated seafood. Fish and fish flavors are so firmly tied to that country's Culinary Identity™ that one would be hard pressed to envision a table full of Vietnamese foods without conjuring the intoxicating scent of the omnipresent fish sauce. This pungent, fermented condiment became a staple in Vietnamese cooking due to the abundance of anchovies it's made from; locals would have been crazy not to utilize them.

Is Traditional the Same As Authentic?

In a word: No. Food culture is a living force that's constantly evolving. In this book, "traditional" and "authentic" have two different yet related meanings. Traditional cuisine refers to the way foods have been prepared through history—the way natives have cooked and presented food and passed those customs from generation to generation. Authentic cuisine is also steeped in history—respectful of traditions but incorporating innovations while still retaining the essential features that impact all our senses—sight (colors, presentations, knife cuts, etc.), smell (the aromas), taste (balance or equation of sweet, salty, bitter, sour, and umami), touch (textural attributes—fat, doneness, etc.) and sound (crunch factor, etc.). Spice pastes have been integral to Southeast Asian cuisines for centuries. Once they were always hand pounded in a mortar. That's traditional. Now, they're sometimes puréed in a blender. Since that's now routinely done by modern practitioners of these native cuisines, it's authentic.

This happens at some level within an Asian country and more so by Asian cooks in foreign lands as they adapt to local conditions, ingredients, and tools. Traditional foods and techniques are sometimes replaced by more contemporary versions—remaining authentic, but updated. The recipes in this book are all as authentic as you would find if you stepped into a Southeast Asian home, restaurant, or market stall today. Some are also traditional—unchanged from the generations-old way they were taught to me.

There are many right ways to prepare something, but there are also wrong ways. These wrong ways create a different dish altogether. It may be delicious, but once you start adding heavy cream as a replacement for coconut milk in a Thai red curry you've lost me—it is no longer an authentic Thai curry. There may be many different recipes for this aromatic mixture, but some key ingredients, techniques, and presentation elements are essential to maintaining a recognizable *standard of identity*. That standard is a touchstone that enables cooks and tasters of that dish all over the world to share an understanding and flavor memory when discussing or preparing Thai red curry (pg. 159). An experienced eater can taste the curry with eyes closed and know it is Thai—whose version is debatable, but the flavor profile is a standard. So, as you look, read, and, hopefully, cook from this book, keep in mind that this is one authentic way to prepare the dish, but not the only way.

Regional Foods Make a Statement

The differences between foods from region to region *within* a country can sometimes be as dramatic as those from country to country. Think of the colorful, complex gumbos of the American South compared with the staid chowders of New England. The ingredients that one area possesses can create unique dishes that are worlds apart from foods of another area, even when they're only separated by a few miles. Comparing the foods of southern Malaysia with the dishes of northern Malaysia could be as dramatic as the difference between France and Spain. This was truer in the past, as modernization has diminished the prominence of traditional regional cuisines, especially in developed countries. Sometimes regions can be as general as north, central, or south. This is still the case of how many look to Vietnamese cuisine, and dialogue regarding the cuisines can reveal the importance of their regional identity. For instance, in the past, northern Hà-Nội locals could be discussing dinner plans to have Phở; there is no need to say Phở Bò (Bò is the word for beef), as it is implied that this northern-style dish is made with beef. Phở Gà made with chicken is common in the south and served in the north as well.

Vietnamese Phở Gà

Chinese Influence

Cooking implements shape food's character as much as ingredient availability does. China's primary cooking vessel, the wok, has infiltrated every country in Asia. Although the wok has been tailored in size, material, and application depending on the region's cuisine, the basic culinary principles of wok cookery remain the same. China's fuel-poor, labor-rich society spawned this versatile cookware, which is used to stir-fry, deep-fry, steam, poach, simmer, boil, and even smoke foods. *Wok hay,* or "breath of the wok," is the Chinese expression for the beloved smoky flavor achieved by stir-frying in the intense heat of a wok. Most of the Chinese immigrants to Southeast Asia came from China's southern provinces, and Cantonese is still the language of the kitchen in much of Vietnam, Singapore, and Malaysia.

Portuguese Heat in Southeast Asia

Of the many European influences in Southeast Asian cuisine, few are as profound as the Portuguese introduction of capsicums (chili peppers) to Thailand in the 1500s. Previously, only peppercorns were available to infuse that stinging bite characteristic of Thai food.

French Finesse in Vietnam

Vietnam was occupied by the French from 1858 until 1954, when the French presence ended with the Geneva Conference. The French, who had used Vietnam as a site for production of tobacco, indigo, tea, and coffee, left a distinct mark on the cooking techniques in the country and were responsible for the Vietnamese fondness for cafés and coffee. Other obvious remnants of the French reign are the omnipresent baguettes ("Bánh Mì" in Vietnamese), which are often stuffed with pâté, sausage, fresh herbs, and chili paste to make a sandwich that is one of the national dishes.

Dutch Takeout

Although the Dutch held Malacca from 1641 to 1806, they had surprisingly little influence on the cuisine there. Their effect is seen more in the region's architecture than in its food. Nutmeg, worth more than gold at the time, was the treasure that drew the Dutch to the Spice Islands. Food influences sailed the opposite way with them, leading to a significant Southeast Asian personality in the cuisine of the Netherlands to this day.

British Service

British colonial presence had the biggest impact on Malaysia and Singapore, taken in 1786 and 1824 respectively. Malaysia got its independence in 1957, and Singapore became part of Malaysia in 1963. That arrangement lasted for only two years, until Singaporeans formed their own country. Singapore has become a gloriously food-obsessed nation. In its short existence as a country, it has successfully incorporated the formal style of service (and British-accented English as a national language), with Asian finesse.

Church in Melacca, Malaysia

Ethnic Diversity

Over the course of history, waves of immigration, such as the Chinese migrations into Southeast Asia, have seeded culinary trends in many countries. Industrialization brought Indian immigrants to developing nations like Malaysia and Singapore to work the tin mines and rubber plantations. These countries remain multiethnic today. Enclaves of ethnic groups often congregate in Little Indias, Chinatowns, Malay towns, or other faux-towns. These enclaves provide a safe haven for Culinary Identity™. As succeeding generations assimilate into the population, they build a fusion of cultures that results in some of Southeast Asia's best foods.

Fusion—It's All Fusion

It's only a matter of time before culinary influences collide, combine, and take new forms. Once a culture (not just a few chefs) has adopted a culinary innovation, it becomes authentic contemporary food (though not traditional). True *fusion cuisine* (as opposed to a fusion dish) occurs when one culture's ingredients, cooking techniques, presentation styles, or complete dishes are adopted by another culture as a whole; they're not simply occurring in a few fine-dining restaurants. The Thai, Vietnamese, Malaysian, and Singaporean cultures all have excellent examples of this within their library of dishes.

Mee Rebus is a fusion of Indian and Chinese flavors

Colorful Indian temples tower above in Singapore

Singaporeé's China town is a blend of old and new

Culinary Etiquette

How one eats can be as important as *what* one eats in defining a culinary experience. It is not only the utensil that matters, but also how foods are assembled. Traditional styles of service can say a lot about a place. Southeast Asia exhibits simpler, and some would say more casual, styles of service than its northern neighbors like China, Japan, and Korea. Typically, dishes brought to the table are to be shared as they are completed.

At the Table

How hot is hot? Our ultra-conservative sanitation sensibilities can induce panic when we arrive in Southeast Asia. Our obsessive food safety laws govern the food supply in the U.S. If foods defined as "hot foods" are held at any temperature below 140°F for more than two hours, the seller is considered in violation of the law and can be fined or, in come cases, put out of business. But in Asia, it's not uncommon to prepare food well in advance and serve it at room temperature hours later. Don't get me wrong, hotel chains, higher-end restaurants, expatriate clientele-based businesses, and multinational companies actually have similar (if not superior) standards of sanitation there than we do here, but much of the Southeast Asian population eats food that would send our stomachs into a tantrum. They are used to it, as you would be if your body was given time to adjust to it.

I eat everything in Southeast Asia and rarely experience any intestinal distress (no more than in the U.S.). Time and temperature are two of the main elements a chef controls when managing food safety. Do realize, however, that many of the foods in this book taste best at room temperature and should not be served chilled. Not only do your taste buds perceive nuances of flavor better at room temperature, but textures change drastically as well. Rice noodles that are cooked and chilled for a salad roll are too firm and lose their prized resiliency.

The Communal Table

The table is a microcosm of a traditional community. Many of the supplies are shared from a central area. Imagine the center of the table as the community center of a town—here one will find a gathering place for shared activities, storage of food, equipment, and the essential well of water. When a family needs water they take a small bucket and go to the well, take what they need, and carry it home to be used sparingly. The Southeast Asian table is not different. At a family-style meal, the foods are placed in the center of the table—the container of rice, the platter of fish, the stir-fried vegetables, and so on. Individuals' plates are brought to the communal center to take a few spoons of the plentiful rice, yet only a small amount of the less-available fish or even vegetables and then returned to their respective spots at the table to be consumed. Metaphorically speaking, each person's place at the table would be like a family's home within a village. Going back to the communal and centrally located well several times in one sitting is expected. The act of lifting a communal service plate and bringing it to your personal plate to take large amounts of each dish is a serious faux pas and is equivalent to trying to bring the entire village well to your house and not leaving that precious resource for others; it's quite rude, self-serving, and disrespectful.

Throughout Southeast Asia, this family style of service and dining is the norm; people share multiple dishes, rather than each guest ordering his own. In Vietnam, *cơm* (steamed rice) is the core of the meal. It's served with crisp vegetables, grilled meats, and pungent sauces, which are sparingly paired with each bite of rice; this is a reflection of economic realities as much as taste. Inexpensive and abundantly available rice anchors the meal and is flanked with a multitude of less-available or more-expensive, smaller dishes. Rice with stewed pork, rice with grilled shrimp—basically the menu is "rice with…" Rice provides the medium, or blank canvas if you will, for culinary artists to paint on with palate-pleasing flavors of all colors and kinds.

The Pecking Order of Service

Guests and elders are served first, usually by the host or younger family members. Service utensils aren't always present at the Southeast Asian table, and the use of personal chopsticks to serve others is common. Soup may even be eaten from a communal bowl, with each guest dipping in with his own individual spoon. If you find yourself in this environment, just relax and go with it. This is how more than 25 percent of the world eats.

Rice is often the foundation of the meal.

The Vorarittinapa family hosted me for an outdoor meal.

Southeast Asian culture may be more reserved than the West, but these folks revel in their food, and eating is not always a silent occasion. Slurping is okay, but proceed judiciously. Southeast Asians don't eat as noisily as the notoriously audible Japanese. They simply celebrate the sounds of saucy noodles as they're sucked into the mouth.

One-Dish Meals in Southeast Asia

Street foods constitute some of the best one-dish meals. For a quick gustatory pleasure on the run in Vietnam, stop in Hà-Nội, for a bowl of *Phở* (pronounced like "fuh"), the classic Vietnamese beef noodle soup. It contains meat, vegetables, noodles, broth, and herbs—a complete meal.

In Singapore, duck into an aroma-packed food court for *Nasi Briyani* for a complete meal of spice-laced, vegetable-studded basmati rice paired with mutton curry.

In Thailand, the beloved *Pad Thai* is a complete meal of chewy rice noodles, crispy bean sprouts, crunchy deep-roasted peanuts, and a sweet-sour-spicy tamarind sauce, usually garnished with shrimp or chicken.

How Eating Utensils Are Used in Southeast Asia

Westerners often incorrectly assume that Asians eat all their food with chopsticks. In most parts of Southeast Asia, chopsticks are reserved primarily for noodle dishes. Those unfamiliar with Southeast Asian culture are often surprised by the unique use of the spoon and fork together to scoop up food as it's eaten. Europeans introduced these implements, and the locals created their own style of use. The spoon is held in the dominant hand, and the other hand holds the fork. Once you've tried this ingenious method yourself, it will become quickly apparent how very practical this utensil adaptation is. Asians tend to avoid putting sharp utensils, such as forks, in their mouths. So the spoon is used to convey the food to the palate.

Most populations in the region once ate with their hands; many people still do. Just as with other utensils, there are rules when using your fingers to scoop up food. Only the right hand is used. The left is reserved for other, nonsanitary functions. The four longer fingers are used to scoop as the thumb assists and then pushes the food into the mouth. The bottom part of your fingers, as well as your palm, should stay free of debris. Sinks are a common fixture in the dining rooms of Malay and Indian restaurants, as this style of dining is more prevalent in these two cultures.

Back to the chopsticks. There are rules: Never poke the chopsticks into a dish and leave them sticking out. This is correlated to a funeral. If you want to take a break from eating, gently set your chopsticks on the rim of the plate or bowl. In formal settings, utilize the rear (handle) end of your chopsticks to serve yourself or others from the serving bowl or platter. When among intimate friends, it's usually okay to serve yourself with the eating ends of your sticks.

Teaw Vorarittinapa with Tom Yum Hot Pot

A noodle bowl can be a whole meal.

Pad Thai noodles

Bamboo chopsticks sun dry after washing.

Beverages

As in the West, Southeast Asians consume beverages before, during, and after mealtimes. But they traditionally drink less *while* they're eating than we do. Drinks are seldom carefully matched with the food, and some of them can actually spoil an otherwise great meal. A cloyingly sweet soda would spoil the flavor of a delicate chicken broth noodle dish. For this reason, soup sometimes serves as the beverage during the repast. A brothy soup is sipped along with other dishes.

Southeast Asian climates are hot, and cool drinks of many types can be found for sale at nearly every street corner. Long, slender stalks of sugarcane are stripped of their tough and off-flavored outer husks, then fed through rollers that compress the stalks and expel a sweet, greenish juice. Poured over ice it's refreshing and not as sweet as you might expect—some like a squeeze of lime added. Fruit stands often sell freshly peeled and cut fruits—carrots, pineapple, oranges, honeydew, watermelon, or even sour sop fruit—and offer juicing services. Try blending orange and carrot juices for one of my favorite vegetable/fruit combinations.

Tea

Tea is a topic so huge there are entire volumes dedicated solely to it, but I do have a few things to say. Chinese tea—primarily black and green—is highly prized. It's the center of highly ritualized tea ceremonies, and copious amounts are consumed at Dim Sum dining rooms, along with small plates of appetizers that constitute an Asian-style "tasting menu." In countries with British history, like Singapore, English-style high tea, complete with finger sandwiches, scones, and clotted cream, is offered in upscale hotels. Tea is also the daily beverage that, crossing all cultural borders, is a common thread throughout Asia.

Each culture also has its own specialized regional tea. In the U.S., the most popular Southeast Asian tea is Thai Iced Tea (pg. 182). It's a concoction of flavored tea leaves (sometimes scented with sesame seeds and vanilla) that is brewed very strong, seasoned with lots of sugar, topped with evaporated milk (American Thai restaurants often use half-and-half), and then poured over crushed ice. In the

Cameron Highlands of central Malaysia, tea is grown and processed into a black tea (using the standard fermentation and drying of the leaves). It's typically brewed and stirred together with sweetened condensed milk. The real specialty there is Teh Tarik, the so-called "pulled" tea. The sweetened tea is poured back and forth from container to container until a bubbly froth is created on top. Vietnamese tea culture is more similar to the Chinese, where it is simply brewed and sipped in small glasses while chatting or eating food.

In Vietnam, Thailand, Malaysia, and Singapore (as well as in other parts of Southeast Asia), coffee gets special treatment. Imagine brewed coffee that is blacker than black. The coffee beans are sometimes combined with sugar and butter while roasting, which gives the brew its characteristic opaque look. Thailand takes it further by adding roasted soy, corn, and sesame seeds to the mix. Creamy condensed milk is added to the brewed coffee, settling at the bottom of the glass and forming a sweet white foundation. Each country has its unique brewing strategy, and each chapter will provide you with the insight and recipe to re-create these energetic brews in your home (pgs. 182, 268, 354) Give the beverage a stir, and that distinct blacker-than-pitch-black color dies and fades as a rich brown color is born and comes to life. It's enjoyed iced as often as it is hot.

Street Food—
Good Food Fast

Street food has been part of food cultures for thousands of years in Southeast Asian lands and is an integral part of their Culinary Identity™. According to the Food and Agriculture Organization of the United Nations (FAO), street food accounts for 20 to 30 percent of household expenditures in urban areas. In Bangkok, more than 20,000 street vendors provide city residents with 40 percent of their meals. Yes, there is Western "fast food" in Southeast Asia, and many chains have had tremendous success in the Asian market. But the authentic, indigenous fast food is found in the market stalls and carts out on the streets.

The food is fast by design, but still prepared with whole, fresh ingredients and minimally processed foods. Often within a few minutes, you can have regional specialty dishes cooked to order by an expert. These masters of their craft have been cooking these dishes their entire lives and sometimes represent the second or third generation of cooks. Their family may have spent years perfecting their own interpretation of vegetable-crunchy, spice-layered, shrimp stir-fried noodles; sesame seed-battered deep-fried baby bananas; or some other specialty.

Malaysian Fried Banana and Tapioca

Curry vendors welcome a motorbike to-go order.

The yoke and basket is still a common sight in Vietnam.

Breakfast in Saigon

Dried squid to grill, tenderize, and dip in sweet chili sauce

Roasting chestnuts with pebbles in Bangkok

It only takes a moment to grab a taste.

Sidewalk vendor selling grilled bananas

I am having breakfast after going to the market in Vietnam.

Singaporean Hawker Centers

Singapore is the best example of a culture that has successfully transformed street food into a sit-down affair. Thailand, Vietnam, and Malaysia have multidimensional places where food stalls are congregated around a common seating area, but they also have stalls everywhere on the streets. Singapore prohibits "hawkers" (the Singapore term for small, independent food makers that make specialty dishes) from setting up shop on the streets. So the people have created palaces of culinary pleasures that cannot be beaten for a breathtaking selection of awesome food at any time of day. The Singaporeans have retained street food culture while also improving the typical hygiene issues and reducing street congestion. In fact, for travelers uncomfortable with lax Asian food-safety practices, Singapore is the best choice, because it's so clean.

At hawker centers, dozens (if not hundreds) of vendors come together from around the city to serve their specialties under one roof. One Singapore classic to seek out at these places is the multilayered *Roti Paratha* (pronounced "prata"), which is twisted in the air into a paper-thin sheet, drizzled with golden ghee (clarified butter), and cooked on a griddle to golden-brown perfection (pg. 286).

Braised Short Rib by Chef Alan Wong while Guest Chef at Humble House of Tung Lok Restaurant Group

The Restaurant Scene

Although this book focuses on traditional cuisines of this region, there is also a sophisticated fine-dining scene in Southeast Asia that rivals any restaurant in the Western world. In my travels through the region, I seldom make much time for these restaurants. Since my time there is only temporary, I seek out specialties at street carts, food courts, coffee shops (actually open-air restaurants), and smaller, independent restaurants.

Prevailing Flavors— Recurring Ingredient Combinations

Certain ingredient combinations tend to repeat themselves and create a familiar flavor profile, which threads its way through many dishes. This enables us to distinguish one cuisine from another—French from Mexican, or Indian from Italian. The flavor base created by the combination of soy sauce, ginger, garlic, and scallions occurs in most Asian cuisines. But this can be an oversimplification.

It may be a combination of spices and aromatics, such as when lemongrass, turmeric, galangal, garlic, and shallots come to the forefront in many Malaysian dishes (pg. 102). Beef *Rendang* (Dry Beef Curry) (pg. 334), Malaysian Chicken Satay (Spice Marinated Grilled Skewers of Chicken) (pg. 310), and *Otak Otak* (Grilled Fish Paste Wrapped in Banana Leaves) all share this flavor base, but they also have other ingredients and methods that make them distinct. Malaysian cooks grind thin slices of the lemongrass into a *rempah*, a spice paste that forms the base of a Malaysian beef curry. *Otak Otak* (fish paste cooked in a banana leaf) is speckled with these same aromatic ingredients.

In Thailand the combination of lemongrass, galangal, shallots, garlic, peppercorns, kaffir lime rind, and shrimp paste is fundamental to numerous curry pastes. Red, green, yellow, and Massamun curry pastes (pgs. 159, 161, 160, 163) all have these ingredients as their base, though they vary in amount. Additional ingredients are added to differentiate

Rows of food stalls fill the Singaporean hawker centers.

Pounding aromatic spices for a Thai red curry paste

the curry pastes, and each color paste is traditionally paired with specific vegetables, meats, and fishes, making each dish unique.

In Vietnam the omnipresent *nước mắm* (fish sauce), lime juice, garlic, sugar, and chilies constitute the main combination of ingredients for *Nước Chấm* (pg. 198), the dipping sauce that shows up everywhere, as well as for Lotus Rootlet Salad (pg. 234), a dressing for Grilled Pork on Cool Noodles (pg. 256), or even the revered Lemongrass Chicken of Vietnam. (pg. 248)

These are examples of how each cuisine evolves over time and how cooks tweak regional spice combinations to fit their dishes while retaining the flavor of the place.

CONDIMENTS: For thousands of years, Asians have relied upon a battery of condiments such as soy sauces, fish sauces, shrimp pastes, chili pastes, and fruit concentrates like tamarind. These condiments often represent that common vein that runs through a country's cuisine and lays that familiar foundational flavor that is indicative of the country or region. The omnipresent fish sauce is at the core of Thai and Vietnamese cuisines, less so in Malaysia and Singapore. They're used similarly to the way we use salt in the West—applied to dishes as a flavor-enhancing seasoning, not to make them taste fishy. Shrimp paste, a mixture of fermented shrimp and salt, is extremely pungent. It's definitely an acquired taste—not for the faint of heart.

The cuisines of Southeast Asia rely on numerous condiments.

Preparing bottles for fish sauce in Phu Quoc, Vietnam

Some people still ferment soy sauce in the traditional clay pots.

HERBS: In Southeast Asia I wander the markets for hours, browsing the stalls of meat, seafood, and spices. I spend the most time perusing fresh vegetables and fruits. So many colors, shapes, and aromas— they beckon you closer to touch, smell, and taste. In Vietnam, stalls have dozens of herbs destined for *Phở*, the aromatic beef noodle soup. Some herbs are quickly recognizable: basil, mint, and cilantro. Others, such as *rau răm* (Vietnamese coriander), are still hard to find here. See the Asian Resource chapter to find some for your kitchen (pg. 362).

FRUIT: Durian, the pungent, prickly-shelled prize of a Southeast Asian tree, is a fruit that deserves respect. Once you pry open the thorny exterior, creamy pods of rich, custard-like fruit tempt. Although each is somewhat accurate, the descriptions of its flavor as fermented onions, sweet mangos, and petroleum (sometimes all wrapped up in one) don't do this delightful fruit justice. OK, it's an acquired taste. I, however, acquired the taste the very first time I ate it. After that, when I got past its smell, I learned to love it. Now, I crave it so much that my travel plans are subject to the timing of durian season.

Durian is known as the "King of Fruits," but mangosteen, the "Queen of Fruits," is equally sumptuous. A thick purple exterior shell with a green crown is pushed open to reveal seedless segments of brilliant white gems, arranged tangerine-like. Pop these in your mouth to release a supersweet, slightly tart juice that will make you weak in the knees.

Other exotic fruits—lychees and their shelled, juicy stone-fruit cousins, rambutans and longans—populate the markets there too. Sample at will. It's a tryer's market.

Table Condiments Rock

Want to spice up the dish? Asians often let their guests decide. The dining tables of Southeast Asia are filled with limes, chili pastes, herbs, sauces, sliced chilies, and fresh vegetables to allow

Longan fruit floats by in the Mekong Delta, Vietnam

diners to customize flavor. Want some more spice with your noodles? Add the bite of a fiery roasted crimson chili powder for a deep flavor, or perk up the dish with pickled chilies. Are those noodles a bit salty for you? Balance the flavor by sprinkling some glistening sugar crystals over the rich, soy-slathered noodles. In Thailand and Vietnam most tables brim with bottles and dishes of sauces even before guests order. And many dishes come with specific condiments.

In Southeast Asia, texture is key. Table salads provide crisp, raw vegetable contrasts to hot dishes like curries and soups. Cool bean sprouts for pho noodle soup are always crisp, and they don't infuse the broth with too much of their flavor. A sour element is added with shaved unripe starfruit and for astringency thin slivers of unripe bananas and figs come into play.

THAILAND

Dining tables across the country have a small frame with four small glass jars: Pickled green chilies (pg. 120), roasted and ground chilies, sugar, and fish sauce with chilies usually fill these flavor enhancers.

Table salads are served with one or more of the following: cucumbers, Chinese long beans, green cabbage, fresh chilies, raw variegated eggplants, and/or whole Thai bird chilies (pg. 152). Other noteworthy condiments include plain fish sauce (pg. 48), fresh chili sauce (pg. 133), and roasted chilies in oil.

Vietnamese table salad of herbs with pickled carrots and onions

Thai table salad served with Laarb

Thai table salad with wedged banana blossoms (in center) and salted eggs

VIETNAM

As in Thailand, the Vietnamese have table condiments at the ready: *nuoc chấm* sauce, fish sauce (*nước mắm*), pickled chilies, and soy sauce. Tables are set with salads containing a few herbs such as Asian basil, mint, saw leaf herb, sliced chilies, and cucumbers (pg. 27). Other noteworthy condiments include lime wedges, salt, and black pepper.

Soy sauce and chilies perch above silky noodles, poached chicken, and tender shrimp in Ipoh, Malaysia.

MALAYSIA AND SINGAPORE

In Malaysia and Singapore, condiments are much more often paired with specific dishes, and so fewer general sauces are left on the table when guests are seated. Chili sambal is served with *curry laksa* and *hokkien mee*. Lime wedges accompany *asam laksa* (Sour Fish Noodles from Penanag) and *mamak mee* (Indian Fried Noodles). Thick soy with chopped red chilies and minced garlic are paired with *bak ku teh*.

Many of the Indian restaurants have three types of sauces to serve to their guests: *Dhal* (a spiced legume stew curry (vegetarian or meat), and coconut chutney (pg. 300) (serve with flatbreads such as *dosai* (fermented rice and *dhal* flatbread).

Rows of green lemon basil destined for a Vietnamese table

Thick soy sauce for pork rib soup

In Malacca, Malaysia, a few places have begun to form the chicken rice into balls and serve with chili-ginger sauce and roasted chicken.

Chopped long red chilies will soon be flooded with soy sauce.

The Southeast Asian Pantry

Thailand • Vietnam • Malaysia • Singapore

Same Building Blocks, Different Models

In the different regions of the world, one often finds similar pantries of ingredients that form the foundation of their cooking. This is true of Southeast Asia. It's a factor of geography, topography, climate, and cultural interaction among indigenous peoples there. Similar pantries do not translate as similar cuisine. Both Mexican and Vietnamese cooking include cilantro, limes, black beans, garlic, chilies, and rice in their pantries, but their cuisines could not be more different. In this chapter you will learn what ingredients are, how they are made, how they are used, and some recommendations of how to buy and store them. Keeping a well-stocked larder of Southeast Asian ingredients will enable (and even encourage) you to whip up authentic meals. Many of the items in this section can be stored for weeks, months, or even years. If you stock the pantry early, you won't find yourself running around for hours, seeking specialized ingredients from myriad markets (pg. 362).

Make Your Pantry Your Own

The evolution of your pantry is like the evolution of a country. Basic ingredients like jasmine rice, fish sauce, lemongrass, and others listed in these pages mark a starting point. But as you expand your repertoire, you bring in new ingredients learned from the people you meet, the places you travel, and the foods given to you as gifts. That special mustard, chili sauce, or spice blend found in a town you visited becomes a new part of your larder. Then, as you mature and move on through life, you adopt more new ingredients. The flavors of your travels become the flavors of your kitchen. Your home-cooked food goes through a metamorphosis and takes on a new identity that reflects who you are and where you've been.

What Brands Do I Use?

I am often asked which jasmine rice I covet. What about rice flour? How do you get the most supple rice noodles? Which naturally brewed soy sauce enriches the color and taste of my stir-fry? The list continues, and it's a very logical line of inquiry. These are the building blocks of flavor, and being able to count on a sauce of consistent viscosity is important, especially for food professionals who try to give their guests the same dish each and every day. Throughout this chapter I have given recommendations on some ingredients when I felt one brand was really superior to the rest; or that using a different brand would give you different-than-expected results (not necessarily bad, just different)—I've named names.

Lost in Translation

Pay attention to what you are buying, and save labels. Often, things are lost in the English translation. Simply because it is labeled "palm sugar," don't assume it's the right type of palm sugar. In my recipes, I specify the characteristics of certain ingredients that come in various forms. Although all palm sugars are made essentially the same way in Southeast Asia, by boiling down the sap of a palm tree (pg. 58), they vary greatly. Thailand and Vietnam have tan-colored sugar (recipes will list light brown palm sugar). But in Malaysia, a very dark brown sugar is produced. (Recipes will list dark brown palm sugar.) Using this Malay sugar instead of Thai sugar would change the flavor profile of Thai Sticky Rice with Mangos (pg. 180) completely.

To guide you in using the right ingredients, the following pages are crafted to enable you to select the right ingredient for the right recipe. When applicable and useful, especially with vegetables, herbs, and spices, the various common English names, the Latin name, a phonetic pronunciation, and the indigenous language are given. In Thailand there are numerous dialects. In Vietnam many foods are called different things in the North and the South. In these cases, I have selected the most commonly used name. Hopefully, this section will not only be used as you cook the recipes in this book, but will also help you decipher recipes from other books that have not given the English translation. Some of my favorite books are from overseas. Seeing a recipe that lists "yam bean" confused me until I learned that here in the U.S. it is always known by its Spanish name, *jicama* (Vietnamese: *củ sắn/củ đậu*). Look to (pgs. 34–93) for other tips on ingredient names.

Reading the pages in this chapter will help you prepare for your journey into the fusion of cultures that have created the culinary treasures of Thailand, Vietnam, Malaysia, and Singapore.

Setting Up Your Southeast Asian Pantry

If you have everything listed below, you can cook a majority of the recipes in this book. Most have a long shelf life (more than six months). Of course, you will need to buy the meat, fish, and produce as needed. Having these staples on hand will enable you to create Asian flavors on the fly. Then, as you try other items, you can bolster the pantry with specialized ingredients like fenugreek seeds, which are used to make curry powders (pg. 158), and other esoteric things.

Recommended brands follow each item in parentheses. When applicable, other quality indicators to look for are listed in the section heading or by each entry.

- Dried goods
  - Neutral-flavored oil, such as soy, peanut, canola, or vegetable
  - Coconut milk (Chaokoh, Maeploy, or 1st Oriental Food New Formula)
  - Soy bean sauces
    - Soy sauce (Lee Kum Kee)
    - Dark soy sauce or mushroom dark soy sauce (Lee Kum Kee)
    - Thick soy sauce (Koon Chun)
    - Brown/ground bean sauce (Lee Kum Kee)
    - Hoisin sauce (Lee Kum Kee)
  - Other condiments
    - Oyster sauce (Lee Kum Kee)
    - Fish sauce (Squid or Golden Boy)
    - Rice vinegar (unseasoned)
    - Distilled white vinegar
  - Chili sauces
    - Thai roasted chili paste in oil—nahm prik pow (Pantainorasingh) or homemade (pg. 132)
    - Vietnamese-style chili paste (Huy Fong) or homemade (pg. 199)
    - Sriracha or homemade (pg. 133)
  - Tamarind paste
  - Sweetened condensed milk (Longevity or Nestlé)—avoid "filled" milk. Look at the ingredient list to ensure there is no oil or other fillers added. It should list only milk and sugar.
  - Dried shrimp
  - Dried red chilies
  - Raw peanuts
  - Dried Chinese black mushrooms (shiitake)
  - Dried spices
    - Coriander seeds
    - Cumin seeds
    - Black and white peppercorns
    - Star anise
    - Cassia (cinnamon)
  - Rice
    - Jasmine (Elephant/Erawan or Rice King)
    - Long-grain sticky rice
  - Rice flour (Elephant/Erawan)
  - Cornstarch
- Rice noodles
  - Vermicelli
    - 1/4 inch wide
    - 1/2 inch wide
  - Cellophane noodles (mung bean)
- Frozen things
  (some bought fresh and stored for later use)
  - Banana leaves
  - Pandan leaves—bought fresh when available or frozen when fresh is not available
  - Cilantro root—to mince later into curry pastes
  - Kaffir limes—to grate directly from the freezer for an intense burst of flavor
  - Galangal—to grate frozen from the freezer for *rempahs* (spice pastes)
  - Lemongrass—for things like iced tea (pg. 36) or grill brushes (pg. 156).

Rhizomes

Ginger is not a root; it is actually an underground stem known as a *rhizome*. Rhizomes represent one of the hidden secrets of Southeast Asian cooking. Originally prized for their many medicinal properties such as being antibacterial, a nausea cure, an anti-inflammatory, a digestive aid, and a cough suppressant, now rhizomes have taken chefs under their flavorful spell.

Ginger, galangal, krachai, and *turmeric* are a select group among the fifty perennial plants in the *Zingiberaceae*, or ginger, family that sport horizontal-growing, underground stems. Stems store food as roots gather it. Rhizomes can be cut into pieces, and each part will then grow into another plant. Rhizomes may look similar on the outside, yet internally each possesses an identity that is uniquely its own. One of the least commonly used yet most intriguing is asafetida (*Ferula assafoetida*), known as hing in Hindi. The Indian culture uses the highly aromatic, garlic-flavored dried gum resin of a rhizome from the carrot family. A small amount goes a long way, as in the coconut chutney recipe (pg. 300).

SHOPPING GUIDELINES:

There are several common things to look for with all ginger, galangal, and turmeric. Look for smooth skin without wrinkles; flesh that does not yield to pressure when pushed with the edge of

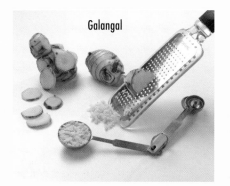

Galangal

See pg 103 for tips on how to use galangal

your fingers; and absence of discolored spots. Look closely for mold beginning to grow in cracks (this means it is old and best left in the store).

STORING SUGGESTIONS:

Many rhizomes may be stored for a week at room temperature (temperate, not tropics) in a dark place. For longer storage, wrap in paper towels and then place in a sealable plastic bag and store in the refrigerator for up to two weeks. Place in an airtight bag and freeze for extended storage. (You may want to grate or slice the rhizome before freezing to make it easier to measure later, as many of the recipes in the book use grated galangal.)

GALANGAL (*Alpinia galanga*)—Greater galangal is most frequently used in Asian cooking. Sometimes called blue ginger, this essential Southeast Asian ingredient has a smoother skin than ginger, with distinct lines around its circumference and a more pungent, camphor-like aroma. Its mustardy, citrusy, earthy nuances add complexity to Thai and Vietnamese classics. Galangal is rarely eaten raw. It's more commonly pounded, ground into curry pastes, or sliced and infused into soups and sauces.

Thai: *kha*; Malay: *lengkuas*; Vietnamese: *riềng* (North) or *giềng* (South)

GINGER (*Zingiber officinale*)—The most commonly available of the group, it's used in most Asian cooking. Unless otherwise specified, most recipes are referring to mature or "old" ginger. When the mature rhizome is meant to be consumed, rather than used for an infusion, it can be minced, shredded, candied, or grated. Ginger can also be juiced for use in drinks, sauces, and marinades. Thick, peeled slices are commonly bruised or crushed to release their flavor and aroma into stocks, broths, marinades, simmering liquids, sauces, and soups. Young ginger, now available year-round, has a more subtle flavor and hence is sometimes eaten fresh, in thin strips. Its wispy, paper-thin skin is translucent, and the bulbs have vivid pink highlights.

Thai: *khing*; Malay: *halia*; Vietnamese: *gừng*

Ginger

Krachai

KRACHAI (*Boesenbergia pandurata*)—This rhizome is sometimes called "Chinese keys," because it resembles a set of keys with one base nodule and a bunch of narrow extending appendages. It's also called "wild ginger" or "lesser Siamese ginger." It's very aromatic and has a mildly spicy flavor. A member of the ginger family, krachai has light brown skin and a yellow interior. This rhizome is prevalent in the cuisines of Thailand, Laos, and Cambodia and is used mainly in fish curries and soup broths. If it is not available fresh, substitute the frozen or brined version, available in jars. Krachai is also available already cut into julienne strips. It is a dominant flavor in the Thai jungle curry recipe (pg. 162).

Thai: *krachai*

TURMERIC (*Curcuma longa, C. domestica*)—Unlike the other rhizomes, turmeric is often used in its dry, powdered form. The fresh leaves can be used to flavor curries. It colors the *Nonya* vegetable curry (pg. 344), and the tender young shoots are used as vegetables in Thailand, usually served with *nam prik* (spicy chili paste). Turmeric is included in almost every commercial curry powder and is an essential element in much yellow rice, since it's much cheaper than saffron. To substitute fresh rhizome, for every 1 tsp. ground turmeric, replace with 1 Tbsp., ½ oz, 14 g. grated fresh turmeric.

Thai: *khamin*; Malay: *kunyit*; Vietnamese: *nghệ*

Turmeric

Turmeric

Fresh Herbs

Copious use of fresh herbs is a hallmark of Southeast Asian cuisine, especially in Vietnam. The Vietnamese serve herbs in quantities that would startle most Westerners. They pile grand platters with herbs, cucumber slices, chilies, beans, and other raw fresh vegetables, which comprise a *table salad* eaten with many meals. Some dishes call for specific herbs, while others pair with the usual array of basil, cilantro, and mint.

SHOPPING GUIDELINES: Look for firm leaves, no discoloration or decay present, and an overall perky appearance.

STORING SUGGESTIONS: Gently wrap the herbs in paper towels, newspaper, or parchment before storing in a sealable plastic bag. You will be amazed how long they last, upwards of a week!

LEMONGRASS (*Cymbopogon citrates*)—an aromatic perennial plant that may be tough on the outside but whose delicately flavored inside is coveted by cooks worldwide. When choosing lemongrass, look for whole stalks whose bottom ends are moist and freshly cut, not dried out or discolored (mold is obviously a no-no). I suggest sticking with fresh lemongrass, since the dried lemongrass products I've tried have lost most of the herb's admirable qualities. Some Asian markets carry a preminced

LEMONGRASS TEA OF SINGAPORE'S SPICE GARDEN

When life gives you lemons, make lemonade. When a recipe leaves you with lemongrass tops, make lemongrass tea. In the center of Fort Canning Park in Singapore, one can find At-Sunrice Global Chef Academy. Here they go through a lot of lemongrass, hence producing piles of tops. The chefs combine 8 cups of water with about 8 stalks' worth of bruised lemongrass (or 16 tops), bring it to a boil, and simmer it for 20 minutes. Remove from the heat and add 1/2 cup of sugar and 2 black tea bags; steep for 20 minutes longer. Strain, cool, and serve over ice. While testing this recipe, I found that a splash of dark rum and a few slices of lime create a brilliant cocktail.

frozen product that is usually of poor quality, yet getting a bunch of fresh lemongrass when you can, slicing or mincing it, and freezing it at home is a great way to get ahead. Go to page (pg. 102) to see a step-by-step photo guide on how to trim and cut lemongrass.

Thai: *takrai*; Vietnamese: *xả*; Malay: *serai*; Tamil: *sera*

KAFFIR LIME LEAVES (*Citrus hystrix*)—One of the defining flavors of Southeast Asia, both the leaves and zest of this lime are used. The juice of a kaffir lime is very bitter and rarely part of cooking. Although an actual leaf of a citrus tree, it is smaller than the leaves of other varieties of lime. This double-lobed leaf is much more aromatic than any other citrus leaves, so don't be tempted to substitute. They freeze very well, so buy them when you can for safekeeping. Dried kaffir lime leaves are available, but in my opinion they are useless. Use whole leaves to infuse broths, soups, and curries. Like bay leaves, these whole leaves are tough and not eaten, and are removed before serving the dish. One exception, however, is when they are

Kaffir Lime Leaves

deep-fried until extremely crispy and used in northeastern Thai dishes such as *Laarb* (pg. 152) or in the Tom Yum Flavored Fried Peanut Snack (pg. 136). Shaved very thin across the narrow width of the leaves (after folding back the edges and pulling out the tough spine), they are sometimes added to curries or served as a table condiment with Pho Ga. Fortunately, kaffir lime plants can be bought at many nurseries now for homegrowing, a worthwhile investment.

Thai: *bai makrut*; Malay: *daun limau purut*; Vietnamese: *chanh kafir*

PANDAN LEAVES (*Pandanus amaryllifolius*)—Although very different in flavor, this herb is sometimes called the "vanilla of Southeast Asia," since it is used as an aromatic in sweets, much as we use vanilla. Pandan supplies the brilliant green color found in many Southeast Asian sweets. It's ground, and its juice is extracted (pg. 350) and added to doughs, custards, sticky rice, and other sweet treats. When used in savory dishes, the long, slender pandan leaves are left whole, usually tied into a loose knot, and bruised with a blunt object to extract the maximum flavor. It is added to rice, imbuing it with a mysterious herbal nuance. Also, the long leaves are tied around marinated pieces of chicken, which are then deep fried. The leaves are peeled and discarded before the chicken is served. In the West, it isn't

easy to find fresh, but it freezes well and is available in that form. If you do find it fresh, buy a lot, wrap it well, and freeze it for later use—it will be more aromatic than frozen imported pandan.

Thai: *bai toey*; Vietnamese: *lá dứa*; Malay: *daun pandan*; Tamil: *rampe*

CURRY LEAVES (*Murraya koenigii*)—Slender thin branches of this herb hold numerous small, pointed, dark shiny leaves that emanate a strong curry-like aroma. The leaves are traditionally used in curries, yet are not a common ingredient in curry powders. They are fried or cooked with *dried lentils* and mustard seeds and then used to top chutneys and stews such as the coconut chutney (pg. 300). Curry leaves are often used in Malaysian in Indian dishes. The leaves become very crisp when fried and infuse dishes with their strong flavor. Like *kaffir lime leaves* (pg. 36), they freeze well, but dried curry leaves are useless.
Malay: *daun kari*; Tamil: *karapincha*

WILD PEPPER LEAF OR BETEL LEAF (*Piper sarmentosum*)—A distant relative to peppercorns, this broad, glossy, heart-shaped leaf has a peppery bite with a prized astringency. The leaves are very flexible and are used to wrap foods, especially various *miang* (snacks) in Thailand (pg. 138). These large leaves

are also stuffed with ground beef and lemongrass for a grilled dish popular in Vietnam: *Bo Nướng Lá lốt*. This same plant also produces a fruit that is often called a "long pepper," an elongated, cone-shaped pepper. It is sometimes marketed as "Balinese long pepper" and is used to season some soups and fried dishes. Do not confuse this leaf with the similarly shaped but much thicker and more bitter Betel leaf that is chewed as a digestif with slaked lime and betel nuts. Thai: *Bai phluu*; Vietnamese: *lá lốt*; Tamil: *bulath*

Curry Leaves

Pandan Leaves

Wild Pepper Leaf

Asian Basil

Basil in Asia

There are three fundamental types of basil used across Southeast Asia, each with specific applications. Generally they're not used interchangeably. In the U.S., where Asian basil varieties are still hard to find, Italian "sweet" basil may be substituted for Thai basil or even lemon basil, but the dish will not have an authentic Southeast Asian flavor profile.

THAI BASIL OR ASIAN BASIL

(*Ocimum basilicum* var.)—This Asian basil is easily recognized by the smooth, pointed leaves attached to its purplish stem (which varies in darkness, but always has a purple hue). The purplish-green flowering tops are even more potent than the delicate leaves and are often left on the herb. The essence of Thai basil is reminiscent of anise and cinnamon. It's used both raw and cooked. When cooking with it, Southeast Asian cooks always add it at the very last moment and remove the dish from the heat as soon as the basil has wilted, preserving its bright, fresh flavor. This is the most widely used basil across Southeast Asia. Thai: *bai horapha*; Vietnamese: *húng quế*; Malay: *daun kemangi*

LEMON BASIL

(*Ocimum basilicum citriodorum*)—As the name indicates, this smooth-skinned, narrowed-leafed basil possesses a lemony taste and aroma. It is used in salads, rice paper salad rolls (sometimes called "summer rolls" or "steamed spring rolls"), and other cold dishes. Thai: *bai manglaek*; Malay: *kemangi*; Tamil: *maduru-tala*

HOLY BASIL (*Ocimum sanctum*)

—Named for its prevalent planting around temples, the dark, small, rounded, slightly furry leaves are added to stir-fries, such as Thai Pad Ke Mao (pg. 176), and to curry dishes. There are two varieties. White holy basil has green stems and a milder flavor. It's used mostly for seafood dishes. Red holy basil has purplish stems (similar to Thai basil) and matches well with meats, poultry and seafood. Thai: *bai kraprow*; Malay: *selaseh*; Tamil: *maduru-tala*

CILANTRO (*Coriandrum sativum*)

—Cilantro is also called "coriander leaf" or "Chinese parsley." It is, in fact, the leaf of the same plant from which the spice, coriander seed, is sourced. It has a lemony, rosy essence and a slight tartness on the palate. It's the most widely used herb in Southeast Asian cooking. Cilantro leaves, stems, and roots are used in various preparations A notable percentage of people perceive its flavor to have an unpleasant "soapy" note. This is a genetic predisposition more that a personal preference and cannot be unlearned. When a recipe calls for chopped cilantro, include the leaves and also bits of the tender stems. Usually the more fibrous parts of the stems, the bottom one inch or

Green Holy Basil

Cilantro

so, are discarded. Whole sprigs are central to the *table salad* in Thailand and Vietnam. Ethnic Indians in Malaysia and Singapore use this tender herb for cilantro chutney. In America, the straggly root is usually cut off at the farm, but some markets carry cilantro with the roots still attached. The root's earthy aromatic character is an essential element in Thai curry pastes (pgs. 159, 160, 161). If it is not available, substitute 2 tsp. of minced stems for every one root. Thai: *pak chee*; Malay: *daun ketumba*; Vietnamese: *ngò*; Tamil: *kothamalli kolle*

VIETNAMESE CORIANDER

(*Polygonum odoratum*)—This powerful, tart, peppery herb has slender, delicate leaves with distinct, V-shaped dark patches. The Vietnamese use cupfuls of the whole leaves in salads, like the Vietnamese chicken salad (pg. 238), also usually served with clams and other shellfish. Malaysians chop it finely and sprinkle it atop bowls of *laksa noodle soup* (pg. 302). Use this herb sparingly, so as not to overwhelm the rest of the flavors of a dish. Thai: *phak phai, phrik maa, chan chom, hom chan*; Vietnamese: *rau răm*; Malay: *daun laksa*

SAW LEAF (*Eryngium foetidum*)

—Called by many names, such as "culantro," "Mexican coriander," "saw tooth herb," "eryngo," and "stink weed," this long, serrated leaf looks sturdier than it is. Its leaves resemble dandelion greens. It has a

Vietnamese Coriander

firm texture, but its short shelf life makes it challenging to keep for more than a few days. The herb leaves grow right out of the ground, so there is a low yield and a high cost. The long leaves are used whole in table salads or shaved finely to be added to noodles and salads such as Thai pork Laarb (pg. 152). Its lemony flavor is reminiscent of cilantro, but more pungent. Thai: *pak chee farang*; Vietnamese: *ngò gai*; Malay: *ketumbar jawa*

MINT—Peppermint (*Mentha spicata*) and spearmint (*Mentha gracilis*) are two of the most widely used mint varieties in Vietnamese food. Mint is part of the *table salad* and finds its way into spring rolls, soups, and other dishes. Peppermint, with its familiar wrinkly surface, is the most common. The smoother, darker green variety, spearmint, has a more assertive bite. Thai: *bai saranae*; Vietnamese: *húng lủi*; Malay: *pohok*; Tamil: *meenchi*

PERILLA (*Perilla frutescens*)— Although it's sometimes referred to as mint, it's a different species. There are two varieties of this strong herb: green and green/purple (whose leaves are two-tone—one side is green and the other purple). Similar to Japanese *shiso* leaves, perilla leaves have a furry

surface, a lemony flavor, and produce a cooling sensation on the palate. In Vietnamese food, perilla is never cooked, but is always used raw. It's a common part of the *table salad*. Guests tug leaves from the sprigs and use them to wrap fried foods before popping them in their mouths. It's also a classic accompaniment to *Bánh Xèo*, a sizzling crepe (pg. 208).

Vietnamese: *tía-tô*

VIETNAMESE LEMON BALM (*Elsholtzia ciliate*)—The brightly flavored, delicate, fuzzy leaves of this herb are never cooked, but always used raw. It is most often left in whole leaves as an element of a *table salad*, but can be shredded and added to fresh vegetable dishes and salads. Vietnamese: *kinh giới*

RICE PADDY HERB (*Limnophila aromatica*)—Named such because it is grown in rice paddies and other shallow water areas in Vietnam, this herb has small, tender, oval leaves with a slightly purple base. Its flavor, reminiscent of cumin and citrus, goes best with seafood and sour fish soups. It is always added at the last moment, and the stems are eaten along with the leaves. Vietnamese: *ngò-ôm*

FISH MINT (*Houttuynia cordata*)—This is definitely a love-it or hate-it herb. Its heart-shaped, sour leaves taste like a combination of anchovies and aluminum. Its strong flavor is often paired with red meats. Personally I like it with nothing (hate it). Vietnamese: *dấp cá*

CHINESE CELERY (*Apium graveolens dulce*)—Leaves of this herb look like a cross between cilantro and a celery leaf. It has a very pungent, celery-like flavor and is used sparingly in soups and salads like the Thai cellophane noodle salad (pg. 146), as its strong flavor is more akin to a powerful herb than a vegetable. Thai: *khun chaai*; Vietnamese: *cần tàu*

Saw Leaf

Peppermint

Perrilla

Vietnamese Lemon Balm

Rice Paddy Herb

Fish Mint

Chinese Celery

Spices

Spices are seeds, roots, rhizomes, bark, and other plant parts, except for the leaves, that are used for flavoring. The leaves of plants are known as *herbs*. Southeast Asian cooks tend to use whole spices, like cinnamon sticks, coriander seeds, and whole peppercorns, rather than the preground spices that are common in the U.S. Each spice is usually dry roasted before use to maximize the aroma and potency. This dry-roasting process, embraced by more and more Western chefs, actually changes the way spices taste.

Annatto

SHOPPING GUIDELINES: Spice quality and cost may vary more than for any other staples in the kitchen. Supermarkets can be ghastly expensive for spices, and less common spices may sit on the shelves for months. Go to your local Asian market, where they're more likely to go through these spices in a reasonable amount of time. Also, shop on line through one of the sources located on page 362.

STORING SUGGESTIONS: Keep spices in a cool, dark place, and use them quickly. A cool cabinet will do, as long as it's far away from your oven or stove. Spices can be placed in a closed cabinet or opaque containers. Spice shelf life is a very subjective topic; some insist that every six months you should trash them all and start over (very wasteful). Yes, toasting them "brings them back to life," but only so much. Bottom line: Smell and taste your spices. If they're not extremely aromatic, toast them. If they're still flat, discard them.

Coriander Seeds

ANNATTO (*Ixa orrellana*)—Called "achiote" in Latin American cuisine, this seed is used to impart brilliant yellow color to foods. The seeds are harvested from tree-borne pods. Each individual odd-shaped, rock-hard, brick-colored seed releases a large amount of colorant when heated. A common technique is infusing oil in the first stage of a dish to gain its color, as with classic beef stew with tomato and lemongrass, Bò Kho (pg. 260) of Vietnam. Some cooks do choose to grind the seeds finely and add them directly to the marinade [recipe pg ref Mi Quang]. But the spice does not contribute much flavor. Annatto is used in the West to color Cheddar cheese, butter, and other products.

Vietnamese: *bột điều màu*

CORIANDER SEEDS (*Coriandrum sativum*)—These are the seeds of the widely used cilantro herb. The seeds appear at the top of the plant when it matures. They possess an almost lemon-like scent. Each orb has ridges that run from end to end. Coriander is a primary ingredient in the curry powders of Southeast Asia (pg. 112).

Thai: *mellet pac chee*; Malay: *ketumbar*; Vietnamese: *bột ngò*

Cumin

CUMIN (*Cuminum cyminum*)—Most would recognize cumin's distinct aroma as a dominant scent found in premixed Indian curry powders. Cumin's pungent aroma can easily be overwhelming so use it cautiously, yet often, in Southeast Asian cooking. Cumin seeds are toasted whole and folded into the Indian lentil fritters on (pg. 298).

Thai: *yira*; Malay: *jintan puteh*; Vietnamese: *ngò ôm khô*

CARDAMOM (*Elettaria cardamomum*)—There are several types of cardamom: green, white, and black. Green are the most common and can be used in spice mixtures. The large black pods are more common for stews and soups such as Vietnamese Phở (pg. 218). The small pods contain about twenty seeds. Each cook has his own preference as to whether to use just the seeds or the whole pod. Grinding the whole pod is most common.

Thai: *kravan*; Malay: *buah pelaga*; Vietnamese: *bạch dậu khấu*

Cardamom

Peppercorns *(Piper nigrum)*

The word "peppercorn" is used in reference to several types of plants. The true peppercorn, *Piper nigrum*, yields what we know as green, white, and black peppercorns. Brown Szechwan peppercorns come from another plant altogether. Up until the 1500s, peppercorns were the primary "heat" in the spicy foods of Thailand. The fiery hot chilies prevalent there now were a New World discovery and came with sixteenth-century European explorers. Thai: *prik thai*; Malay: *lada*; Vietnamese: *tiêu bột*

GREEN PEPPERCORNS—These are the immature berries. In Southeast Asia they are available fresh, and that is how they are often used. They're frequently left in bunches, as they grow naturally, so that they infuse into the dish. Guests can break off a few at a time to eat along with the food. Fresh green peppercorns are not sold in the U.S. The closest substitute sold in the U.S. is available brined in glass jars. Canned versions are also available. Pop them into your mouth along with the Vietnamese crispy pork belly (pg. 250).

WHITE PEPPERCORNS—Ripe berries are soaked in water, husked, and then sun-dried. The spiciest of the lot, white peppercorns are used whole, crushed, or ground and are especially useful in Thai curry pastes.

Fresh Green Peppercorns

Large bags of peppercorns in a Vietnamese market

Black Peppercorns

White Peppercorns

Green Peppercorns in Brine

BLACK PEPPERCORNS—The immature green peppercorns are fermented slightly and then dried in the sun to achieve their characteristic wrinkled appearance. Their bite was the leading contender for the spice title until chilies arrived. Singaporean Black Pepper Crab (pg. 316) takes advantage of more than one full tablespoon of coarsely ground black pepper per crab.

Five Spices Come Together as One Flavorful Seasoning

CINNAMON VS. CASSIA

The vocabulary of most chefs contains only "cinnamon," and there is no distinction between *Ceylon cinnamon* and *cassia*. This is as great a culinary over-simplification as if we were not to distinguish between onions and shallots in a recipe. Either would work in the same amounts, yet the resulting flavor would be enormously different.

TRUE CINNAMON (*Cinnamomum zelanicum* or *Cinnamomum verum*)—Best suited for sweet applications, although it can work in some savory dishes or spice mixtures. This is the variety you may see labeled "Canela" or "Mexican cinnamon." Cassia (*Cinnamomum aromaticum* or *Cinnamomum cassia*) is a close relative of true cinnamon and is the primary cinnamon used in the cuisines of Asia. It is right at home in savory dishes like Sweet Spice Scented Braised Pork, *Se bak* (pg. 320), a Malaysian braised delicacy with a salty-sweet, soy-based broth redolent of cassia, star anise, and ginger. Unbeknownst to many cooks, most of the ground cinnamon sold in the U.S. is actually ground cassia.

Oh, yeah—forget about labeling. They can both be labeled as cinnamon. To tell the difference by eye, you need to buy the whole quills, or curled pieces of bark. Cassia is much thicker and, if in a quill shape, is most commonly rolled as a scroll with its two edges rolled inward. *Cinnamomum zelanicum* sticks are thin, brittle, multilayered rolled quills. Thai: *op cheu-ay*; Malay: *kayu manis*; Vietnamese: *quế*

CLOVES (*Syzygium aromaticum*)—The unopened buds of a flower are dried to create this pungent spice, whose essential oils are much more powerful than most other spices. As a result of their intense potency, they're used sparingly. Thai: *kaan ploo*; Malay: *bunga chinkeh*; Vietnamese: *dinh–hương*

ANISE SEEDS (*Pimpinella anisum*)—Also known as simply anise. This licorice-flavored seed color varies from green to brown. Indian restaurants are known to have them available after dinner as guests exit as a breath freshener; occasionally these are candied. Fennel seeds are a common stand-in in five spice powder. Thai: *yira*; Hindi: *patli saunf*; Malay: *jintan manis*; Vietnamese: *hạt hồi*

SZECHWAN PEPPERCORNS (*Zanthoxylum piperitum*)—This tongue-tingling spice is not related to the true peppercorn family, *Piper nigrum*, but Szechwan peppercorns are named such due to their heat. Copious amounts are used in the Szechwan region of China. They have the unique ability to create a numbing sensation on your lips and tongue. They are actually the bud of a bush and are one of the ingredients in Chinese five-spice powder. Each bud consists of two distinct parts: the hard, gritty seed and the crispy, exterior husk. The seed and its husk are roasted whole and then ground very fine. Coarse grinding will leave a gritty texture in the finished dish. Thai: *prik thai say chwan*; Vietnamese: *tiêu tứ-xuyên*

STAR ANISE (*Illicium verum*)—This eight-pointed spice is a key ingredient in five-spice powder and a primary aromatic in *Phở Bò*, Vietnamese Beef Noodle soup (pg. 218). It's similar in flavor to licorice and anise seeds, but is no relation. Thai: *poy kak bua*; Malay: *bunga lawang*; Vietnamese: *hoa hồi*

Five Spice Powder Components

Cinnamon · Szechwan peppercorns · Star anise · Anise seeds · Cloves

Chilies

In the five hundred years since Europeans discovered chilies in the New World, these spicy pods have become one of the defining ingredient categories of Southeast Asia. They are bold and diverse in flavor, and they're amenable to lending their flavor, color, and heat to nearly limitless incarnations. Pounded into pastes, sliced and floated in fish sauce, crushed into salads, or minced and added to soy sauce to punctuate foods with that fiery bite, they have become indispensable throughout the region. Each variety has its own flavor, level of capsaicin (the compound that determines heat), and implicit function. To reduce the heat of a chili, cut out the seeds and inner white membrane (also called the ribs), since these components contain the majority of the capsaicin (pg. 110).

Although hot chilies are sometimes used interchangeably, most recipes call for a specific variety. The reason may be color, thickening properties, spice level, or the floral note that a given chili contributes. Speaking of floral, most cooks in Southeast Asia leave the "crown"—the base of the flower bud that connects the stem to the fruit. It adds a special aroma. But these chefs do snip off the stem. The list that follows represents the most commonly used chilies in Southeast Asia, but it's by no means an exhaustive list.

SHOPPING GUIDELINES: As with most produce, firm, taut skin and stems that are not dried out are clear signs of freshness.

STORING SUGGESTIONS: Once you get them home, they'll keep at room temperature for a few days. But I usually keep them in a loosely covered container or paper bag in the refrigerator. Freezing them is a great way to preserve their flavor and color. Their texture is lost in freezing, but for pastes and cooking that is not an issue.

FRESH CHILIES

THAI BIRD CHILI—aka "bird's beak" or "dragon's eye chili"—These medium-hot chilies are used red (ripe) or green (immature) and are about 1 to 1¹/₂ inches in length. They have a distinctly crooked shape, are very versatile, and are one of the most commonly used chilies in this book's recipes. They are sometimes served whole at the table, where guests take bites between morsels of food. Thai: *prik kii nuu sun yaew*; Vietnamese: *ớt hiểm*

LONG RED AND LONG GREEN CHILIES— aka "Holland chilies" or "long hot chilies"—These brilliant green or red curved chilies are 3 to 4 inches in length. Very smooth skinned and shiny, they are only mildly spicy. They are often used as ornamental chilies, whole or cut into flower shapes. In cooking, they're used as a flavor and color element in mild chili sauces. They lend a vivacious red color to dishes, and hotter specimens are added for heat at the cook's discretion. These are fundamental to Malaysian *sambals* (chili sauces), where they are used by

Dried Chilies

the dozen and still yield a sauce that doesn't sear the palate. Thai: *prik chee fah*; Malay: *chili merah*; Vietnamese: *ớt đỏ / ớt xanh*

BIRD'S EYE CHILI—aka "chili padi" or "mouse shit chili"—This slender powerhouse, usually ¹/₂ to 1 inch in length, will turn red when ripe, as most chilies do. They're most commonly used for curries, soups, and *nahm prik* (fresh chili sauces) of Thailand, or chopped or sliced as table condiments in Vietnam, Singapore, and Malaysia. They are some of the hottest chilies used in Southeast Asia. Thai: *prik kii nuu suan*; Malay: *chili padi*; Vietnamese: *ớt xiêm* ("from Thailand")

ORANGE CHILI—A thicker fleshed chili, this is used in Thailand's "southern curries." In Vietnam, it's often sliced thin and served as a table condiment. Somewhat sweet and sour in flavor, it could be characterized as medium-hot. These chilies are uncommon outside of Thailand. They are about 3 cm. long, thin fleshed, and possess extraordinary heat. Long chilies can be substituted. Thai: *prik leuang*; Vietnamese: *ớt*

SUBSTITUTIONS: Bird's eye chilies (*chili padi*) and Thai bird chilies (*dragon's eye*) are fiery buggers (bird's eye chilies are hotter; usually the smaller the chili the hotter it is) that are relentless with their heat. The closest you will get is a serrano. Habaneros are too hot and relentless. Jalapeno chilies, those that are most readily available, can be used in place of any fresh green chili in this book, but the heat will not be there, and the flavor will be different. Add some ground dried chilies to add back the bite.

Long red and long green chilies, often labeled as "Holland chilies," are becoming more commonly available. If unavailable at your market, ripe red jalapenos are the best approximation, albeit with a slightly greener flavor and much tougher seeds. Next in line are ripe Fresno chilies. Recently, I have spotted some ripe serranos, which work well and have a fiery bite (they're hotter than their distant cousins, the long chilies). For long green chilies, I have even used long green Anaheim chilies with a few Thai chilies thrown in for their bite.

DRIED CHILIES

Dried chilies add a depth of color and flavor to foods that is extremely different from fresh chilies. With the drying process comes a slight fermentation, which intensifies the flavor. As the chilies are dried, their color darkens and evolves. Chefs dry roast them, toast them in a pan, or fry them before incorporating them into soups, stews, or other dishes. Sometimes they're pulverized before use. In most cases, cooks reconstitute dried chilies by soaking them in room temperature water for thirty minutes or longer. Reconstituted chilies can be used to make spice pastes, purées, or seasoning blends. I always use cool water to reconstitute dried chilies, as warm or hot water leaches out too much flavor.

When chilies are dried, they're harder to identify by sight than fresh chilies are. Smaller chilies are usually hotter and have a brighter red color, and the longer, more wrinkled chilies have a deeper brick-red color, and are slightly milder. To moderate the heat, break open dry chilies and shake out the seeds and ribs. Often, smaller chilies are fried whole and used as garnishes, or they're pan-toasted and pulverized into powders for use as a spice. Longer chilies are used for spice pastes.

SHOPPING GUIDELINES: As with spices, shop in markets that have a high turnover of chilies, such as a busy Asian market or Latin market. Chilies' colors vary drastically between varieties, each supplier, and even within batches. This is due to their color when raw, drying techniques, and storage conditions. Yet they should be a homogeneous red color with some "orange-ish" patches (but mostly red).

STORING SUGGESTIONS: Refer to spices section [SEA pantry pg ref].

SUBSTITUTIONS: The two varieties listed below can be found in Latin stores or international aisles of supermarkets. They are acceptable substitutes for the Asian-sourced chilies. No, their flavor is not identical, but the nuances will not be noticed by most.

Japanese—The relatively straight chilies are 1 to 2 inches in length, have a shiny, smooth skin, and sport fiery heat and a bright red color.

De Arbol—These longer-stemmed dark red chilies are 2 to 4 inches in length. They are the most versatile type for Southeast Asian cooking. When in doubt about which dried chili to use in Southeast Asian cooking, reach for these.

Thai Bird Chilies

Birds' Eye Chilies

Orange Chilies

Long Green and Red Chilies

Thai Bird Chilies

The Onion (Lily) Family

SCALLIONS (*Allium fistulosum*)—A lot of confusion arises from the names "spring onions" and "green onions." Available in any U.S. market, the long, slender members of the allium family we call scallions have thin, diminutive bulbs. They are sometimes called "spring onions" in the U.S., and routinely called "spring onions" in Britain. But the less common, pudgy-bulbed "real" spring onion has a thinner skin and more narrow greens. It's actually a bulb onion, harvested young, whose greens have not been trimmed, so they come to a point. These are sweeter, juicier, more aromatic, and are the green onion of choice in Southeast Asia. Both the green and white portions are used, although some recipes call for only one part or the other. If you can't find true spring onions, use scallions. Thai: *ton hom*; Vietnamese: *hành lá*; Malay: *duan bawang*; Tamil: *lunu kolle*

GARLIC CHIVES (*Allium tuberosum*)—These delectable, grass-like herbs are also called "flowering chives" or "Chinese chives." Their rather thick, firm, elongated narrow leaves have a flavor that is a cross between scallions and garlic. They are used in large pieces, rather than finely chopped as Western chives are, and they are treated more like scallions, as an aromatic base for stir-fries. They're often seen poking out from one side of a Vietnamese Salad roll (pg. 206) and are added at the last moment to the classic Thai noodle dish of Pad Thai (pg. 172). The Chinese treat them as a vegetable, quickly stir-frying them and serving large platters full of them. They are a favorite flavoring in dumpling fillings. Sometimes, snowy white, pale yellow, or lavender flowers and buds adorn the tops of these chives. There's no need to discard these handsome flowers—they are delicious. Thai: *kui chaai*; Vietnamese: *hẹ*; Malay: *kucai*

SHALLOTS (*Allium oschaninii*)—Although European shallots, familiar to most Westerners, are available in American supermarkets, they are larger and closer in flavor to onions than Asian shallots. The drastically different size can cause major flavor variances when using a foreign book in your home, especially if the recipe has fifteen shallots, like the Malaysian chicken stew (pg. 322). Southeast Asian–style shallots are small, with a redder skin and usually have only one bulb, about one inch in diameter. They're transformed into crispy shavings (pg. 119), which are a favorite garnish for anything from fried rice to noodle soups. Raw shallot slivers are tossed into salads, or pounded into semifine pastes that act as thickeners for sauces and soups.

Thai: *hom dang*; Vietnamese: *hành củ tím*; Malay: *bawang merah*

GARLIC (*Allium sativum*)—Garlic may be the most universally used aromatic around the world. It's certainly integral to the flavors of Central and South America, Europe, North Africa, and Asia. But there are many varieties of garlic. The garlic cultivated in Southeast Asia is different from that in the U.S. Its smaller cloves pack quite a punch. Ounce for ounce, they're much more potent, so Southeast Asian recipes calling for garlic may have to be adjusted up to attain an authentic flavor.

Thai: *kra tiem*; Malay: *bawang puteh*; Vietnamese: *tỏi*

Spring Onions in Vietnam

Garlic

Shallots

Garlic Chives

47

FISH SAUCE

The most universal seasoning in Vietnam and Thailand is a salty, pungent clear brown liquid flavored with fermented fish. In Vietnam it's called *nước mắm,* and in Thailand it's called *nahm pla*. It's used in all types of dishes, regardless of whether or not they contain seafood. The sauce is primarily made with a species of small fish known as the long-jawed anchovy. Actually there are two to three varieties of the *Stolephorus* fish: *Baccaneeri, Miarcha,* and *Purpureus,* which is often referred to as an anchovy, but is not the familiar anchovy of the Mediterranean (*Engraulis encrasicolus*).

The fish are layered with salt in wooden vats—two parts salt to one part fish by weight—and fermented there for six to eight months. To avoid mashing the fish, which would cloud the sauce, a spigot at the bottom of the vat or a sunken "extraction well" allows the amber juices to be tapped. The first draining of this liquid gold is the most prized premium grade, labeled *nhi* in Vietnam. For those produced in Thailand, look for the Thai Department of Export Promotion (DEP) emblem from their government, which oversees the quality levels. After the first draining, water is added, and the mixture is fermented again for a lower quality, less-expensive second run. As with fine olive oils, you get what you pay for. The best fish sauce costs only a few dollars more than the mediocre second run, so don't skimp here. Fish sauce is often the fundamental flavor in a dish. Like most cooks, I have favorite brands. Some of my favorites are Golden Boy and Squid Brand. Generally, Vietnamese fish sauce is of higher quality than Thai brands, but it's hard to find here in the U.S. Look for *nước mắm nhĩ* on the label of Vietnamese brands, as this term designates it comes from the first draining of liquid.

In my work as a research and development chef, I am fortunate to have some direct access to background information, mostly from my friend Dan Goral, about the properties of ingredients that give them their character. The first measure of quality in fish sauce is the total protein content that directly relates to the nitrogen content, which is expressed in degrees, the higher quality sauce earning a 25- to 35-degree score. A 30- to 35-degree fish sauce sells for almost double the price and frankly is worth every penny, as the flavor impact is drastic. I even

Sea Salt

sampled a 40-degree fish sauce on a recent trip to Vietnam. The lower-rated sauces are usually made by diluting the higher quality sauce with water, or come from second or third extractions of the same fish, as discussed above.

The protein content indicates the umami impact of the sauce and how it will affect the overall flavor of the dish. But how the fish were processed is an equally important factor. The cleanest flavor is achieved when the fish are salted at sea immediately after being caught. This is generally the practice in Vietnam and halts microbial growth that creates off-flavors. Some manufacturers wait until the fish land on shore before salting them.

What can be learned from observing the color of a fish sauce? The color is determined by two main factors: the degree of amino acids, and the exposure to air that the sauce has experienced. When fish sauce is exposed to air, it darkens in color. You may have noticed this in your own home. Once opened, the color of the fish sauce darkens over time. The flavor changes slightly, but usually not noticeably in the final dish. If you are really concerned, transfer the sauce to progressively smaller bottles as you use it and keep it in a dark place. Refrigeration is optional, but not essential.

Wondering about the crystals that sometimes form in bottles of fish sauce? As fish sauce ages, the salt it contains may crystallize in the bottle. It's no cause for alarm. It won't affect the quality of the sauce.

Stolephorus Fish

Fermenting

Soy Sauces

SOY SAUCES and other ready-made flavor building blocks are often used in small amounts, so they stay on shelves and in your refrigerator for quite some time. There's no reason to worry, since most of them will be stable for upwards of a year, ready to add flavor to your next dish.

SHOPPING GUIDELINES: Experienced cooks rely on certain brands and varieties of condiments to get the flavors they know. See "Setting Up Your Southeast Asian Pantry" (pg. 33) for my brand recommendations.

STORING SUGGESTIONS: Unless otherwise stated (it's sometimes hard to spot), it is not necessary to refrigerate soy sauce or other salty condiments after opening. Storing them in a cool, dark area is best. These things do change with time. As the sauce is exposed to air, the area on top will darken, especially fish sauce. But for most recipes it will not make a substantial difference in taste.

Soy-Based Flavorings

The importance of soybeans in the cuisines of Southeast Asia cannot be overstated. The myriad fermented sauces made from dried soybeans includes products that are sweet, salty, savory, intense, delicate, paste-like, and water-thin, among other characteristics. A few of the essentials follow.

SOY SAUCE—With more than 3,000 years of presence in Asia, soy sauce is integral to all Southeast Asian cooking. In Malaysia and Singapore, more so than in Thailand and Vietnam, this is due to the high percentage of ethnic Chinese and the cuisines they have introduced. The term "brewed" soy sauce is important, yet somewhat misleading. The Chinese version of the sauce is not brewed or cooked like beer, but it is naturally fermented with whole soybeans. Thin soy sauces should never be colored with caramel color. Its presence is a sign that shortcuts were taken to achieve the dark color that usually takes months to develop as the soybeans ferment.

Soy Sauce Types

REGULAR SOY SAUCE "AKA light soy or thin soy" (listed as soy sauce in my recipes)—This is the main soy sauce used in much of the world. It adds not only desirable saltiness to foods, but a wallop of *umami,* the coveted meaty, savory flavor discussed in more detail on page 53. Soy sauce plays the role of marinade, dressing, braising liquid, table condiment, and more.

DARK SOY SAUCE—The dark color and extra viscosity comes from the addition of caramel color (a product of cooked sugar). Some manufacturers also use a vacuum-dehydration process to concentrate the sauce. Not only does dark soy have a desirable, slightly bitter flavor, but its jet-black color enables it to be used as a coloring element in dishes like stir-fried noodles without adding too much soy flavor. See (pg. 336) for the Malaysian Stir-fried Rice Noodles with Shrimp *char kway teow.* A drop will add a rich brown color to a soup, stew, or sauce. There is also one variation available—mushroom dark soy sauce—that is traditionally made by infusing dark soy sauce with straw mushrooms. Some manufacturers have switched to using the more savory and widely available Chinese black (shiitake) mushrooms for a more intense flavor.

THICK SOY SAUCE—This gooey black soy sauce has molasses added to it to achieve its jet-black color. It is used to marinate meats before stewing them, as in the Malaysian *pong teh* (pg. 322). Do not confuse it with the much sweeter Indonesian *kicap manis.* Not very salty, thick soy sauce has a bitter flavor and a little goes a long way.

MSG—An Impartial Assessment

During the development of this book, some really core beliefs of my cooking career came to the table to be evaluated. For years I've had an internal battle over whether to use monosodium glutamate (MSG) in my cooking. The struggle began more than a decade ago when I really began to understand Southeast Asian food. I avoided using it, since as a classically trained Western chef, I was taught it was cheating and unnecessary to achieve really good food (actually true). But the challenge is that the food I've loved so much when I've traveled tasted so different from what I would make in my kitchen stateside. I realized there was no question that the prevalent use of MSG in restaurants and by street vendors of Southeast Asia was a significant factor affecting the flavor. I have ventured into hundreds of kitchens in Southeast Asia over the past twenty years. Most use MSG in one form or another. I have decided to address what most cookbook authors avoid—the topic of monosodium glutamate.

I've studied, interviewed, experimented, and argued—at home, at school, and on trips—to discover authenticity. One such research mission happened a decade ago, when I was in Malaysia. I contacted Ajinomoto, one of the leading producers of MSG. I simply picked up the phone and dialed my way into the place, talking to a series of folks to get the right person. I explained that I was a chef and wanted to see what they do. They graciously granted me a tour. As part of my thirst for knowledge, I really needed to see, firsthand, what this was all about. MSG is commonly produced through the fermentation process of tapioca starch, corn, sago palm, and sugar from beets, cane, or molasses. The fermentation process converts molasses to glutamic acid. Through a heated evaporation process, a crystalline substance is created. This mixture is then liquefied, so that it can be neutralized and decolorized. It is then dried into white crystals. MSG contains about 12 percent sodium, while table salt contains almost 40 percent.

DON'T SHOOT THE MESSENGER

Before you toss this book in the trash, thinking that I condone the use of MSG and you do not, hear me out on this. I do not recommend nor disapprove of its use. The reality is that a majority of the kitchens in Southeast Asia use it. In the U.S.A. "No MSG added" is a common restaurant claim. But while the cooks may not have added MSG in its pure form, they probably still use sauces that have it added at the factory. Many cooks exclaim they do not use MSG, but frankly many do not even realize that they do. Regardless of your viewpoint, gaining an understanding of what nature's glutamic acid is, how it contributes to the development of flavor, and where it exists can help you create more flavorful food.

Some cooks buy the MSG crystals in bags and add it straight to the food. Others use ingredients that have MSG added to it already, such as chicken bouillon powder, oyster sauce, or other ready-made condiments. On the shelves of American supermarkets we find MSG branded as Accent seasoning. In Asian markets, it's called Aji-nomoto. It's also known as *vetsin* in Vietnam, *may jing* in China, and *ji-no-moto* in Japan.

I believe much of the modern-day use of MSG in the foods around Southeast Asia is a cost-cutting measure. Making a rich broth for a dish like Vietnamese Imperial Spicy Pork & Beef Soup with Shrimp Dumplings (*Bún Bò Huế*) requires pounds of bones and meat. But a similar flavor can be achieved through the addition of MSG to a weaker broth. Hence, the use begins. It is simply less expensive to cook with it, and it tastes good. That stated, MSG is a relative newcomer to Asian cookery, having been in use for just over one hundred years. Although I was not around two hundred years ago, I'm sure there were amazing, vibrant, flavorful foods long before MSG's invention.

Many believe that MSG causes adverse reactions, such as numbness, heart palpitations, headaches, chest pain, and asthma attacks. These symptoms are often referred to as "The Chinese Restaurant Syndrome." According to the American College of Allergy, Asthma and Immunology, MSG is not considered an allergen. Also, the U.S. Food and Drug Administration has not found any long-term, serious health consequences from consuming MSG. Since 1959 it has been grouped with the category of food additives Generally Recognized as Safe (GRAS), along with sugar, salt, pepper, baking powder, and vinegar. Some assert that there is no such thing as "The Chinese Restaurant Syndrome," but that it is actually a case of mistaken identity, attributing the alleged reactions to the high levels of sulfites and histamines that are present in some Chinese food.[1]

IT'S UP TO YOU

The question still remains: Should you use MSG. when you cook? That is a decision for each cook and chef to make. From a cook's perspective, there are many ways to maximize flavors without adding MSG. The first, simple step is to use ingredients that are naturally high in free glutamates, such as mushrooms, ripe fruits, cured meat, seafood, and fermented sauces.

I have included some Web sites where you can get more information (pg. 363). Just like any other ingredient, I like to understand what it is, where it's from, and how best to use it. Many prepared condiments contain MSG, as do most premade broths (if you want to avoid MSG, buy low-sodium broth, which usually doesn't have any). If you choose to use MSG, just as with any other ingredient, do so in moderation.

[1]Maeder, Thomas 2001. "A Clean Bill of Health." www.redherring.com

Shrimp Pastes

There are numerous regional variations of shrimp paste, all made essentially the same way. Small shrimp are pounded or ground, combined with salt, and then fermented. The Vietnamese version is the runniest, the Thai variety is a bit pastier, and the Malaysian type is so dry that it forms a sliceable block. The different varieties of shrimp from each area and the varying moisture contents of the pastes give each of them a unique flavor. They really should not be used interchangeably if avoidable.

The Thai version, called *gkapi,* is a pungent, thick, dark paste with a slightly pink tint that's almost always included in Thai curry pastes. Wrap a 1/4-inch-thick amount of it in wild pepper leaves, banana leaves, or aluminum foil, and then toast it over an open flame before using it (pg. 111).

Vietnamese shrimp paste, known as *mắm ruốc* or *mắm tôm,* is essentially the same purplish paste as Southern Chinese fine shrimp paste. It is so important in Vietnamese culture that when looking for an article of clothing, one might ask for *mắm ruốc* color, since its purple hue is favored by ladies across Vietnam. *Mắm ruốc* is used in the central and southern parts of Vietnam and is made from very small shrimp, while *mắm tôm* is a more northern style made from larger shrimp.

Malaysian/Singaporean *belacan* is an almost crumbly shrimp paste. It is so pungent that it should be wrapped in multiple layers of plastic to prevent everything in your refrigerator from taking on its smell. Malaysians also toast the *belacan* over a medium fire [recipe pg. 284/tech. pg 111] for a couple of minutes before using it; I usually sandwich a spoonful between two layers of foil, push down to flatten it, and put it directly on a low flame for ten to twenty seconds on each side.

Shrimp Pastes

Vietnamese   Thai   Malaysian

Thai Shrimp Paste

Other Soy-based Sauces

BROWN BEAN SAUCE—aka ground bean sauce—This is the mash that is left over after producing soy sauce. Called *tau cheong* in Chinese, it is widely used in Malaysia and Singapore, where its deep brown, rich and salty ground bean essences add unparalleled depth to stews and stir-fries such as the Malaysian *Chap Chae* (pg. 346). Thai: *dtao jee-ao*; Vietnamese: *tương bột*

HOISIN—This sauce's name, erroneously translated literally as "sea freshness sauce," is misleading. It's not often used with fish or seafood, and it contains no fish or seafood. What it does contain is soybean paste, sesame, spices, garlic, sugar, sweet potato starch, cornstarch, and wheat flour. This dark brown sweet-and-salty Chinese condiment is an essential element in Asian preparations of roasted meats. It's part of the classic Chinese dish, "Peking Duck." In recent years it has also become a staple sauce served with *phở*, the spiced beef broth noodle soup of Northern Vietnam (pg. 218). Vietnamese: *tương đen*

YELLOW BEAN SAUCE—This is a Vietnamese sauce, produced in a way similar to soy sauce. Traditional versions of peanut sauce and other dipping sauces for the beloved Vietnamese salad roll were made from yellow bean sauce, but it is now commonly replaced by the much darker and sweeter hoisin sauce. Thai: *dtao jee-ao kao*, Vietnamese: *tương bần*

HOW LEE KUM KEE SOY SAUCE IS MADE

The three main types of soy sauce used in Southeast Asia are *light soy, dark soy,* and *thick soy.* All are produced using the same basic technique, with only slight variations. The cleaned, dried soybeans are soaked to soften and rehydrate them. These soaked beans are then cooked and cooled.

The next stage is where the alchemy begins. A revered strain of mold, *aspergillus orzyae*, is added. The mold has been cultivated on sterilized wheat bran, which remains with the mold as it is mixed with wheat flour and then used to coat the soybeans. The coated soybeans, which become white in appearance, are transferred into large troughs in a climate-controlled room. The temperature, humidity and airflow are all precisely managed to maximize the mold's growth.

An enzymatic fermentation process begins, and the complex *umami* (sidebar pg. 50.) flavors begin to develop. After two days the soybeans are deep green-brown and ready to be fermented. They are ground, combined with saltwater, and placed in fermentation vats. The breakdown of proteins into deep brown soy sauce takes three to six months. During this time the contents of the vat are active; they're bubbling, propagating yeasts, producing alcohol, and developing color (a function of the Maillard Reaction).

Once the soy sauce has been drained off, the soybean mash left behind (by itself known as "brown ground bean sauce") is utilized in the making of various other sauces (such as *hoisin sauce*). Alternately, saltwater is sometimes added to this mash, and the mixture is fermented again for a less-costly soy sauce.

The fermented soy sauce is moved to sedimentation tanks to remove excess particles, then strained and heat-pasteurized to kill the live culture. This heat process ensures that the sauce does not continue to ferment and change in flavor. The sauce is filtered again to remove any residual sediment, and then it's transferred into the final packaging.

southeastasianflavors.com Go to...

OYSTER SAUCE

One sauce that is now fundamental to meat marinades, vegetable stir-fries, bubbling clay pot chicken dishes, and verdant plates of Chinese broccoli is oyster-flavored sauce. Invented little more than a century ago, it has become inextricably linked with the cuisines of Southeast Asia. Vietnamese: *dầu hào*; Malay: *Sos tiram*

It Began in a Restaurant

In 1888 Mr. Kum Sheung Lee, a restaurateur in the coastal village of Nanshui in southern China, was preparing oyster soup. At the end of the night he left, forgetting to tend to the soup. The next morning he returned to an aromatic kitchen to find a pot with a thick dark sauce at the bottom. This mistake was the inspiration for the Lee family to become the pioneers of all modern-day oyster-flavored sauce.

In 1902 Lee's company, Lee Kum Kee, moved production to the island of Macau so that it could be close to the source of the sauce's integral ingredient—fresh oysters. On a recent trip to Hong Kong, I discovered that the sauce is made the same way today as it was over a hundred years ago. In the beginning, customers would bring their own bottles to be filled. The popularity of this unique seasoning continued to grow. As the Chinese emigrated, they could not do without this essential ingredient in their kitchens, so export was inevitable. The first foreign market was San Francisco's grand Chinatown. By 1932 transport of raw materials had become efficient enough to allow Lee Kum Kee to move its headquarters to Hong Kong, where it remains today.

How It's Made

Each batch begins by simmering freshly shucked oysters down to a thick purée, which is strained to create a consistent-flavored oyster extract. Lee Kum Kee's oyster-flavored sauce is made by simmering a mixture of oyster extract, sugar, water, modified cornstarch, wheat flour, and caramel color. Since the best oysters are so important to creating a high-quality sauce, Lee Kum Kee has aquaculture farms that grow their oysters to their specifications. The Premium Oyster Flavored Sauce has the highest percentage of oyster extract. There are also excellent, less-costly alternatives with less extract. For vegetarian cooks seeking the intense umami essence of oyster sauce without actual seafood, the company has developed a vegetarian oyster-flavored sauce which uses shiitake mushrooms in place of oysters, yielding a deeply flavorful, savory sauce.

Infinitely Versatile

In marinades, sauces, soups, vegetable stir-fries, dips, and even dressings, oyster sauce is a versatile ingredient. It's now used extensively across Southeast Asia in Thailand, Vietnam, Malaysia, and Singapore. The sauce can be used right out of the bottle. If you have ever been at a *dim sum* lunch and ordered *gai lan* (Chinese broccoli), you know that it's typically piled high on the plate like a brilliant green mountain and then drizzled with pure oyster sauce. Malaysian chefs anoint stir-fried lettuce with spoonfuls of the sauce. The salty, slightly sweet, glistening sauce is a perfect *yang* to the crisp *yin* of steamed greens.

Photo Courtesy of Lee Kum Kee

Oyster sauce imparts a deep, savory flavor when marinating meat and seafood, and it also tenderizes. The sugar and salt in the sauce act as a quick "cure," while the cornstarch helps lock in moisture in the intensity of the wok. When these items are grilled, the marinade caramelizes to create intense new flavors.

I considered oyster-flavored sauce my secret weapon (not anymore) for ground meat mixtures—dumpling fillings, pâté forcemeats, and even American-style hamburgers and meat loaf. All gain layers of complexity when oyster-flavored sauce is added. Moderation is the key with this application, as the sauce should be used to increase the umami taste, not create "oyster-flavored burgers."

It fascinates me how an ingredient with just over one hundred years of history can become such an integral part of a cuisine that has evolved over thousands of years. Incorporating oyster sauce into your cooking can add a depth of flavor, a savory aroma, and a rich brown color. Try out these two recipes: Vietnamese grilled pork with cool noodles (pg. 256), and Thai stir-fried pork with basil and oyster sauce (pg. 176).

Photo Courtesy of Lee Kum Kee

Photo Courtesy of Lee Kum Kee

Chili Pastes and Sauces

Although Americans have become accustomed to using fresh and dried chilies in Mexican cuisine and other Latino cooking styles, the new kids on the spicy block are exotic, complex Asian chili pastes essential to Chinese, Thai, Vietnamese, Malaysian, and Singaporean cooking. There is no single national chili paste, yet in each culture one type of chili paste has taken center stage. Some are made from dried chilies, others from fresh chilies—all use sun-ripened red chilies. Consistencies vary from chunky purées (such as Indonesian *sambal oelek*; Vietnmese *ớt tỏi băm*) to smooth purées (like *Sriracha* chili paste; Vietnmese *tửởng ớt/đỏ*). As ingredients, condiments, or dips, these fiery pastes are essential elements in creating authentic Asian foods. Let's take a look at the most popular chili pastes of Asia.

SAMBALS—There are many styles of coarse chili paste called *sambal*. Probably originating in Indonesia, it has become a prominent condiment in Malaysian and Singaporean cuisines. Sambal is a broad term that includes many chili-based condiments. The most common ingredients are chilies, garlic, shallots, and sugar. Many also contain shrimp paste, salt, and tamarind. The Indonesian name for pestle is *ulek ulek*. This is why one of the leading brands coined the name *Sambal Ulek*. *Sambal belacan* (pg. 284) in Malaysia and Singapore also has shrimp paste (*belacan*) added; it is served as a condiment to soups and noodle dishes such as Hokkien mee (pg. 338).

SRIRACHA CHILI SAUCE (pg. 133)—This Thai chili sauce was traditionally used as a table condiment, but it has become one of the most used sauces in fusion foods. It's also been adopted by Vietnam and other Southeast Asian cultures. Originating in the Southern seaport village of Sriracha, Thailand, just north of Pattaya, it's made from sun-ripened red chilies, which are flavored with garlic, sugar, and salt. Some versions also contain fish sauce (*nahm pla*). Americans have readily incorporated this new-style chili "ketchup" into daily life, and most professional kitchens have at least one bottle at the ready. Nontraditional uses include adding a spoonful to an equal amount of mayonnaise for a spicy sandwich spread; squeezing it right out of the bottle for a spicy hot dog; or dipping fries in this instead of ketchup. (Too spicy for you? Mix with an equal part of ketchup to tame the flame.)

NAHM PRIK POW (THAI ROASTED CHILE IN SOYA BEAN OIL OR ROASTED RED CHILI PASTE) (pg. 132)—Also referred to as "chili jam," palm sugar gives this moderately spicy paste a sweet taste with a cloying quality. Garlic, shallots, dried shrimp, chilies, and galangal (a ginger-like rhizome, see (pg. 34) are each independently fried or grilled and then combined with oil, shrimp paste, palm sugar, and tamarind pulp and simmered until a thick jam is produced. All that preparation leads to a harmonious chili paste often used as the base to Thai hot-and-sour soups. Stir into a cool noodle salad for a roasted spicy sensation.

VIETNAMESE CHILI-GARLIC SAUCE (pg. 199)—It can be seen on many Vietnamese restaurants' tables. It's a blend of fresh chilies, garlic, and vinegar combined and coarsely puréed (or, in Vietnam, pounded in a mortar). It's the perfect cure for bland soup, which is one of the many dishes it's stirred into on Vietnamese tables. Vietnamese: *ớt tỏi băm*

Left to right: Sriracha Chili Sauce, Sambal, Roasted Chili Sauce, Thai Sweet Chili Sauce, Vietnamese Chili-Garlic Sauce

Sweet and Sour Flavorings

ROCK SUGAR—These jewel-like, transparent, jumbo sugar crystals are used for sweet dessert soups as well as simmered meat dishes. In sauces they are thought to impart a certain shine, and their flavor, less processed-tasting than granulated sugar, is more rounded. Rock sugar varies in shape and color, from uniform, perfectly clear gems to uneven, amorphous amber crystals. I prefer the latter, which have more flavor. Thai: *nahm than gloo-ut*; Malay: *gula batu*; Vietnamese: *dường phèn*

TAMARIND (*Tamrindus indica*)—Widely known as "asam," which translates as "sour," tamarind has the unusual propensity to taste tart without being very acidic. It also has distinctly sweet undertones. Used extensively in Southeast Asia for soups, noodles, sauces, and even as a hair tonic, it can also be found in South American candies and drinks. It grows as a tree pod with a thin, brittle shell. Fresh pods and the paste made from them should be hydrated (reconstituted in water) before use. If tamarind is unavailable, substitute other sour ingredients such as lime juice, lemon juice, or vinegar. The flavor will be different but acceptable. Avoid buying the processed liquid forms of tamarind—their flavor is lackluster. The paste is usually labeled as seedless. This is a half-truth, since the seeds are not in the paste, but the fibrous seed pods are, making it necessary to process them to attain a smooth pulp (pg. 109). The recipes in this book call for measurements of processed pulp. Thai: *makahm*; Malay: *asam*; Vietnamese: *me*

Rock Sugar

Tamarind

Tamarind Paste

Palm Sugar

Although all coconut sugar is a type of palm sugar (coconut is a palm tree), not all palm sugar is coconut sugar. Most of the prized Southeast Asian palm sugar is crafted from the Asian Palmyra palm tree, *Borassus flabellifer*, whereas coconut sugar is from the *Cocos nucifera*, or coconut tree. Palm sugar is used in Thailand, Malaysia, and Singapore. It's used to a much lesser extent in Vietnam. Although coconut and palm sugars are made the same way and are used interchangeably by most cooks, Thai dessert specialists prefer coconut sugar for its more subtle taste.

Sap is extracted by cutting the flower buds at the top of the tree. Containers are strapped on and left to collect the sap. Shaved wood of the *Shorea* genus is left in the sap buckets to prevent souring. The day's sap is combined with cane sugar of varying amounts—less cane sugar is considered better quality—and then the mixture is boiled down in large woks until it becomes an aromatic syrup. After cooling, it is either poured into jars to solidify (the Thai way—this version usually has a slightly fermented flavor), or it's stirred vigorously until it crystallizes and is then spooned into large disk shapes (typical in Thailand and Vietnam). In Malaysia the sap is boiled at higher temperatures until it's deep brown. It's then poured into bamboo molds to make their signature cylindrical shape. If you're ever fortunate enough to end up in a palm sugar–producing area, seek out a local dessert that's sure to be offered: reduced sap served over shaved ice.

BUYING PALM SUGAR: Essentially there is light brown and dark brown palm sugar. The light brown palm sugar made and used in Thai and Vietnamese cooking is sold in two forms: in a jar (how the coconut palm sugar is sold) or small discs as seen in the photo here. The dark brown palm sugar used in Malaysia and Singapore is much darker due to the cooking process and is then formed into cylindrical pieces. Traditionally it is poured into cut lengths of bamboo as molds while the sugar crystallizes and firms. Most of the imported dark brown palm sugar in the states is from Indonesia.

WORKING WITH PALM SUGAR:

Grating the dark cylinders and light brown disks is the most accurate way to measure an amount for recipes. To use the sugar sold in a plastic tub, open it and scoop off the waxy paraffin layer sometimes present as a preservative technique. Soften it in the microwave in twenty-second intervals until it's pliable. The hard disks are best tackled by grating them on a sturdy box grater. The palm sugar can then be measured accurately by gently packing it into a measuring cup.

Thai: *nahm dtahn bpeep/buk* (coconut sugar), *nahm dtahn mapra* (palm sugar); Vietnamese: *dường thể thốt-nốt*; Malay: *gula malacca*; Indonesian: *gula jawa*

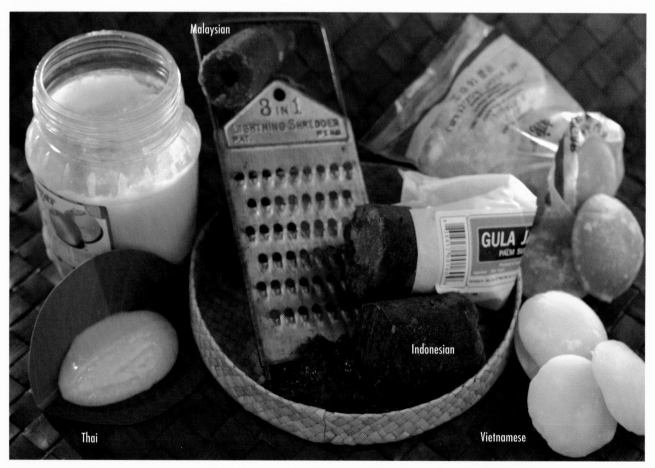

Step 1

Step 3

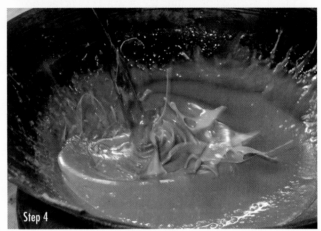

Step 4

Step 2

Step 5

Coconut *(Cocos nucifera)*

Like buffalo to the Native Americans, no part of the coconut palm goes to waste in Southeast Asia. The tree yields everything—sap for sugar, sweet potable water for refreshing drinks, rich milk for curries, fronds that are woven into rice packets and thatched roofs, coconut husks for fire fuel (or cheesy touristy souvenirs), and even beautiful wood for utensils. Of course, the coconut meat has many culinary uses of its own.

As the coconut matures on the tree, the water inside diminishes and the white flesh firms. This white meat is used for coconut milk or is shredded for culinary uses. It's what most Westerners would associate with sweetened coconut for candy or macaroon cookies. In Southeast Asia the meat is grated and toasted as part of the sauce for Malaysian *beef rendang curry* (pg. 334) or used fresh to encase the Nyonya *ondeh ondeh* (molten palm sugar pandan balls) (pg. 350). Green, immature coconuts are sold chilled as refreshing drinks across Southeast Asia. The Vietnamese have developed recipes where pork belly and hard-boiled eggs (pg. 246) are simmered in the juice. They also use chunks of green coconut in their sweet snack, *Chè* (pg. 195). Vietnamese: *dừa*; Malay: *kelapa*

COCONUT MILK—Coconut milk has become an iconic ingredient of cooking in Thailand, Malaysia, Singapore, and, to a lesser extent, Vietnam. It is a rich and creamy cooking liquid that forms the base for many sauces, soups, and stews. Coconut milk is made by combining water (not milk as many books suggest) with grated coconut meat. The mixture is squeezed through mesh to yield the creamy milk. It's pleasingly unctuous texture and sweet undertones can be decadent (in a good way) in desserts, such as when it's used as a topping for Thai Sticky Rice with Mangos *mamuang khao Nieo* (pg. 180). Thai: *nam gla ti*; Malay: *santan*; Vietnamese: *nước cốt dừa*

FRESH COCONUT MILK—(please see page 114 for detailed preparation technique). There are two distinct types of coconut milk: thick and thin. They come from different stages of the same process, just as extra-virgin and regular olive oil come from different pressings of the same olives. Thick coconut milk is prepared by combining shredded coconut with warm water, massaging or blending the mixture, and then squeezing it to expel thick coconut milk. This process is repeated with new water to produce a second flush, which is the thin coconut milk. Generally, thin coconut milk is used for simmering, and the thicker, richer coconut milk is added at the end of the cooking process. Again, the similarities to olive oil are significant: Italians generally cook with second-pressing olive oil and finish dishes with extra-virgin, first-pressing oil. There are exceptions. Thai cooks use thick coconut milk to start some of their curries. They boil it until the coconut milk separates ("breaks," in cook's jargon) to yield pure coconut oil. Curry paste is roasted in this oil, and thin coconut milk is added later to stew the curry ingredients. Additional thick coconut milk may be added at the end to reinforce the rich coconut flavor.

Vietnamese woman at a market in Huế wacks off the outer shell with a machete.

Bangkok street vendors husk, fire-roast, and ice coconuts for sale to passersby. They puncture a hole with an ice pick, insert a straw, and hand them to buyers. In the tropical heat of the city, it's one of life's great pleasures to savor this icy-cold, smoky, lightly sweet coconut water. If you've indulged in this treat, don't neglect to hand the coconut back to the seller, who will swiftly crack it open with a large knife and fashion a spoon for you with a piece of the shell so you can devour the roasted young coconut meat.

CANNED COCONUT MILK—When not in Southeast Asia, I usually use canned coconut milk. I'm very selective about the brands I use, and I use it in ways that give results that are as close to fresh as possible. Large manufacturers sell very different versions under the same brand name. Characteristics vary widely. I recommend only three brands that consistently have the best overall flavor: Chaokoh, Mae Ploy, and 1AF (this newcomer to the market has proven itself worthy of inclusion in my recipes).

Heat thick coconut milk over medium heat, stirring often. The water will evaporate slowly. A roasted flavor will develop from the browning of the milk solids at the bottom of the pan. Continue cooking until the coconut fat begins to separate from the creamy milk. It is this semibroken mixture that is used to roast the curry paste when making authentic Thai curry dishes. Only frying in this medium will bring out the full aromatic quality of the spice paste. This critical stage is what gives some Thai curries puddles of fat in the sauce (in this case, a desirable trait). Look to the Thai chapter for more on coconut milk usage in Thai curries (pg. 158).

Malaysian men mechanically shred coconut to be sold at the daily market.

Grated for Milk

Grated for Toasting

Shredded for Desserts

Canned Coconut Milk

Nuts

Some nuts and seeds are more perishable than others, but all are best stored in airtight containers in a consistently cool, dark place. In humid, hot locales, refrigerate them.

PEANUTS (*Arachis hypogaea*)—The diminutive peanuts used in Southeast Asia are sometimes labeled "red peanuts" or "Spanish peanuts." Yes, the larger variety are also used, especially in Chinese cooking, but this smaller variety, usually sold with the papery skin still on, has a sweeter, drier meat. Please see page 109 for a full description of the proper technique for roasting peanuts for recipes in this book. Thai: *tua li song*; Malay: *kacang tanah*; Vietnamese: *lạc (Northern)/đậu phộng (Southern)*

CANDLENUTS (*Aleurites moluccana*)—Native to Malaysia, this hard, oily nut is slightly bitter. It's used primarily as a thickening agent in Malaysian dishes. The most common substitution for this hard-to-find item is macadamia nuts. I find that peeled almonds also work well. Unlike macadamia nuts, however, raw candlenuts are slightly toxic to humans, causing digestive distress. They must be cooked before being eaten. They're usually cooked into the spice paste fried at the beginning stages of soups and curries. Their peculiar name originates from their oil being highly flammable (it was once used as candle oil). Over the years in my cooking classes I have illustrated this point by holding a flame to one end for about twenty seconds. Once removed, the nut continues to burn with a small flame all by itself. Malay: *buah keras*

Noodles

In the next few pages, you will find a summary of the most popular noodles found in Thailand, Vietnam, Malaysia, and Singapore. There are many other regional varieties, even some made specifically for one particular dish, but these noodles make up the majority of the dishes.

Wheat Noodles

FRESH WHEAT NOODLES—In the Chinese-speaking world, fresh wheat noodles are referred to as *mein*. Most are made by combining wheat flour, salt, water, and sometimes egg and then kneading the mixture into a smooth dough. The dough is rolled into sheets and then cut, just as Italian pasta is. These noodles are sometimes (though less often) extruded through dies into strands of various shapes and sizes. Often, coloring is added to get that distinctive yellow color.

Wheat noodles are available in mainstream markets and freeze fairly well before they're cooked.

Retailers sell fresh noodles in small packages, usually about a pound. It is natural for the noodles to have a white powder on them. This is usually cornstarch, which is dusted onto them to prevent sticking. What is *not* natural is discoloration, usually in the form of graying or small dark-gray dots the size of vanilla bean specks. Do not buy or use noodles with these. They are past their prime.

EGG NOODLES—Although egg noodles may go by numerous names ("Cantonese noodles," "dan mien," Chinese egg noodles," "wheat noodles," and "lo mein" to name a few), most are made the same way as Italian pasta is made. Wheat flour, eggs, water, and salt are combined and kneaded into a dough, rolled out by hand (or now more commonly by machines), and then the dough is cut or extruded into noodles. Asian egg noodles range from 1/16 inch to 1/4 inch thick. Most fresh egg noodles are refrigerated; they can also be frozen. Although it's not so common in Asia to use dried egg noodles, having them on hand can help a chef out in a pinch.

It's not unusual to see an Italian-style pasta machine strapped to the side of a street vendor's cart in Malaysia. He uses it for *wonton mee*, a Chinese dish of super-thin egg noodles, which are boiled quickly; tossed with soy sauces, cooked greens, and white pepper; and topped with slivers of roast pork. These soy-slathered noodles are always served with a bowl of light chicken broth garnished with boiled, pork-filled wontons. Slurp some noodles and then wash them down with the broth. Occasionally, pluck some of the pickled green chili slices from the side dish and crunch them with the noodles.

THAI BA MII—These are egg noodles that vary from about 1/8 to 1/16 inch in diameter. *Ba mii* are one of the few wheat-based noodles used in Thailand, where rice noodles are much more common.

THAI MEDIUM FLAT NOODLES—Rolled thinner than *ba mii,* these are about 1/8 inch thick and cut 1/4 inch wide. These noodles are used for dishes like Thai *Kao Soi* (pg. 178).

HAND-PULLED NOODLES, a specialty of northern China, deserve mention, especially if you have seen a chef begin with a large mass of dough and begin to pull, twist, and fold it into noodles. A skilled pair of hands can yield fine strands within minutes. This craft is best left to the experts of noodle making. The rest of us can buy high-quality noodles (or, if really inspired, make some noodles with a rolling pin and knife or pasta machine). I have not included a section for dried wheat noodles, as they're rarely used in Southeast Asian cooking. Instant noodles, however, have become as common there as they have on college campuses across the U.S.

VIETNAMESE MI—These are usually 1/6 or 1/8 inch in diameter, with one significant exception. The *cao lầu* noodles of Hội An in Central Vietnam are not only 1/8 inch thick and 1/4 inch wide, but they also have a slightly yellow color, owing to the addition of ash to the dough that causes a desired chemical reaction.

WHEAT NOODLES OF MALAYSIA AND SINGAPORE (*Mee*)—Egg noodles are more prevalent in these two countries than in Thailand and Vietnam, probably due to the larger percentage of Chinese in their population.

FINE NOODLES are about 1/16 inch (2 mm) in diameter. When raw, these yellow egg noodles have a very firm bite. They are first boiled for less than a minute, cooled in water, and then boiled again to reheat and improve their texture before being added to the dish.

MEDIUM NOODLES are about 1/8 inch (3 to 4 mm) in diameter when raw. They are the most all-purpose noodle, and resemble spaghetti. They're sometimes known as *lo mein.* These noodles are often boiled ahead of time, rinsed, and drained for later use.

LARGE NOODLES are sometimes called *Fujian mien* (Malaysia). They're about 1/4 inch (5 to 6 mm) in diameter when raw. Thick and resilient, these can take upwards of 10 minutes of boiling to cook. Often, they are parboiled and then cooked once again in a rich soy gravy, as in *Malaysian Hokkien mee,* Stir-fried Noodles in Thick Soy Gravy & Crispy Pork (pg. 338).

Fresh Rice Noodles

Since rice is so abundant in Asia, it was inevitable that a variety of noodles would evolve using rice as a base. Fresh rice noodles are prepared from a thin batter rather than a dough. The noodles are then formed by either steaming or boiling the batter.

Traditionally, the rice can be simply whole, long grain rice that is soaked in water until soft and then ground until a fine paste is made. Alternatively pre-milled rice flour is becoming a more popular choice. The flour is combined with water to reach the desired thickness. Some add tapioca starch or wheat starch to add elasticity.

For steam-formed noodles (steaming method) made in sheets, *chow fun* in Cantonese, the watery batter is ladled onto a piece of cloth, over a cauldron of boiling water, and steamed to create sheets. The sheets are dried and cut into noodle shapes. These supple rice noodle sheets, left whole, are used to wrap ground pork, minced wood-ear mushrooms, and diced shrimp in the Vietnamese dish *bánh cuốn* (pg. 212). The tender roll is topped with mint leaves, crisp-fried shallots, and a drizzle of *nước chấm* (the quintessential local dip of fish sauce, garlic, sugar, water, lime juice, and shredded carrots (pg. 198).

For boil-formed noodles, (extrusion method), the batter is made thick enough to be extruded (forced through a die). Noodles are often extruded directly into boiling water. After such cooking, they are rinsed until cool and made into decorative bundles ready to be incorporated into a bowl of steaming broth.

Fresh rice noodles are referred to as *Kway Teow* in Malaysia and Singapore. The most common dish in these countries is *Char Kway Teow* (pg. 336), in which the scorching-hot wok is used to fry bean sprouts, scallions, coarsely chopped garlic, and noodles until they begin to brown and get a bit chewy. They are tossed to one side of the wok and the chef quickly drizzles a thin stream of oil to coat the exposed wok. Next, an egg is broken into the wok and fried to be tossed together with the browned noodles. It is then scooped onto a plate and served with a chile *sambal*.

BUYING FRESH RICE NOODLES: In Southeast Asia, fresh rice noodles are made by small producers all over the region and are delivered daily. This is not so here in the U.S. Fresh rice noodles have a shelf life of only a few days. Large Asian stores have them delivered fresh each morning. Place your hand on the package—they may be warm (I always smile when this is the case) or at least soft with a resiliency that will give when poked and bounce right back. That's a sign they've never been chilled. When stored in the refrigerator, they become hard. Look for packages that show the noodles clearly, without any grainy appearance or milky liquid (both signs of spoilage). When I get them home, I always open the package, take a whiff, and taste a small piece to make sure they are not sour. Rice noodles are sold in 12 oz. to 2 lb. packages. Sometimes they are folded into large sheets; others are cut into varying width noodles, ranging from 1/4 inch to 3/4 inch wide. Remember, you can always make your own with the recipe on page 117.

Fresh Rice Noodles

MALAYSIA/SINGAPORE

Kway Teow—Made by the steaming method and cut into 1/2-inch-wide strips (though sometimes cut more narrowly), Kway Teow is used for stir-frying or in broth-based noodle bowls. Used in this book on page 336. *Char Kway Teow,* Stir-fried Rice Noodles with Shrimp and Chinese Sausage . I've always wondered why Malaysia primarily uses fresh *kway teow* (wide rice noodles) but dried *bee hoon* (rice vermicelli). Thailand does the opposite.

Hor Fun—This wide, flat rice noodle is made by the steaming method and cut into 1/4-inch-wide strips. The central Malaysian town of Ipoh is famous for making these super-supple rice noodles paired with a chicken broth, which I always devour in minutes.

Laksa—aka rat tail or silver pin—Round noodles created by the extrusion technique. *Laksa* noodles are so called since they are made for Penang-style Laksa Soup. Some makers add tapioca starch to the recipe, giving them a more translucent appearance and resilient bite.

Chee Chow Fun—A specific dish as well as a classification of noodle. The supple rice noodle rolls are made to order, found in the U.S. in dim sum restaurants. Bits of dried shrimp, scallions, or roasted pork are often found within the tender sheets of noodles that are rolled up and doused with a slightly sweet-and-salty soy sauce.

VIETNAM

Bún—Made by the extrusion method into round threads about 1/8 inch in diameter, these are sold fresh and also dried (as "rice vermicelli"). These are the most common noodles in the Vietnamese kitchen, used for salad rolls, soup noodles, and usually for *Bún Thịt Nướng*—Vietnamese Grilled Pork on Cool Noodles (pg. 256).

Bánh Hỏi—These are made by the extrusion method into very fine threads about 1/16 inch in diameter. They are uniquely packaged in almost sheets of threads; small swatches are to eat items like *Chạo Tôm*, grilled shrimp paste on sugar cane (pg. 242), or other grilled items like pork and beef. Look for them packed on trays instead of in plastic pouches like most noodles.

Bánh Phở Tươi—Made by the steaming method into 1/8- to 1/2-inch-wide strips, they are also sold dried. They look like Italian fettuccine. These are most often used for the famous Vietnamese soup *Phở Bò,* beef noodle soup (pg. 218).

THAILAND

Sen Kuaytiaw—Made by the steaming method and cut into 3/4-inch-wide strips. Primarily used in broth-style noodle bowls.

Sen Lek—Made by the steaming method and cut into 1/4-inch-wide strips. Primarily used in broth-style noodle bowls.

Khanom Jin—Round noodles the diameter of spaghetti, these soft noodles are made from a rice that is sometimes slightly fermented, giving them a unique flavor that isn't sour, just a bit tangy. Since they are rare, not available fresh outside of Thailand, other similarly shaped and textured fresh rice noodles, like bún from Vietnam, are the best substitutes.

Dried Rice Noodles

Dried rice noodles are usually made with the extrusion method, boiled, or steamed in large commercial pressure steamers. They're made using a similar method to fresh noodles, but are taken to a second stage of drying. Drying not only provides a longer shelf life, but also alters the texture and flavor of the noodles. In Southeast Asia, texture is often viewed as the most important characteristic of a food, and so noodle textures vary widely to create specific effects. Drying is one method of creating different texture in noodles.

DRIED THIN RICE NOODLES— Often called *rice sticks*, *mee hoon*, or, when ultra-thin in Vietnam, *vermicelli* or *bánh hỏi*. Wider dried rice noodles with a 1/4-inch width are easily recognized in the famous *Pad Thai* (pg. 172), a dish of stir-fried noodles with bean sprouts and peanuts. They're also the most widely used noodle for the national dish of Vietnam, *Phở Bò* (pronounced "fuh") (pg. 218). Vietnamese noodle soup often consumed for breakfast, originated in Northern Vietnam. It begins with a rich beef broth, scented with cinnamon, star anise, charred ginger, and onions. This aromatic broth is poured over cooked rice noodles, thinly sliced onions, and beef.

RICE VERMICELLI—Very fine "angel hair" rice noodles that are used for salads, salad rolls, soups, and stir-fries. When deep-fried, they transform into a light, brilliant white nest of crunchy noodles and are used as an edible garnish. Thailand—*sen mii*; Vietnam—*bún*; Malaysia/Singapore—*mee hoon*

FLAT RICE NOODLES—These dried rice noodles are sometimes called "rice ribbons." They vary in size from 1/8- to 1/2-inch-wide flat strips. Used in soups and stir-fries, they are the iconic noodle of the classic Thai dish *Pad Thai* (pg. 172) and are the dried noodle of choice to replace the fresh *banh pho tuoi* in the classic Vietnamese soup *Phở Bò*, beef noodle soup (pg. 218). Thailand—*sen kuaytiaw*, Vietnam—*bánh phở*, Malaysia/Singapore—*kway teow*

BEAN THREAD NOODLES— Referred to by many names, such as *mung bean noodles*, *cellophane noodles*, or *glass noodles*, these filaments are made from the starch of ground mung beans. They are used in Thai Cellophane Noodle Salad, *Yum Woon Sen* (pg. 146), incorporated into spring roll fillings, or as a textural treat in soups. Buy them packed in small bundles, as they are much easier to manage. Large packs need to be cut with scissors, and inevitably small pieces fly around the kitchen. They are cooked by pouring boiling water over them, completely covering, and letting them soak for five to eight minutes until they are elastic and transparent. Drain and rinse them under cool water before serving. In contemporary kitchens they are often deep-fried while still dry into light, brilliant, white nests of crunchy noodles for an edible garnish. Thailand: *woon sen*; Vietnam: *miến*; Malaysia and Singapore: *tung fen*

Rice Vermicelli

Flat Rice Noodles

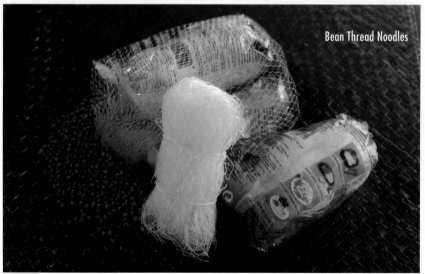

Bean Thread Noodles

Dough-Based Spring Roll

Spring Roll Wrappers

The Chinese began the tradition of making spring rolls during the Chinese New Year celebration. They were rolled into bar shapes resembling gold bars that represented prosperity. Since the New Year usually happens around spring, they became known as "spring rolls."

In Southeast Asia, there are three types of spring roll wrappers: homemade, craftsman-made, and factory-made.

POH PIAH (HOMEMADE)—In Malaysia and Singapore, these fresh spring roll wrappers are made a few at a time from a batter of wheat flour, eggs, water, oil, and salt. They're similar to French crêpes. See the recipe on page 294 for a detailed description of the preparation of these. I hope you will be inspired to prepare the whole recipe, filling and all.

DOUGH-BASED SPRING ROLL (CRAFTSMAN-MADE)—The Chinese perfected this awe-inspiring technique. A very sticky, soft wheat dough is held in the hand, rubbed onto a hot griddle in a circular pattern, and then quickly snapped back off, leaving only a very thin film on the griddle. Within seconds the dough is peeled off with a spatula, and a super-thin spring roll wrapper is ready. These fresh versions can be eaten as they are or rolled up around a filling and deep-fried into a multilayer crispy spring roll.

BATTER-BASED SPRING ROLL (FACTORY-MADE)—This is what most of us know as spring roll wrappers,

bought in the freezer section of the market. It's a mass-produced product. A thin, wheat-based batter is applied to rotating, heated drums, which cook the batter on contact. The large sheets that roll off the drums are then cut into round- or (higher yielding) square-shaped wrappers, stacked, and vacuum-packed. Some of the better brands include Spring Home from Singapore and Menlo from Hong Kong.

MUNG BEAN STARCH

Called *salim* in Thai, this starch is extracted from the tiny green mung bean and is used to make cellophane or glass noodles. It is also used as a thickening agent and in making sweet steamed cakes and small noodle-like threads for a Malaysian shaved ice treat, *chendol.* Vietnamese: *đậu xanh*

Rice Paper *(Bánh Tráng)*

Rice paper, with its cross-hatched bamboo markings, has become one of the most utilized Vietnamese ingredients in Western kitchens. Cooks and chefs are finding all sorts of creative ways to fill them with nontraditional ingredients.

In Southeast Asia, rice paper is still often made using age-old traditional methods. (Some imported brands still buy these, but factory imitations are quickly filling the shelves.) As they're made in Vietnam, a thin batter is prepared with pulverized whole rice (as described for rice noodles), water and salt. The soaked rice is added to the small hole on top as the entire round stone is rotated. As it moves downward, the rice paste through the stationary stone on the bottom and the top rotating stone and comes out very fine wet paste.

A thin piece of cloth is stretched over the top cauldron of boiling water (the fire is usually fueled by rice husks and peanut shells). As the steam seeps through the cloth, a ladle fashioned from a coconut shell is used to pour some batter on top of the cloth and quickly spread it out into a paper-thin disc. A cover is used to deftly trap in steam, which cooks the thin batter disc into a rice noodle sheet. Makers use a flat bamboo stick to skillfully lift up the sheet and transfer it to a drying mat. The mat is a lattice of bamboo strips that leaves the characteristic pattern on the rice paper sheets as they sun-dry for a day.

These uneven-edged sheets can be used as they are, but for export they are sent to a processing plant, quality checked, and cut to even the edges. They're then repacked into plastic packages that help prevent the brittle sheets from being destroyed in shipping. For details on using these rice paper sheets, see page 206.

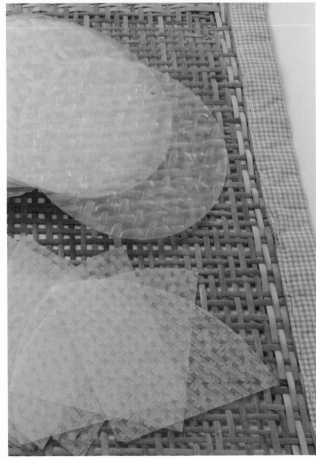

Rice (Oryza sativa)

Rice has earned the title of "staff of life" in Asia. Cultivated there for more than four thousand years, it has provided sustenance for billions. In Southeast Asia rice is not considered a side dish, but often the center of the meal. In Thailand, a popular way to greet people is to ask whether they have eaten rice.

There are more types of rice than can be addressed in this one chapter. Colors span from stark white, light red, dark brown, and deep purple to jet black. Each has its own character of taste and texture. Cooking methods vary and so do the treatments applied after cooking. Sometimes grains are simply soaked and then steamed. The term steamed is sometimes misleading, because most of the time, rice is actually simmered. Sometimes rice is actually set in a dish above a measure of simmering water and truly steamed. Other times, rice is cooked with copious amounts of water until it dissolves into a silky porridge called *congee*. An excellent volume about the myriad types and preparations of rice is *Seductions of Rice* by Jeffrey Alford and Naomi Duguid (Artisan Press 1998).

Although rice cultivation began in Asia, it's now grown all over the world. Some of the best quality rice is grown in the U.S. California leads the charge, now producing some excellent Southeast Asian strains, including long, short, and aromatic varieties such as jasmine and basmati. Once you find a brand you like, stick with it: each brand cooks differently, even if it's the same variety. Here are some of the varieties used in Southeast Asia.

JASMINE RICE—This prized fragrant Thai rice has a naturally occurring floral aroma. This aromatic long grain rice is thought to have been first propagated in Thailand. It has the highest concentration of the aromatic element found in all rice, so as it cooks it releases a sweet scent into the kitchen. It's most often cooked using the *absorption method*, commonly and mistakenly referred to as "steamed rice"—see page 106 for cooking tips and techniques. Thai: *kao hom mali*; Vietnamese: *gạo thơm*

BROKEN RICE—The fractured grains of jasmine rice cracked during processing are considered lower quality in Asia. It is used at less- expensive eateries and mostly kept within the borders of these countries. It happens that certain dishes in Africa have evolved using these cheaper rice "seconds." Vietnamese: *gạo tấm*

LONG GRAIN RICE—This is the most common rice in theChinese kitchen. It is the blank canvas onto which the aromatic dishes of the cuisine are applied. The grains stay somewhat individual, especially after cooling, so it is chosen for fried rice preparation. Thai: *kao san*; Vietnamese: *gạo hột dài*

BASMATI RICE—This extra-long grain white rice, used in Indian cuisine, is not sticky and tends to stay separated into individual grains. Sometimes Indians employ a technique that is literally boiled rice, where rice is cooked in copious amounts of water, like pasta. Unfortunately, this method washes much of the nutritional content from the rice. Vietnamese: *gạo Ấn*

STICKY "GLUTINOUS" RICE—The word "glutinous" is in quotation marks because rice does not contain any gluten. Only wheat contains the two proteins glutenin and gliadin that, when combined and kneaded with moisture, form a network of elastic protein that we call gluten. What this type of rice *does* contain is a high percentage of the starch amylopectin, which yields a sticky and flexible texture when cooked, with a chew that resembles the feel of gluten. Glutinous rice is frequently wrapped in palm- or banana-leaf packets with flavorful garnishes and then steamed or boiled for a long time to produce the beloved sticky rice preparations of Asia. Thai: *kao neaw*; Vietnamese: *gạo nếp*

LONG GRAIN GLUTINOUS RICE—More commonly used than the shorter variety of sticky rice, it's especially popular in northeast Thailand. Long grain glutinous rice is soaked in cool water for up to six hours before being steamed over pots of simmering water, traditionally packed into a conical bamboo steamer. It takes thirty to forty-five minutes to yield the clear, long, chewy rice grains. This rice is usually eaten with hands by grabbing a small amount, kneading it into a small ball or disk, and using it to scoop up other foods. Thai: *pin khao*; Vietnamese: *gạo nếp hột dài*

Broken Rice

Basmati Rice

Short Grain Glutinous Rice

Jasmine Rice

Black Sticky Rice

Long Grain Glutinous Rice

SHORT GRAIN GLUTINOUS RICE—Vietnam uses mostly the shorter variety of sticky rice, but it's prepared the same way as in Thailand, by soaking and then steaming. Very often, it's combined with mung beans and then steamed and eaten with grated coconut, peanuts, and sesame seeds for breakfast. This variety is also used to prepare glutinous rice flour (see above) and Chinese porridge (*congee*). Vietnamese: *gạo nếp hột tròn*

BLACK STICKY RICE—Also called "purple rice" or "black glutinous rice," this is long grained and unhulled. Since the coloring, which resides in the hull, seeps out when cooked, the rice appears black when raw, but is transformed into a beautiful purple color when cooked with coconut milk. As it is rather tough, it is usually soaked before being cooked. When cooked, it attains a wet porridge-like consistency. Try the delicious Malaysian sticky rice with coconut milk on page 348. Thai: *kao neaw dum*; Vietnamese: *gạo nếp than*; Malay: *pulut hitam*

Beans and Legumes

MUNG BEANS (*Vigna radiata* var. *radiata*)—Often called "green beans" (especially in Vietnam), these are sold in two different forms: peeled (and hence yellow) or husk-on (green). These are the same beans used to make bean sprouts. Probably the most common legume used in Southeast Asia, in savory items such as dhal stews, they are also ground and made into dumplings. They are used in the Vietnamese sweet snacks, *che*, and are also dry-roasted to garnish Thai sticky rice with mangos (pg. 180). Thai: *tua keaw*; Vietnamese: *dậu xanh*

URAD DHAL (*Vigna mungo*)—Black skinned with a beige center, these are most commonly used as part of the batter for dosai, appam, or other Indian flatbreads. Buy them already hulled. The soaking and peeling process is tedious. Thai: *tua dum*

SOYBEANS (*Glycine max*)—There are actually five colors of soybeans grown: white, green, brown, red, and black. White and black are the most commonly used in Southeast Asia. White soybeans make up the majority and are used to make soy sauce and other soy-based condiments, tofu, and soy milk. Black soybeans are used in stews such as Malaysian black bean and pork stew. Vietnamese: *dậu nành*

ADZUKI BEANS (*Vigna angularis*)—These small, oval, red beans are boiled and made into paste for dumpling fillings, boiled into sweet soups, or cooked and used in the shaved ice snacks of Malaysia and Singapore. Thai: *tua dang*; Vietnamese: *dậu đỏ*

Soybeans

Mung Beans

Urad Dhal

Adzuki Beans

Soybean Products

All the following soy products begin with dried soybeans, which are blended with water and then strained to yield soymilk. Some soy products are made from raw soymilk, but most also contain a coagulant, such as calcium sulfate (gypsum), to encourage the proteins to bind together. Further processes define the final texture and taste of the end product. Countless products with countless textures can be crafted from soy. These include the familiar bean curd (tofu) in varying firmnesses, dried sheets that are used as spring roll skins or wrappers, chewy snack foods, resilient meat or fish substitutes, and more. Some of the most widely used include the following:

DOFU—Known in the West by its Japanese name, *tofu*, this bean curd is sometimes spelled "tau fu." I discuss dofu into two categories: silken (not as common in Southeast Asia) and curd, because they're used for different purposes. Curd dofu is made when the coagulated soymilk is stirred into curds, and then molded and pressed to remove some of its liquid. Vietnamese: *đậu phụ*

PRESSED DOFU—These extra-firm, small, flat squares of processed dofu are cut into fine strips and then added to soups and stir-fries such as Pad Thai (pg. 172). Some are seasoned, usually with Chinese five-spice and soy. To press curd dofu, transfer the drained dofu to a plate, top with another flat item, and then weigh down with 1 to 2 lbs. (you can use anything: cans, jars, etc.). Within thirty minutes you will have expelled some water. Pressed overnight, dofu could actually reduce its weight by 20 percent.

DOFU POUCHES—Large blocks of curd tofu are deep-fried until excess moisture is forced out, forming deep brown cubes with spongy, slightly chewy interiors that are full of holes. These porous pouches are excellent at absorbing rich soups like Malaysian *Curry Laksa* (pg. 281). While savoring the soup, diners select pillows of dofu, place them on the tongue, and slowly bite down. A rush of spicy soup is released across the palate. (Whew! What a rush!) Another great use for these pouches is to slit their sides and stuff them with fish paste, and then poach them to make Malaysian *young tau foo*. Vietnamese: *đậu phụ bao*

BEAN CURD SHEETS—Dried, it is sold as "dried bean curd sheets" or "tofu skins" and is used as a wrapper for rolls of various types. A higher moisture-content variety is sold in the freezer section. As with cows' milk, when soymilk is heated, a film forms on top. This film can be lifted off and dried to form firm sheets of bean curd. Sold dry, they have a mustard yellow appearance and can be brittle and slightly flexible at the same time. This depends on age and the manufacturer. When brittle, they are soaked in cool water to soften and then used to wrap various fillings before being boiled or deep-fried. They can be added to vegetable dishes such as the Nyonya Mixed Vegetables (pg. 346). They make quite a spectacular spring roll wrapper. Vietnamese: *đậu hũ ky*; Cantonese: *fu chok*

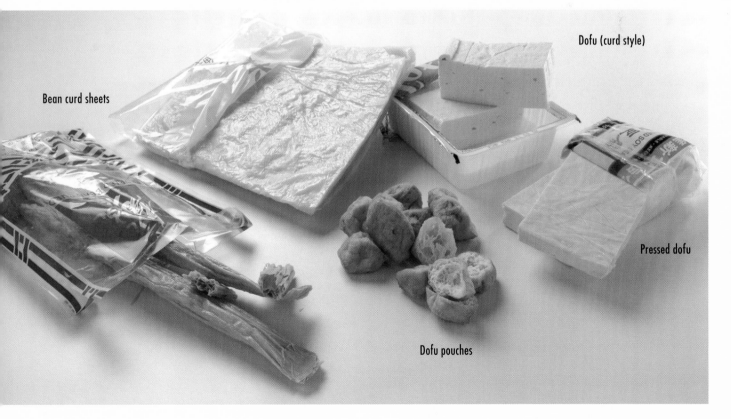

Dofu (curd style)

Bean curd sheets

Pressed dofu

Dofu pouches

Vegetables

BOK CHOY FAMILY—There are many varieties of this vegetable, which is part of the *brassica* (cabbage) family.

BOK CHOY *(Brassica rapa* subsp. *chinensis)*—Crisp, white stems and deep green leaves characterize this celery-shaped vegetable, which is common in the U.S. It is used primarily in ethnic Chinese dishes and is especially popular in Malaysia. Thai: *bok choy*; Vietnamese: *cải trắng*

Bok Choy

BABY BOK CHOY—Also called "Shanghai bok choy," this diminutive vegetable is not really a baby anything, but a smaller, three- to six-inch–long relative of bok choy. A "jade" variety has a beautiful pale green hue, and other varieties have the traditional milky white stems of bok choy. Its leaves are commonly left whole and used as an edible garnish for other dishes, arranged around the perimeter of the platter. Thai: *luuk bok choy*; Vietnamese: *cãi trắng thượng-hải*/or *dàu-loan*

Baby Bok Choy

CHOY SUM *(Brassica rapa* var. *parachinensis)*—This brassica is also called "flowering cabbage" (Yu choy sum). It's used extensively in brothy noodle dishes. Typically, it is blanched in advance, squeezed to remove excess water, cut into 2- to 3-inch lengths, and then added straight to the bowl when assembling the dish. One such dish is Prawn Mee (pg. 304). Thai: *pahk kwang thoong*

Choy Sum

WATER SPINACH *(Ipomoea aquatica)*—Sporting other names like "morning glory," "hollow heart spinach," "ong choy," and "Kangkong," this very popular green grows in shallow water all around Southeast Asia. When consumed raw, it's frequently shaved into fine threads with a razor blade. In this form, it's often included as part of a *table salad* (pg. 27). I feel that the best way to cut it is to deconstruct it into pieces with one inch of stem and a whole leaf. Shrimp paste, garlic, and chilies pair well with the earthy flavor of this vegetable in Malaysian stir-fried water spinach with garlic (pg. 342). Thai: *pahk boong*; Malay: *kangkung*; Vietnamese: *rau muống*

Water Spinach

Water Spinach

Cabbages

GREEN (*Brassica oleracea*)—Common green cabbage is used in some Chinese-based stir-fries such as the Malaysian *Chap Chae* (pg. 346). It's also thinly shaved to garnish *Vietnamese un Bo Hue Soup* (pg. 226). Thai: *ga lum plee*; Malay: *sayur kubris*; Vietnamese: *bắp-cải*

NAPA (*Brassica rapa* subsp. *pekinensis*)—This is also primarily used for ethnic Chinese dishes and does not play a leading role in foods of the indigenous peoples of Malaysia, Thailand, or Vietnam. Still, since Chinese cuisine has so much presence in the region, Southeast Asian markets usually carry napa cabbage in both its round heads and longer, barrel-shaped forms. Lemony Vietnamese cabbage salads often feature this crinkly-leafed, light green cabbage. Thai: *pahk ghat kao*; Vietnamese: *cải bắc-thảo*

CHINESE BROCCOLI (*Brassica oleracea* Alboglabra)— This thick-stemmed brassica has thick, deep green leaves and occasionally small white flowers, which are not necessarily signs of over-maturity. These antioxidant-rich heads are so flavorful on their own, that they are simply boiled or steamed and served with a drizzle of oyster sauce in dim sum restaurants in Malaysia and Singapore. Slice the stems and tear the slightly bitter leaves before adding them to a stir-fry. Thai: *pahk kah nah*; Cantonese: *gai lan*; Vietnamese: *cải-làn*

LETTUCE (*Lactuca sativa*)—Primarily loose leaf, rather than head lettuce, is used in Southeast Asia. Some green-leaf and red-leaf varieties, similar to American strains but with firmer leaves and a more bitter flavor, are cultivated in the hot tropical climate. Softer leaf varieties are used to wrap hot foods and as a filling in Vietnamese rice paper salad rolls (*gỏi cuốn*) (pg. 206). These fresh salad rolls not only have some leaves on the inside but also each roll is laid into a leaf along with herbs then dipped in a dipping sauce, adding a layer of flavorful crunch. Lately, an iceberg variety is becoming common. Local chefs shave it very thinly and combine it with herbs and other vegetables atop steaming bowls of noodle soup. Firm-ribbed loose-leaf lettuce is frequently stir-fried and served as a hot vegetable. Vietnamese: *xà-lách*

Green

Napa

Chinese Broccoli

EGGPLANTS (*Solanum melongena*)—Dozens of varieties of this nightshade are cultivated in Southeast Asia. They come in a seemingly endless array of shapes, sizes, colors, and textures. Some are supple and creamy, others crisp and bitter. Each is employed in a way that highlights its special characteristics. Thailand is by far the largest consumer of eggplant among the countries in the region. Thai: *ma keuua yao*; Malay: *terung pipit*; Vietnamese: *cà tím*

CHINESE EGGPLANT—Eight to twelve inches long with one-to-three-inch diameters, the lavender Chinese eggplant is usually deep-fried or steamed. These techniques are the first steps to maximizing this variety's velvety rich texture.

Chinese Eggplant

SMALL PURPLE EGGPLANT—This 1- to 3-inch variety comes in various shapes and is used for many purposes. Used as a common vegetable in a large range of dishes, the flesh is somewhat firmer than the common Western black eggplant. Since they have a higher skin to flesh ratio than American eggplant, they hold together well in stir-fries.

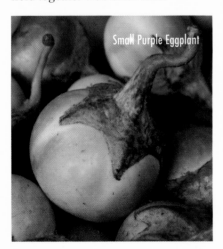

Small Purple Eggplant

VARIEGATED GREEN EGGPLANT (*Cà-pháo xanh*)—These 1- to 2-inch round eggplants with a green and beige pattern are packed with tough seeds. One of the only eggplants that is primarily eaten raw in Thailand, it's used to scoop up fiery chili dips or as a component of a *table salad*. They're also cooked into green curries.

THAI PEA EGGPLANT (*Cà-pháo Thái*)—As small as peas, or sometimes as big as small, these tough-skinned, bitter eggplant are used solely in Thailand, where they are added to vegetable dishes and curries. After they're cooked, they practically pop in your mouth, releasing their flavorful natural juices and adding complexity to the many dishes they enhance.

Variegated Green Eggplant

WHITE EGGPLANT (*Cà-pháo*)—This ancient variety, one of the first known, is the size, shape, and color of a hen's egg, hence the name "eggplant." The smaller, 1-inch miniature variety is pickled in Central Vietnam and eaten alongside pork and seafood dishes.

White Eggplant

Thai Pea Eggplant

Roots

LOTUS ROOTLETS—Outside of Southeast Asia this part of the lotus plant is a rare find. If fresh can't be found, rootlets packed in brine are a reasonable substitute. Although only about ¼ to ½ inch in diameter, they retain the unique interior pattern of the full-grown lotus root. They are primarily used for salads, such as the Vietnamese *Gỏi Ngó Sen* (pg. 234). Vietnamese: *ngó sen*

LOTUS ROOTS—When sliced, each sausage-like, connected segment of this cylindrical tuber reveals a gorgeous pattern of oval and circular channels. The root, usually 2 to 3 inches in diameter and segmented into 4- to 6-inch-long sections, is able to retain its crunchy texture even after it's been simmered for an hour or longer. Sliced thinly and blanched, it's often added to stir-fries. Sometimes the long, internal channels are stuffed with a ground meat mixture, simmered, and then sliced for a spectacular presentation. Thai: *rahk bua*; Malay: *ubi teratai*; Vietnamese: *củ sen*

BAMBOO SHOOTS (*Bambusa vulgaris*)—The pointed, cylindrical shoots are young growths from a specific, edible variety of bamboo. Eaten raw, they are quite caustic and cause an unpleasant reaction, so they must be cooked. Buy them fresh, cut off the top third, and then trim the outer circumference to get rid of the tougher leaves. Boil the peeled shoots in salted water until cooked through. They should yield easily when pierced with a skewer. If not cooking fresh, use high-quality, store-bought bamboo shoots that are packed in airtight bags with a little brine. You pay for the quality, but their superiority over the lackluster canned ones makes it worth a few bucks' difference. Thai: *naw mai*; Malay: *bamboo redang*; Vietnamese: *măng*

LONG BEANS (*Vigna sesquipedalis*)—Sometimes called "yard-long beans" or "Chinese long beans," these whip-like vegetables never reach a full yard, but can reach up to two feet in length. They're presented in one of two ways: cut into shorter lengths and added to *table salads* (pg. 151) in Thailand and Vietnam, or cooked whole to be served as a snack or vegetable dish. Boasting a deep green bean flavor and enviable sweetness, they're great stir-fried with ground pork and chili sauces. Thai: *tua fak yao*; Malay: *kacang tunggak*; Vietnamese: *đậu đũa*

Long Beans

Bamboo Shoots

Lotus Rootlets

Tubers

JICAMA (*Pachyrhizus erosus*)—This round, squat tuber is known in Asia as a "yam bean" or sometimes simply as "turnip." Unlike in Latin America, where it is frequently served raw, in Southeast Asia it is cooked, especially as a filling for *Po Piah*, the Malaysian Spring Roll (pg. 294). It retains a pleasantly gentle crunch even after extensive simmering. For some recipes, such as the filling for Chinese dumplings, they are an excellent substitute for water chestnuts. Thai: *mun kaaew*; Malay: *seng kuang*; Vietnamese: *cû dâu*; *củ sắn* (Southern)/*củ đậu* (Northern).

TAPIOCA (*Manihot esculenta*)—Used throughout North and South America, Africa, and Asia, the tapioca root goes by names such as cassava, manioc root, sago root, and others. The starch of this tuber has a unique gelatinous quality that imparts an elastic texture to foods. It is this property that makes it so essential to certain dumpling and noodle recipes. Combined with rice flour, it makes a dough with a firm bite yet still some chewiness to it. The raw tuber is sometimes grated for use in cakes. In Malaysia it is cut into large strips, steamed, and served with a mixture of grated fresh coconut, sugar, and salt. Thai: *man sahm bpa lang*; Malay: *ubi kayu*; Vietnamese: *khoai mì*

POTATOES (*Solanum tuberosum*)—In their potato-laced stews and curries, Southeast Asians use mostly the somewhat waxy varieties of potatoes, like our White Rose or Yukon Gold varieties. The Vietnamese don't use potatoes very much. The Thais use them in dishes like Mussamun Curry (pg. 168). But in Malaysia and Singapore, potatoes are more widely used, especially in ethnic Indian and Malay cuisines. Thai: *mun farang*; Malay: *kentang*; Vietnamese: *khoai tây*

SWEET POTATOES (*Ipomoea batatas*)—True sweet potatoes, with a pale yellow flesh and firm texture, are used in Southeast Asia the same way that taro is used: They're simmered in coconut milk, sometimes fried as thickly battered slices, or fried alone until crispy throughout. Thai: *mun taeht*; Malay: *keledek*; Vietnamese: *khoai lang*

Tapioca Pearls

These small pearls are made from tapioca starch.

Kabocha Squash

Jicama

KABOCHA SQUASH (*Cucurbita maxima* var. *akehime*)—This squash is often referred to as the "Japanese pumpkin." These extremely hard-skinned squash are most commonly used in Thailand. In savory recipes, such as Pumpkin and Pork with Scallions (pg. 170), its starchy, orange flesh lends a comforting heartiness. Another popular presentation is to hollow out the pumpkin of its seeds, steam it to tenderness, fill the cavity with a custard mixture, and then steam it again until the slightly sweetened custard sets firm. The finished pumpkin custard is then sliced into wedges for service. Thai: *fahk tong*; Vietnamese: *bí đỏ*

AVOCADO (*Persea americana*)—In Southeast Asia, this newcomer is used for sweets or eaten out of hand. It's received an especially warm welcome in Vietnam, where avocados are used for delicious, decadent smoothies (pg. 266). Vietnamese: *quả bơ*

CORN (*Zea mays*)—Corn varieties in Southeast Asia are tougher and starchier than the tender sweet corn familiar to Americans. Southeast Asians prefer types more similar to what we would use for livestock feed corn. Vietnamese cooks slice it thinly from the cob and use it in *che bap*, a thick sweet corn soup with coconut milk drizzled on top. In Malaysia and Singapore, shaved iced snacks (pg. 280) feature canned corn, often creamed. Thai: *kao pohd*; Malay: *jagung*; Vietnamese: *bắp*

CUCUMBER (*Cucumis sativus*)—Small, thin, tender-skinned cucumbers are widely used in Southeast Asia. The closest substitute is the Kirby variety, sometimes referred to as the "pickling cucumber." Cucumbers are often simply sliced and then served as an accompaniment to fatty dishes like roasted pork belly. Southeast Asian cooks are much more likely to serve crisp, cool, raw vegetables alongside hot, savory foods than we are in the West. Cukes are served as part of Vietnamese and Thai *table salads*. They're also stir-fried as a hot vegetable. Thai: *thang gua*; Malay: *timun*; Vietnamese: *dưa leo*

PRESERVED CHINESE GREENS—There are many names for this Chinese pickle used throughout the ethnic Chinese communities of Vietnam, Malaysia, Singapore, and Thailand. They're called "preserved mustard greens" and "swatow mustard cabbage," among other things. Sold in vacuum-packed plastic pouches, these salty greens are primarily used in soups. After draining their brine, give them a quick rinse to remove excess salt before cooking with them. Vietnamese: *dưa cải chua*

Cucumbers

American (Standard)

English

Kirby (preferred)

PICKLED RADISH—This preserved vegetable is also called a "preserved turnip." Prepared by drying daikon radishes in a series of stages, this crunchy pickle can be used as an ingredient in dishes or as a side dish with rice. Pad Thai noodles (pg. 172) are inauthentic without salty bits of this fermented radish. It is used sparingly. Look for small flat plastic bags about 8 oz. each, with straggly bits of brown radish pieces. Vietnamese: *củ cải muối*

Preserved Chinese Greens

Pickled Radish

Fungi

Fungi, by definition, stand on their own in this world. They're separate from plants or animals. They're a kingdom unto themselves, which, when analyzed, is closer to fauna than to flora. What we call a mushroom is actually the fruit of the living organism, *mycillium*, which grows below ground (or within the fibers of decaying wood). Fungi rely on a host, which they devour slowly as they grow. Oyster mushrooms (*Pleurotus ostreatus*) are a favorite in Thailand, where they're batter-fried. Chinese black mushrooms (shiitakes) are most common.

Drying mushrooms can actually improve their flavor and texture for some recipes and increase the available naturally occurring glutamate. See page 98 for more details on glutamate and their umami impact. Also look to page 110 for critical techniques in the preparation of fresh and dried fungi.

CHINESE BLACK MUSHROOMS
(*Lentinula edodes*)—Called "dong gu," in China, these are the shiitake mushrooms (actually the Japanese name) mushrooms that are widely available, fresh and dried, in American markets. Quality levels of these flavor powerhouses vary widely, especially among dried (better-quality dried mushrooms can be four times the price per pound of the lowest quality). In Southeast Asia quality is assessed by the thickness of the cap, (thicker is better), the texture of the cap, and the color of the gills underneath the cap. Much of this is determined by the growing conditions of the mushrooms. The coloring is mostly a result of the technique of drying them. The best quality mushrooms have thick caps with visible cracks and pale, still-intact gills below. It's worth the money to get high-quality mushrooms, since their thick, meaty texture and deeper flavor can make or break a dish. The stems of dried black mushrooms are edible, but so tough that they're used only for flavoring stocks and broths. Thai: *het hom*; Malay: *cendawan*; Vietnamese: *nấm hương/nấm đông-cô*

STRAW MUSHROOMS
(*Volvariella volvacea*)—These mushrooms get their name from where they grow: on rice straw. They're rarely found fresh outside of Asia. Harvested when the mushroom is still immature, they sometimes still have a solid oval shape, like a grape. When their outer veil is cut, a mushroom is revealed inside, waiting to break through, with the classic cap-and-stem shape of a mushroom. Canned straw mushrooms, while no flavor match for fresh, actually have an appealing texture. Straw mushrooms are great bite-size garnishes for soups such as the Thai Hot and Sour Soup, *tom tum goong* (pg. 144). The entire mushroom is edible. Thai: *het fahng*; Malay: *cendawan*; Vietnamese: *nấm rơm*

Chinese Black Mushrooms in Thai Market

WOOD EAR (*Auricularia polytricha*)—Also called "black fungus" or "cloud ear," these are available both fresh and dried. These very thin, gelatinous-textured fungi grow on tree trunks. Each side has a different texture and, when dried, a distinctly different color. The top side is smooth and dark in color. The bottom side is almost felt-like in texture and, when dried, turns an almost-beige color. Make sure to cut off the tough nodule where the fungus was attached to the tree; it's hard and woody. These soft, supple fungi are cut into bite-size pieces or strips for stir-fries like the Malaysian Nonya style mixed vegetables, *Chap Chae* (pg. 346), soups, and sweet stews. Thai: *het hoo noo*; Malay: *kuping tikus* or *cendawan telinga kera*; Vietnamese: *nấm mèo/ mộc nhĩ*

Chinese Black Mushrooms

Wood Ear

Fresh Straw Mushrooms

Fruits

The myriad fruits found in Southeast Asia are more than enough to fill a library, let alone a book. This section addresses some of the main varieties that are used in their food and that can be found in markets across the U.S. and in other countries outside of Southeast Asia.

Citrus

Citrus plays a starring role in the Southeast Asian culinary scene. Flavorful sweet-sour juices are essential to creating dressings, dipping sauces, and beverages. Lime wedges are a mainstay on the table, adding balancing acidic notes to broths, brightening seafood dishes, and dissolving salt and chilies into instant sauces. The aromatic zest of regional citrus fruits, especially of the kaffir lime, is critical for Thai curry pastes. Segments of giant Vietnamese *pummelo* fruit are served at the end of meals to cleanse the palate or separated into glistening shards to create intriguing *pummelo salad* (pg. 240). As in the West, citrus is squeezed into tea. Finger bowls of citrus-laced water are offered at the end of a seafood meal to rinse seafood odors from the hands.

Lime *(Citrus laifolia)*—Sometimes called a Persian lime, this is the citrus workhorse of the Southeast Asian kitchen. It is juiced for soups, salads, and sauces or cut into wedges Southeast Asian style (pg. 108). You will see the following entries on limes is extensive, and each posseses its own flavor. This is a lime variety that you can find in any market and rely upon for the floral citrus acidic flavor. Malay: *limau*; Vietnamese: *chanh*

Key Lime *(Citrus aurantifolia)*— These small, smooth-skinned limes have a sweet flavor and are used in beverages and as table condiments. They are the variety from the Florida Keys that lend their name to the classic custard pie of that area. Thai: *manao*; Malay: *limau nipis*

Calamansi Lime (*Citrus microcarpa*)—This smaller, diameter variety of lime becomes orange when ripe and brings a unique floral aroma to foods. These are available only rarely in the U.S. Substitute the standard lime, or to emulate its flavor combine other ingredients. See southwesternflavors.com for what to use. Thai: *ma euk*; Malay: *limau katsuri*; Vietnamese: *chanh calamansi*

Kaffir Lime (*Citrus hystrix*)—Sometimes called "makrut" or "wild lime," this 1½- to 2-inch diameter lime has an unmistakeably gnarly/ bumpy skin. The outer green zest of this lime is used in Thai and Vietnamese dishes, but the juice is very bitter and rarely part of cooking. Although it's used throughout the region, the Thais rely on it most strongly. It is in almost all Thai curry pastes. The whole fruits freeze well. When zest is needed, it can be shorn off the frozen limes using a grater/ rasp. The rest of the lime can be refrozen in a tightly sealed bag for later use. Thai: *luuk makrut*; Malay: *limau purut*; Vietnamese: *chanh kafir*

Calamansi Lime

Kaffir Lime

PUMMELO (*Citrus grandis*)—As I complete a tour around Vietnam in September it's the season, and they are everywhere. Stacked on roadsides, pouring out into the streets, piled high in baskets on motorbikes, and on altars in homes and restaurants, this thick-skinned citrus has a pith that can be as thick as one inch, revealing inside a grapefruit-like interior. There are red and pale greenish-yellow varieties. Each has mildly sour, subtly sweet citrus segments. The tough encasing membrane is peeled off before serving as the end to a meal, or the individual juice sacs are pulled apart into clumps and used as the bulk of a Pummelo Salad (pg. 240). Thai: *som ob*; Malay: *limau bali*; Vietnamese: *bưởi*

Pummelo

ORANGES (*Citrus sinensis*)—
Due to the hot climate, oranges grown in Southeast Asia have a green exterior. Only with cold weather does the green chlorophyll leave the rind. The interior is very pale orange and not very flavorful, lacking that characteristic sweet and tart flavor of Florida- and California-grown varieties. The variety most similar to the types used in Southeast Asia is the *Shaddock* orange. Thai: *som*; Malay: *oren*; Vietnamese: *cam*

TANGERINE (*Citrus reticulata*)—
Also known as the mandarin orange, this celebratory fruit is brought home across Asia during the New Year celebrations to wish the receiver good luck, fortune, and happiness. Not often used as part of a dish, they are eaten out of hand and the peels are dried to infuse flavor into stir-fries, soups, and sweet soups. Thai: *som keaw wahn*; Vietnamese: *quít*

Tangerine

Oranges

MANGOS—Asia has the greatest variety of mangos in the world. Fresh mangos like the Tommy/Atkins are available all year, and other types' availabilities peak in certain times of the year. As a chef, I look to the difference in flavor and texture as the two main factors when choosing a variety. The Haden's flavor is what most Americans are familiar with. It is large with lots of firm, usable flesh. The Ataulfo is what I reach for when making the Thai dessert of Fresh Mangos, Coconut Sticky Rice and Crispy Mung Beans (*mamuang khao nieo*) (pg. 180). These mangos have a quinine flavor that Asians love. Ripe mangos are seldom used in savory foods. Green mangos, immature and unripe, are used extensively in Thai, Vietnamese, Malaysian, and Singaporean cuisine. They are shredded into salads with salted shrimp, chilies, and fish sauce, and large chunks are often dipped with salty, spicy shrimp paste and then eaten as a snack or tossed with salads. Thai: *ma muang*; Malay: *mangga*; Vietnamese: *xoài*

BANANAS (*Musa sapientum*)—Like mangos, Southeast Asian bananas come in all shapes and sizes. Ripe bananas are eaten out of hand as snacks. A favorite treat is to coat them in sesame batter and then deep-fry them. In Vietnam, unripe bananas are shaved thin and used as an astringent accompaniment to salads and noodle dishes. Smaller varieties are sliced lengthwise, and larger varieties are slivered in thin discs. While the familiar Cavendish variety we know in the U.S. has been bred so that its seeds are nothing more than tiny specks, some smaller Southeast Asian varieties actually have sizable seeds. The blossoms of banana trees are also important to Southeast Asian cooking. Thai: *gloo-ay*; Malay: *pisang*; Vietnamese: *chuối*

Bananas

BANANA BLOSSOMS—These reddish-purple, elongated, teardrop-shaped flowers may look inedible at first, but once you peel back the pliable, plastic-like petals, it all makes sense. One flower grows during the life of the banana plant (not botanically a tree), and it is solely for reproduction. Under each petal grows a hand of miniature banana flowers. As it grows forward and down, each of these forms one hand of bananas, like the ones you're familiar with buying in the market. This continues, and the plant produces tens of pounds of bananas along a single stalk. Vietnamese: *hoa chuối*

Banana Blossoms

MANGOSTEEN (*Garcinia mangostana*)—Known as the "Queen of Fruits," this absolutely succulent fruit has just made its debut in the U.S. Topped with a green crown of leaflets, this billiard ball-sized fruit has a thick purple skin that encases opaque, white segments of honey-sweet flesh. These delicate gems yield to the slightest pressure, and almost dissolve on the palate as they relinquish their mango/pineapple-like flavor. On the bottom of each fruit, a green, spoked "nib" indicates the number of segments inside. Browning on the exterior is not indicative of their eating quality. Be careful of the colorful sap that the skin exudes, as it stains fabric. They are always eaten raw and are not used in cooking. Prohibited for decades from entry into the U.S., they have finally been granted access in two ways. Imports from Thailand are deep-frozen and then thawed for sale. These are not worth buying, because freezing destroys the delicate texture of the fruit and causes the skin's pigment to taint the snow-white flesh. But fresh specimens, imported with new regulations or grown in tropical U.S. territories, have reached maturity and are being legally sold in specialty markets on the mainland. They're an expensive rarity right now, but will someday be accessible to all. Thai: *mung kuut*; Malay: *manggis*; Vietnamese: *măng-cụt*

Mangosteen

DURIAN (*Durio zibethinus*)—
Known as the "King of Fruits," this
giant, thorny pod is revered by some
(including me) and despised by
others. It has a powerful aroma,
detectable several feet away. Its odor is
so strong that hotels, buses, and
airplanes routinely forbid patrons to
carry it. This is made clear with
prominent signs posted at entrances,
bus stops, and subway stations. The
fruit is quite large, 2 to 8 lbs (1 to
4 kilos), and its shell is covered with
pointy spines. Inside, the custard-like
flesh is segmented into lobes, each
studded with large, light brown seeds.
The creamy fruit tastes like a
combination of sweet mango, overripe
pineapple, and fermented onions—it's
actually very addictive. Thai: *tu rien*;
Malay: *durian*; Vietnamese: *sầu-riêng*

JACKFRUIT (*Artocarpus
heterophyllus*)—The world's largest
tree-grown fruit, the jackfruit can
weigh upwards of 20 lbs. The bumpy
green skin peels back to reveal bright
orange, striated pods with large,
mahogany-colored, oval seeds. The
pulp surrounding the seed is about
1/4 inch thick and has a unique
resilient, bouncy texture. The flavor
is reminiscent of Juicyfruit Gum. The
seeds are also edible and taste terrific
when boiled for about 20 minutes.
They're delicious eaten with a mixture
of sweetened grated coconut seasoned
with salt. Jackfruit strips are used in
shaved ice snacks and beverages.
Thai: *khanoon*; Malay: *nangka*;
Vietnamese: *mít*

PINEAPPLE (*Ananas comosus*)—
The main variety of pineapple in
Southeast Asia is slightly different
than our familiar Hawaiian variety.
It's smaller, less tart, less juicy, and
less dense. In fact, it's so much less
dense that there are often actually air
pockets inside. Nothing is wasted in
the traditional culture of Southeast
Asia, and labor is plentiful. Instead
of hacking off the exterior peel and
1/2 inch of the fruit below, only the
thin outer membrane is removed.
Grooves are then cut to remove the
hard, seed-containing divots. Pineapple

is often served with ground dried
chilies and salt. The pairing of these
spicy, salty, and sweet fruity flavors
illustrates the balancing of tastes,
layers of flavor, and love for spice that
characterize Southeast Asian cuisine.
Thai: *supparoht*; Malay: *nanas*;
Vietnamese: *dứa/thơm/khóm*

Pineapple

"No Durian," a sign on a Singaporean bus

Durian

Jackfruit

Jackfruit

STARFRUIT (*Carambola*)—This fruit is named for its five-pointed star appearance when cut into cross-sections. Its flavor ranges from tart to barely sweet, and it always has a light astringency that causes the mouth to pucker. In Vietnam, unripe green starfruit are sliced very thin and used as a tart flavoring with pan-fried foods like "sizzling pancakes," *Bánh Xeo* (pg. 208). Carambolas ripen to canary yellow and sometimes exhibit a slight orange hue. It is at this level of ripeness that they are eaten as a fruit or juiced for a beverage. Although the fruit is irresistibly attractive when sliced into decorative star shapes, it's actually more delicious to chomp along the elongated ridges of the whole fruit, yielding long, seedless, juicy pleasures. Thai: *mah fu-eung*; Malay: *belimbing*; Vietnamese: *khế*

RAMBUTAN (*Nephelium lappaceum*)—These brilliant magenta orbs can vary in hue, leaning toward yellow, red, orange, or a combination of these colors. They're about 1¹/₂ inches in diameter and have bristly, flexible hairs protruding all over. Their flesh is reminiscent of firm grapes, and it clings to a large, black, shiny, inedible seed. Use your thumb to depress and crack the shell, pull back half of the skin, and then grab the entire jewel of fruit into your mouth with your teeth, stripping the sweet, subtle fruit from the smooth pit. Other Asian fruits such as the longan and the lychee are eaten the same way. Thai: *ngaw*; Malay: *rambutan*; Vietnamese: *chôm-chôm*

PAPAYA (*Carica papaya*)—Because they're so easy to grow, papayas are found in most home gardens of Southeast Asia. Papaya is used both as a vegetable and a fruit depending on its ripeness. The variety grown and used in Southeast Asia is known in the U.S. as the "strawberry papaya." It grows much larger than most other varieties, commonly 5 lbs or more. The immature fruit is green, and its tart flesh is shredded for salads in both Thailand (pg. 148) and Vietnam. Small pickled slices can be found in dipping sauces and soups. Raw, unripe papayas contain papain, an enzyme that is used as a meat tenderizer. Thai: *ma ra gaw*; Malay: *betik*; Vietnamese: *du-đủ*

DRAGONFRUIT (*Hylocereus undatus*)—Native to central Vietnam, this wild-looking cactus fruit is getting a lot of attention due to its shocking appearance. The outside is a hot pink oval bud, with narrow flat puddles extending in a symmetrical pattern around the fruit. The interior is a crisp pulp of flat white, with thousands of tiny, jet-black seeds, not unlike a kiwi. There are two varieties, each with the same bland flavor. The texture is slightly grainy and is easily bruised under slight pressure. Malay: *buah kaktus madu*; Vietnamese: *thanh-long*

Starfruit

Papaya

Rambutan

Dragonfruit

Fats and Oils

Fats and oils are the medium that convey heat from flame to food, allowing cooks to achieve various textures, colors, tastes, and developing flavors. They can be divided into two categories: those rendered from animal sources and those extracted from nuts and seeds. Generally, lipids that are solid at room temperature are called "fats," and those that are liquid at room temperature are called "oils."

Animal Fats

PORK FAT—Rendered pork fat (lard) is used for frying noodles, whipping up stir-fries, and drizzling on top of soups right before the feast begins. The most efficient way to render fat is to start by covering small pieces of fat with water and boiling until the water evaporates and the fat melts. The solids left behind when fats are rendered (cooked until they melt) are called *cracklings*, and are also highly prized for their crunchy texture (pg. 121).

BUTTER—Although dairy was not part of Southeast Asian cooking before the colonial era, Europeans introduced it, and now butter has become part of the Southeast Asian pantry. Unsalted butter is used, but primarily salted butter is used in foods except when preparing *ghee* (clarified butter).

GHEE (pg. 285)—Butter is clarified by melting and then boiling it until all of the water and milk solids (whey) have evaporated and the clear butterfat begins to lightly brown. The ghee is then strained to remove any particulates. It's primarily used by ethnic Indian cooks in the region, whose cuisine is integral to the character of Singapore, Malaysia, and parts of Thailand. It's used for cooking items like *Roti Paratha* (pg. 286). The term *usli ghee* indicates that it has been made from pure butter, and no vegetable oil has been added.

There are three main advantages to ghee over whole butter: It can be stored without refrigeration for weeks, can be heated to a high temperature without smoking, and its roasted flavor is delicious. If you don't want to make it yourself, good-quality ghee can be purchased in the ethnic food section in many American grocery stores and in Indian and Asian specialty markets.

Vegetable Oils

The bottle labeled "vegetable oil" may actually contain any number of processed oils such as safflower, corn, soybean, cottonseed, and others. Canola oil, made from rapeseed, a relative of cabbage and broccoli, is produced almost exclusively in Canada (hence, the name) and has become one of the most common cooking oils in the West. It is a neutral, all-purpose cooking medium. Malaysia is the leader in the production of palm oil, a commonly used oil whose health attributes can be argued on both sides. Store-bought coconut oil is almost solely used in Indian cooking. The This, however, also render a fragrant coconut fat from thick coconut milk as a primary step to creating many curries. Some refer to this as "cracking the coconut milk."

PEANUT OIL is neutral in flavor and has a high smoke point because it is created by a process of cooking and chemical treatment (the same way most neutral vegetable oils are made). This makes an excellent choice for stir-frying. Peanut oil has an enviably high smoke point and a very clean taste, making it the oil of choice for high-heat wok cookery. Peanut oil that's labeled "expeller pressed" is made through a completely mechanical process. While this is more natural, the result is strong peanut-flavored oil that is only for seasoning, not for cooking.

MARGARINE is used not only in recipes for sweet doughs and crusts but also on sandwiches and in flatbreads. In the Singaporean flatbread *roti paratha [recipe pg ref]*, margarine is slathered on the dough balls to keep them separate. When stretched and cooked, the margarine absorbs less than ghee would. It is similar to jarred mayonnaise, and many people have developed a liking to its unique flavor and have become accustomed to using it instead of butter—another unfortunate example of the Western-world influence in Southeast Asia.

SESAME OIL is made of roasted sesame seeds that are pressed until they expel deep golden aromatic oil. To preserve its unique flavor it tends to be used toward the end of the cooking process. Like peanut oil, there are neutral sesame oils. We will not use those oils in these recipes. Always look for bottles that indicate Asian toasted sesame oil. It should be the color of dark maple syrup, not light like corn oil.

Preserved Seafood

DRIED SHRIMP—Small shrimp are salted and sun-dried to create a bright orange, salty-sweet ingredient essential to cuisines in this region. Every Southeast Asian country uses dried shrimp in its own way. In Thailand they are pounded and then used in salads such as the Thai green papaya salad (*som tom*) (pg. 148). In Vietnam they're used to top small rice cakes with crispy pork and dried shrimp, *bánh bèo* (pg. 214). And in Malaysia they're used to enhance the broth of Malaysian Coconut and Lemongrass, *curry laksa* (pg. 302). Although they possess a heady seafood aroma, these chewy seafood treasures can be addictive, so much so that I snack on them when using them in recipes. Look for bright orange, supple specimens. They are pounded into pastes, thrown raw into salads, and infused into broths.

DRIED WHITEBAIT—These small dried fish, also sold as dried Chinese anchovies or *ikan bilis*, are not the same as the salty anchovies used in Italian cooking. Whitebait are boiled in saltwater at sea and then dried in the sun. Many countries make them, and their salt content varies according to which country they come from. In Southeast Asia they're heavily salted. In Japan and Korea the fish are only lightly salted, and the anchovies are then mostly used for broths. They come in various sizes and quality levels. In the U.S., the Japanese company JFC distributes a good-quality product that can be used in most Asian cuisines. See page 330 for preparation techniques.

Dried Shrimp

Dried Whitebait

KG $7.

Techniques for Building Southeast Asian Flavors

INGREDIENTS

PRESENTATION

Authentic Recipe

TECHNIQUES

BUILDING SOUTHEAST
ASIAN FLAVORS

Guidelines for Using the Recipes in This Book

You can trust these recipes…they work. I have tested them numerous times. If followed, they will provide you with authentic flavors of Southeast Asia. That said, ingredients vary, and their overall flavor attributes such as color, taste, and texture are not standardized (thank goodness). In addition, each kitchen is different and variables such as the heat output on each stove differs. The cookware we have is shaped differently and made of different materials, so the cooking that results is not consistent, even if you follow every step. That's okay; just use your common sense and the food will come out tasting delicious as you adjust your cooking techniques and seasonings to your liking.

This book will enable you to become a better cook, and this chapter builds a foundation for making you a better cook who can adapt to the environment. Each person's dish will look and taste different. But hopefully the extensive research, testing, writing, and photography in this book pave the road for your stress-free cooking pleasure.

Read Recipes Before You Begin Cooking

This will give you a heads-up about what order items should be prepared in to save time and maximize flavor development. I find it useful to gather equipment I will need at the beginning, ensuring a more fluid, enjoyable time cooking. It is easier to cook if you are already familiar with the terrain.

Follow the Recipe . . . at Least the First Time

Cooking is an art that is performed by each cook in his or her own way. There are many ways to make a salad, sauce, or soup, but some techniques change the recipe completely. Personal preference is another story, especially where the heat level of chilies is at issue. The recipes were developed with a Western palate in mind: spicy when traditional, but not "Thai spicy." For instance, the green papaya salad, *som tum* (pg. 148), uses two green chilies. I have seen upwards of ten added on the streets of Thailand. Increase or decrease the amount according to your taste. It may be different than what you taste on the tropical island of Koh Samui, Thailand, but after all, who are you cooking for? Those at your table—cook for them!

"How and Why" and Other Forms of Chef Tips in My Recipes

My recipes include not just the basic steps to make a dish, but some added details that fine-tune it. Each recipe has a section titled "How and Why." An illustrative photo usually accompanies these tips on critical points in a recipe, along with an explanation of why I've chosen that particular technique. It may be as simple as the shape and cut of the meat (as this can determine the tenderness).

When the texture of a pounded spice paste is just right, it not only flavors a curry but also thickens the sauce and adds a fine desirable texture. The heat of the wok or sauté pan for a stir-fry must be adequate, or the characteristic charred flavor and browned edges of the dish will not result. The recipes in this book spell out these details for you. I include tips not just because "it's always been done that way," but because it's the way to achieve authentic flavors of Southeast Asia in your home kitchen. To my professional culinarian colleagues: You know what to do to adapt the recipes for the professional kitchen!

Don't Be Afraid to Innovate . . . They Do

Those less familiar with these foods and their cooking techniques should stay on course. As you begin to understand the cuisines, go for it and experiment as do the cooks in these lands. I appreciate and revel in the traditional foods, but there is nothing wrong with finding new uses for traditional ingredients and flavor combinations. I have found myself incorporating new vegetables into dishes, using sauces for non-Asian foods, and cross-utilizing leftover sauces as marinades for a barbecue the next day. After all, it's just food—respect it, enjoy it, and don't be over-analytical.

Finding the Right Ingredients Is Getting Easier

Since the popularity of Southeast Asian food is on the rise, previously hard-to-find ingredients are showing up in supermarkets, especially in ethnic enclaves. If you live in a more secluded area, don't fret—an Internet connection will solve your culinary hunting woes, connecting you with fresh kaffir lime leaves, a mortar and pestle, or even a bag of Thai tea with a special sock-like filter, delivered to your doorstep in days. Look to page 362.

Substitutions Can Be Appropriate . . . If You Know What You're Looking For

Be flexible and substitute ingredients as needed. Produce varies. Especially in chilies, spiciness is inconsistent, even on the same plant. The essential oils in one lime may be less concentrated than another, as is its acid level, so taste and adjust as you go. Before you get started, you may want to read The Southeast Asian Pantry chapter (pg. 30) about the unfamiliar items and how they are used. However, it is imperative you make conscious adjustments as you do so. See page 114 for how I have adjusted canned coconut milk to serve as both traditional types of coconut milk used in Southeast Asia (thick and thin).

Fresh rice noodles are hard to find, so dried ones may be made to work in their place. Fresh straw mushrooms are still not grown here, so canned will suffice. Sourcing the best-quality ones is essential, because the bad ones are better done without.

Just because you don't have a Thai sticky rice steamer doesn't mean you can't steam the rice. Yes, bamboo Thai steamers (pg. 101) impart some flavor, but a stainless steel steamer will work fine. In most recipes, various size and shape pots and pans can be exchanged—although the heat may need to be adjusted.

Use your own judgment. For instance, palm sugar has a unique flavor due to the sap of the tree it is made from and the way it was made (pg. 58). Brown sugar can work. It will be different, though. How different depends on its role in the recipe. If a recipe for a curry that serves four to six people calls for one tablespoon of palm sugar, brown sugar is the next best thing. But for the molten palm sugar dumplings (pg. 350), it would be best to choose another recipe if you can't find real palm sugar. Come back to that recipe later.

Sample Intermittently As You Cook . . . Flavors Evolve

At first, fish sauce may seem to have a foul aroma and an overwhelming taste, but not for long. When used in conjunction with other foodstuff, the alchemy begins and the combination is greater than the sum of its parts. As ingredients move through the preparation and cooking process, their flavor evolves, and they adapt to their environment. Think garlic—raw garlic's flavor can be overwhelming; mince and combine with fish sauce, sugar, and lime juice and a lovely dresing is born; stir-fry the garlic with some greens and heat has transformed the sharp raw edge into a rounded savory flavor; or take whole cloves of garlic and simmer them for an hour, and the natural sweetness is revealed.

Since flavor is more about aroma than taste, not only should you taste a curry paste as you pound aromatics into a smooth red mixture, get your nose in there and smell what's happening. Adjust where you feel the need.

It's Just Food. Really!

Don't be intimidated! Remember, we are just cooking. There is no shame in mistakes—only learning opportunities. This is about enjoyment in both creation and consumption. Plus, I am here to guide you through it.

Bamboo Thai Steamers

Umami— The Fifth Dimension of Taste

Special thanks to Dan Goral for his constant mentorship in this field of study.

Umami may sound mystical, but it really isn't. You have craved this fifth taste since the day you were born. It is only recently that the majority of scientists have come to an agreement that the tongue not only perceives sweet, salty, sour, and bitter but also a fifth taste sensation called umami, roughly translated as deliciousness, savory, or meaty. We have an innate affinity for sweetness and umami[1]. Of the twenty amino acids in breast milk, glutamic acid is the most abundant. Glutamate receptors on your palate sense the free glutamate in foods as a delicious taste.

The theoretical, but widely accepted, postulation is that each taste we perceive helps us survive, mostly by helping us be selective about what foods we eat. This was especially important when humans lived in hunter-gatherer societies. The umami taste is essentially the indication that the food has protein. We need protein to live. This taste is responsible for a majority of the cravability of foods: the urge to pull that dark roasted bit of meat off the end of a roast; to bite down into a crusty baguette; to yearn for the sautéed mushrooms atop your steak; or to close your eyes and revel as you savor aged cheeses. Asian foods are particularly high in umami. Umami is a Japanese term, though the taste exists in foods from every part of the world. What makes umami different from the other four tastes is that umami has longevity. The savory, satisfying taste lingers on the palate much longer than sweet and salty tastes, which dissipate first. Sourness and bitterness lag off next, leaving

umami residing the longest. Umami also changes the mouth feel. Lower-fat foods high in umami actually feel more satisfying, as though they were thicker and remained in your mouth longer.

Where Can Glutamates Be Found?

Glutamic acid is one of the twenty amino acids that make up protein. Our bodies actually produce about 50 mg of glutamic acid daily. MSG is the salt of glutamic acid: $C_5H_{10}NO_4$ *(Glu)*. This may be a valuable shortcut to better flavor, but not really needed. I have addressed this hot-button issue in The Southeast Asian Pantry chapter. Amino acids that serve as neurotransmitters include glycine, glutamic and aspartic acids, and gamma-amino butyric acid (GABA). Glutamic acid and GABA are the most abundant neurotransmitters within the central nervous system and especially in the cerebral cortex, which is largely responsible for such higher brain functions as thought and interpreting sensations[2].

Naturally occurring glutamate is found in both plant and animal proteins and in many varieties of foods that we take for granted. However, to affect flavor the glutamate must not be bound to other amino acids, hence the term free amino acid. The amount of free amino acids increases as fruit ripens, meat ages, and through fermentation; hence the improvement of flavor during these processes.

Fermented fish sauces similar to the sauces used in modern-day Southeast Asia (pg. 48) were consumed in ancient Greece and Rome. The fermentation process creates a sauce that has a high free glutamate content. Even ingredients used for natural flavorings, such as maltodextrin, malt extract, and whey protein, contain significant amounts of glutamate. It's everywhere, but as with most things, moderation is the key.

TRY IT YOURSELF: YOUNG CHEDDAR VS. AGED CHEDDAR

As cheese ages, the umami quality increases. A quick example can be made comparing cheese of different ages. A young cheddar versus an older, aged cheddar will show you this. Taste a piece of a mild cheddar cheese—chew it well and pay attention to what you perceive on your palate over five minutes. The flavor will begin to dissipate. Now eat a same-size piece of aged sharp cheddar. The flavor will linger for much longer.

Roasted Pork's savory aroma fills the Thai market aisles.

[1] Steiner 1987. *Umami: A Basic Taste*, pp.97–123,. Marcel Dekker, New York, NY.

[2] "Neurotransmitter," *Microsoft® Encarta® Encyclopedia 99*. © 1993–1998 Microsoft Corporation. All rights reserved.

It Is Not All About Glutamate

Briefly, there are two other major elements responsible for the umami taste in foods, and they work synergistically with amino glutamic acid. Peptides are small chains of amino acids in mostly plant sources, and nucleotides are the building blocks of nucleic acid that make up the fundamental genetic material DNA in proteins like seafood and meat. When combining these essential elements (glutamate in soy, peptides in mushrooms, and nucleotides in chicken), we achieve a full-flavored savory dish, like the Malaysian chicken and mushroom stew on page 322. This may also be why a traditional Chinese stir-fry, which enables you to get a small bit of each element, tastes so good.

How to Create Umami-Rich Foods in Your Kitchen

In the cuisines of Southeast Asia, there are general categories of ingredients that bolster the umami taste: raw ingredients from animal, plant, and fungi sources; crafted food products such as fish sauce, soy sauce, oyster sauce, and shrimp paste; and manufactured ingredients like MSG, yeast extracts, and hydrolyzed vegetable proteins. Choosing the choicest ingredients is critical to success in the kitchen. High-quality fermented fish sauce and soy sauce lay foundational flavors. Shrimp paste is made of only shrimp and salt, but after months of fermentation the flavor intensifies.

Yes, cooking creates umami. Cooking also breaks down protein into higher-impact taste elements.

Dry-heat methods of cooking like stir-frying, grilling, or roasting create layers of caramelized flavors. The intense heat of these methods sparks the Maillard reaction, a complex chemical reaction between free amino acids, sugars, and other carbohydrates that causes browning. It simply tastes good (think roasted meats, brown crusty bread, coffee beans, and even chocolate). The roasted pork belly on page 250 is a prime example of how deep brown colors represent deep, round flavors. Moist-heat cooking like curries, stews, and long-simmered broths (Vietnamese beef noodle soup (pg. 218) showcases how long, slow cooking also breaks down meat proteins into more readily available flavor.

Umami is now a known entity—something we all crave. In the flavors of Southeast Asia, we find our quarry. For more details on umami, see the Web site **www.southeastasianflavors.com.**

Vietnamese Spit Roasted Pork Belly

Browning Vietnamese Pancakes

Tools

With each trip to Southeast Asia I am more astounded at how the most minimally equipped kitchens (some of which are barely kitchens at all) turn out the most mind-blowing food. Every cook has some tools that he simply can't do without. Novice cooks soon discover certain pieces of equipment that become their friends, confidants, and partners. These are the implements that become associates in transforming a few vegetables into a vibrant salad or a few aromatics into an inspired marinade.

Although my kitchen is admittedly filled with electric gadgetry, pots and pans, countless knives, and steamers, I find myself grabbing the same fundamental equipment whenever I settle into a Southeast Asian recipe. You will build your own battery of kitchen weapons that will help you survive your personal kitchen adventure.

Tool: The Wok

This ingenious cooking vessel evolved in China where labor was plentiful and fuel was scarce. The word "wok" is simply the Cantonese term for "pot." The concave, circular-shaped device not only uses fuel very efficiently, but it is also the most versatile cooking implement known to humankind. Not only can you stir-fry in the wok; you can also steam, simmer, deep-fry, and even smoke foods in a covered wok.

A wok is different from a Western pot in many ways. The primary feature that creates its versatility is its concave design. This shape, working with gravity, pulls items to the center, allowing diverse amounts of food to be cooked in the same pan. As opposed to a sauté pan (skillet), where flat bottoms create the need to alter the size of the pan with the size of the food being cooked, a wok has the ability to caramelize foods regardless of their size or amount (it's limited only by the size of the fire below it). With wok cookery, the intensity of heat is adjusted according to the amount of food and the desired color and texture.

What about all that fire that you see engulfing the woks at your local Chinese restaurant? Yes, an intense heat source is required for really successful stir-frying in a wok, so much so that years ago I bought one of those outdoor gas burners designed for the large pots used for deep-fried turkeys. I use it as my wok burner. Gas stove strengths are rated in British Thermal Units (BTUs). A standard home gas burner is rated at between 7,500 and 12,000 BTUs for each single burner. A restaurant wok burner is rated at between 110,000 and 160,000 BTUs. Even considering that the restaurant is preparing larger batches of food than cooks at home would, the ten-fold heat intensity of the professional burner reflects the need for extreme heat in some wok cookery. The complex combination of smoky, caramelized, seared, concentrated flavors that are created in the rocket-engine heat of a wok is collectively known as *wok hay* (pronounced as it looks). See sidebar for a complete description of this flavor phenomenon.

Can a home cook achieve the same *wok hay* flavor in stir-fry on a small burner? Frankly, without intense heat, you cannot exactly replicate it. But you *can* get close by changing the cooking technique. But if you've taken the extra step and acquired a high-intensity wok burner (more and more home ranges are coming equipped with these), then you can master wok cookery like the Southeast Asians do it.

Take a walk through a serious Asian equipment shop like The Wok Shop in San Francisco, and you will quickly become confused about which type of wok to buy. If you are going to own only one wok for occasional use, I suggest a 14-inch flat-bottomed wok made of carbon-steel with two handles. One handle is large, like the handle on a skillet, and the other is a small loop on the opposite side to

WOK HAY

Wok hay or "breath of the wok," is what the Chinese call the familiar flavor achieved in the intensity of wok cookery. It's part smoky sear, part caramelization, and part that complex alchemy of essences that build up in the invisible pores of a vessel seasoned by long, loving use. The term is fast becoming one of the buzzwords in the industry—so much so that Grace Young has written a dynamic book titled *The Breath of a Wok,* with fantastic photographs by Alan Richardson. It's required reading for any serious cook interested in Asian cuisine.

This high heat–based flavor has migrated and can be found in stir-fries across much of Asia. Regardless of where you taste this intriguing flavor, you can be sure that it is fleeting. Shortly after food leaves the wok, its wok hay diminishes measurably. In minutes, it's gone.

Some cooks argue that only a traditional carbon-steel wok will elicit wok-hay—no Teflon-coated imitations here, please. Begin with a smoky hot wok, cook your food quickly, and serve it immediately. Once you have tasted cooking over that extreme heat, there's no turning back!

help lift heavier loads. Actually a hybrid of the large northern Chinese single-handled wok and the small southern Chinese two-handled wok, it will work over both gas and electric burners and not require too much special care.

Tool: The Wok Utensils

Both the long-handled, short-headed wok spatula (the *chuan*) with its rounded edge and the long-handled, broad, shallow wok ladle (the *hoak*) evolved in the fiery heart of the wok world. The spatula's rimmed edge sweeps through the wok, following the contour of the side.

Open-kitchen Chinese restaurants offer a window into a world where vegetables and noodles twist and turn effortlessly and a plethora of sauces are dipped and poured all day long in flame-engulfed woks. The ladle draws seasonings from counter to cookware on the fly. Buy both utensils for home use. Fourteen-inch handles are my length of choice. These tools are so intuitive that they may insinuate their way into all your cooking, not just Asian.

For an in-depth look at selection, seasoning, and use of the wok, consult Grace Young and Alan Richardson's *The Breath of a Wok* (Simon & Shuster 2004), or the late Barbara Tropp's *The Modern Art of Chinese Cooking* (William Morrow and Company 1982). These books are must-haves for any serious wok cook.

Tool: Frying Pans

The sloping-sided pans that most chefs would call sauté pans (*sauteuse* in French) and most home cooks would call skillets have become a common fixture in the kitchens of Asia. In the Western kitchen, they can be cross-utilized to stir-fry with excellent results. A large surface area makes for maximum food contact, and shallow sides allow excess moisture to evaporate. The main factor that will change when switching from a wok to sauté pan is the amount of oil needed: due to the wide, flat bottom, more oil is needed to achieve similar results.

Inexpensive plastic-handled pans that most of us would turn up our nose at are what is found in the kitchens in Southeast Asia; in reality, it is more about the cook than the pan. That said, I think it is worth the investment to spend the money on a heavier gauge pan that will retain some of the heat as foods are added to it. Cast-iron or anodized alloy, both with textured cooking surfaces, help grip the foods and brown them, achieving some level of wok hay.

Tool: Steamers

No single type of steamer is used by everyone. Stacking bamboo steamers are common. They require only boiling water, and you can stack, one, two, three, or up to ten high. The stainless steel stacking steamers are sanitary and easy to clean, but they lack the unique flavor that bamboo imparts into the food. Professional kitchens have gas-fired steamers that look like chests of drawers. Larger operations have pressurized steamers that cook in seconds. If you don't have the stacking steamers that are occasionally called for in this book, you can place a rack (or a few crisscrossed chopsticks) in the bottom a wok to create a shelf for a plate. Set the plate with the items to be steamed onto this rack, put water in the wok, cover, and *voilà!* You have a makeshift steamer.

Sticky Rice Steamers

Sticky rice is addictive. Its chewy, opalescent grains stick together, making the rice easy to handle and helpful in scooping up spicy salads, fiery curries, and palm sugar syrups. Steaming the soaked rice over a cauldron of boiling water allows each grain to remain separate yet retain its stickiness. The northeasterners are especially fond of conical bamboo steamers used for preparing this unique long grain rice. One favorite recipe is sticky rice with fresh mangos (pg. 180).

Tool: Miscellaneous Pots

Your kitchen is probably already equipped with pots and pans that would be fine for making the Southeast Asian dishes in this book. Broths, curries, and stews in the modern kitchen are often prepared in straight-sided pots such as small stockpots or Dutch ovens.

Aluminum alloy, enameled cast-iron, and stainless steel pots are simmering up some of the Asian world's best dishes. Because of the poor economies in most of these countries, homes are usually equipped with inexpensive, thin-gauge pans. Many kitchens have only one or two cooking pots, which are used over and over for numerous dishes in a single meal. It's not as limiting as it would seem, since there isn't that much stove space either. Standard kitchens have little more than a "portable" two-burner propane stove. Once one dish is complete, it's transferred to serving plates, and the next one begins. The food is usually served all at once, often at room temperature.

I am all for tradition, but I also want to make good use of my time. I use all four burners. Heavy-gauge pans transfer heat more evenly, so foods don't burn as easily. This allows for more multitasking. The most versatile pans for this book are 2½-quart and 4½-quart saucepans. A two-gallon Dutch oven and a three-gallon stockpot will enable you to cook most of the soups, sauces, and curries in this book.

Rack for steamer set-up in wok

Thai Sticky Rice steams in a alley kitchen

1. Peel off hard outer layer

2. Cut in half lengthwise

3. Cut out core at base

4. Slice very thin for tender pieces

Pound before for the infusion technique

Techniques

Technique: Trimming and Cutting Lemongrass

HOW DO I CUT IT?

Once you know how to cut this imposing-looking stalk, you can begin to experiment with its intriguing flavor. The first step is to cut off the bottom half of the stalk, the tenderest portion, which is most commonly used in cooking. Reserve the top portion for another use. Next, peel back the older, outer couple of layers.

To slice it thinly or mince it, first cut the stalk lengthwise in half and trim off the exposed root end.

• For thin slices to be used in pastes or directly in salads, cut the stalk *very* thinly into semicircles. Cutting across the grain this way makes this fibrous, aromatic grass tender.

• To mince it, cut the halves into julienne strips, then turn 90 degrees and cut again to create minced lemongrass.

Some recipes will call for the bottom portion of the stalk to be bruised with a blunt object to enable more flavor to infuse broth. It's then cut into about 3-inch pieces, which are added directly to broth or curry to infuse its flavor. This is how some Thais prepare Hot and Sour Shrimp Soup (*Tom Yam Goong*). The lemongrass pieces are usually left floating in the broth or curry and simply not eaten—many American restaurants remove the pieces before serving, since the uninitiated guest may unsuspectingly bite down into the tough stalk.

These illustrations demonstrate how the same ingredient is used in context within three unique recipes.

Vietnamese

INGREDIENTS
Lemongrass
Caramelized Sugar
Black Pepper
Shallots

Authentic Bun Thit Nuong

PRESENTATION
Lemongrass Eaten with Pork
Contrasting Temperatures
Layering of Textures

TECHNIQUES
Lemongrass Minced for Meat Marinade
Grilled

recipe page 256

Malaysian

INGREDIENTS
Lemongrass
Galangal
Turmeric
Coconut Milk

Authentic Beef Rendang

PRESENTATION
Lemongrass Becomes Part of Sauce
Serve with Nasi Lemak
Room Temperature
Eaten with Hands

TECHNIQUES
Lemongrass Ground Into Spice Paste
Long Cook Time
Coconut Added Early
Cooked Until Dry

recipe page 334

Thai

INGREDIENTS
Lemongrass
Galangal
Kaffir Lime
Fish Sauce
Chilies
Lime

Authentic Tom Yum Soup

PRESENTATION
Lemongrass Floats in Soup
Lime juice Clouds Broth
Often Served in Hotpot

TECHNIQUES
Lemongrass Bruised
Infused in Broth
Short Simmer Time

recipe page 144

Technique: Working with Rhizomes

Galangal, krachai, and turmeric can be sliced, chopped, minced, or grated. (Note: All spice pastes in this book call for grated rhizomes. It is the most accurate measurement method since the diameter of each piece varies and calling for slices is subjective.) Grated or chopped rhizomes can be squeezed through cheesecloth for flavorful juice (or can be juiced in a juice extractor). In many recipes they're added to slow-cooking foods in slices or large bruised chunks to infuse their flavor, aroma, and color into the food. Chefs either remove them before serving, as with a bay leaf, or leave them in as a decorative garnish.

TO PEEL, OR NOT TO PEEL?

That depends on the age of the rhizome and its intended use. The younger the rhizome, the thinner and more tender the skin is. When rhizomes' flavors are being infused into a dish, the rhizomes are generally not peeled. It's also unnecessary to peel rhizomes that will be used in a marinade. In most other cases, many cooks like to peel off the papery skin. Use the edge of a spoon to scrape away the peel effortlessly. Hold the rhizome in one hand and choke up on a spoon with the other. Use the edge of the spoon to strip off the skin, getting into the crevices. This method avoids waste created by peeling with a paring knife.

To infuse the flavor of rhizomes like ginger and galangal into slow-cooked stews, sauces, and soups, there are two approaches: For longer-cooking stocks, crush pieces of the rhizome by striking it with the side of a cleaver or the back of a small pan; simmer the crushed piece in the dish to release its flavor. Alternately, for quick-cooking soups, broths and dishes, slice the fresh rhizome into 1/4-inch slices, drop them into the soup, and simmer them for a quick infusion. *Tom kah kai*, Thai Coconut Chicken Soup (pg. 142), uses the latter technique.

For recipes that call for the rhizome to be diced, julienned, or minced, it's imperative to cut across the tough fibers to avoid a stringy texture. Each rhizome has visible rings that go around its circumference. The tough fibers run through the center of these rings. Jutting fingers of the rhizome change the fiber direction, branching out from the center core. Without wasting too much, the best first step is to peel a rhizome, then slice it into slabs about 1/16 to 1/8 inch thick. Stack two or three slabs at a time and crosscut them into 1/16 to 1/8-inch-thick- julienne pieces. Mincing these only takes one more set of cuts; turn the stack of strips 90 degrees and crosscut again. For extra fineness, chop through this mince a few times.

Even rhizomes to be chopped in a food processor should be cut across the grain first to avoid a stringy mess. When making a paste, thinly slice the rhizome into 1/8-inch-thick slices across the grain of the fibers, as one would do with meat. Next, transfer the slices to a mortar and pestle, food processor, or blender to pulverize. As for grating or juicing, the rasp that has become quite in vogue

Fresh turmeric and young ginger

nowadays works well to grate the rhizome, or the Japanese make a grater especially for ginger—usually made of metal with small, sharp teeth. Squeeze the grated rhizome through some cheesecloth or a strainer for juice.

Each region incorporates ginger into its cuisine in favorite cuts such as grated, planks, diced, julienned, or minced. Used judiciously, it can add an illusive fragrant note, such as in Malaysian chili sauce for Chicken Rice (pg. 319). When used profusely, it can actually add a spicy note that punctuates a dish, as the diced pieces used in Thai Savory Bites (pg. 138).

To substitue fresh turmeric: For every 1 tsp. ground turmeric, use 1 tbsp./1/2 oz/14 g. grated fresh turmeric.

PREPARATION TECHNIQUES

Peeling is optional. For use in a broth, simply wash and slightly smash a ginger bulb or slice it and simmer it with chicken and scallions for a simple stock.

There are three common ways to peel it: A knife, a sharp vegetable peeler, or a spoon. I find that using a spoon is the best—it is efficient, safe, and makes it easy to get into the nooks and crannies of this glorious aromatic ingredient

"Planking" means cutting the ginger into flat pieces in preparation for a julienne or fine dice. Stand the ginger on its widest side on a cutting board. Cut off 1/16 to 1/8-inch slices, or slabs. These slabs' thickness determines the final size of your strips—mince or dice. Restack in groups like a deck of cards and then cut into strips to make julienne, crosscut them to make fine dice.

Technique: Using a Mortar and Pestle . . . and How to Use a Blender Instead

POUNDING PURE POTENCY

The technique of making a paste using a mortar and pestle is a labor of love—not so common in today's modern electric gadgetry-packed kitchens. There remain, however, many devotees to these ancient tools, which transform fibrous aromatics into fragrant spice pastes. Understanding how traditional mortar pounding is done, and the rationale behind why it works so well, will enable modern cooks to achieve similar results (in most cases) with modern machines. I still sometimes use a mortar and pestle because the rhythmic pounding is a comforting sound that brings me down to earth. But most of the time I use blenders, electric spice mills, and food processors, which allow me to produce food in a shorter time. This is a reality of my life as a busy twenty-first–century chef.

Hand pounding with a mortar and pestle is the way to get the best results when creating flavorful Thai curry pastes. Hand-pounded pastes have longer shelf lives and thicken

Completed green curry paste

Clay mortar for Thai papaya salad

the sauce more effectively. David Thompson of Nahm restaurant, the Michelin-star Thai restaurant in London, swears by the method. His cooks' workstations have up to three mortars that are used for dressings and pastes, which are pounded to order throughout dinner service.

It seems simple enough: Add ingredients and pound away, using every ounce of energy in your soul to pulverize the aromatics into a flavorful paste. Yes . . . and no. This ancient kitchen tool is not as simple as it may seem. Which type of mortar and pestle you use, which ingredients you select, when they are added, and your technique with the pestle, all contribute to the result.

CHOOSING A MORTAR

Mortars come in all shapes and sizes. A hard material such as granite takes the hard pounding best. Old, traditional mortars from Asia made of clay are used with a wood pestle. Those are used primarily for *som tom*, the fiery green papaya salad of northeast Thailand (pg. 148). Beware of Mexican and Central American mortars, called *molecajetes*, which are made of lava rock. Although the coarseness of this stone is ideal for mashing soft ingredients for guacamole, the brittle lava rock can chip when pounding seeds and hard spices for Asian pastes, resulting in gritty pastes and chipped teeth.

The mortar should be deep enough to accommodate all of the recipe's ingredients in the bottom third of its bowl. I use mortars that are 5 to 7 inches in diameter. If the mortar is too small, the ingredients fly all over the place during pounding. Err on the side of larger, rather than smaller. Like a wok, the design allows for small amounts of paste to be created in a larger mortar.

A stone mortar is like a seasoned pan. Water-washing is fine, but soap is not. If you need to remove some excess material from the mortar, pound some raw rice in it until it becomes a fine grind. The rice will absorb any oils and flavorings that may be stuck in the nooks and crannies. Rinse the mortar well.

THE WAY TO POUND

Before adding any ingredients to the mortar, make sure they're cut the right way for pounding. Chop large, tough ingredients to aid in their pulverization. Items like galangal, ginger, shallots, and garlic should be peeled. Slice fibrous rhizomes like galangal and ginger across their grain into 1/8- to 1/4-inch-thick slices to shorten the fibers. Chopping or slicing garlic and ginger will save a lot of pounding time. Trim tough chili stems, but do not get rid of all of them. Instead, cut the stem just above the crown where it meets the fruit. This will enhance the aromatics of your paste by releasing the full fragrance of the chili. Toast spices individually and cool them before adding to the mortar. Many curry paste recipes call for ingredients to be toasted or roasted. This draws out fragrant essential oils, boosts flavor, and adds a smoky nuance. Think about the end result when adding ingredients.

GET BOTH HANDS INVOLVED!

Are you left-handed or right-handed? Place the pestle in your dominant hand. Next, take your other hand and cover the mortar, leaving a gap between your thumb and forefinger to pound through. This prevents things from flying out during the first few strokes. Once the paste gets going, you need only do this if you are getting splattered.

Rehydrated ingredients such as reconstituted dried chilies can become a soggy mess in the mortar. Be sure to squeeze out as much water as possible before adding them. Excess water will make for splashy pounding and result in more spoilage-prone curry paste (higher water content enables bacterial growth).

THE RHYTHMIC SOUNDS OF THE KITCHEN

Don't be afraid to use some elbow grease! Stabilize the base of the mortar by setting it onto a damp cloth. This will protect the surface below and eliminate slippage. The mortar should always be used on a well-supported surface. These tools can be heavy, and a good deal of force will be exerted downward during the pounding. Position the mortar on a corner of the table for a solid backing and a quieter experience.

Relax the wrist and aim for the bottom sides rather than the middle with your strokes. This combination of a relaxed wrist and off-center striking will result in a sliding-crushing action against the curvature of the bowl, which drags the ingredients against the inside of the mortar, maximizing the abrasive effects of each action. The pounding will split ingredients into fibers, which aid in thickening your final product. This is especially important when pounding dried shrimp or fish to produce a wonderfully light, flaky texture. Scrape down the sides of both the mortar and pestle occasionally with a spoon as you work.

Begin with drier, tougher ingredients. Usually start with the hardest ingredients to break down. This does not *always* literally mean the hardest ingredients first; while a black peppercorn is much harder than a dried chili, it is much easier to break down into a paste. I tend to grind the spices finely in the dry mortar, take them out, add the chilies, and pound until fine. Then I add the spices back. The dried chilies are added with any salt the recipe contains as it will act as an abrasive aid in the pulverization, saving you time and energy. Next, move on to lemongrass, galangal, and other similarly textured items. Continue to add ingredients one at a time, waiting until each ingredient is fully incorporated before adding the next. Next the higher moisture items like shallots and garlic get pounded. A coarse or fine paste may be desired, depending on the dish.

I warned you it wasn't going to be easy! Take your time and enjoy the beat (music helps); pound with strong blows as they are much more efficient. This simple yet labor intensive traditional method will result in a flavorful and aromatic low moisture curry paste (and an exhausted pounding arm). A concentrated consistency can only be achieved using this traditional method, since no water is needed as it would be with a blender or food processor.

MAKING A SPICE PASTE BY MACHINE

Making a paste in a blender (preferred) or a miniature food processor can also yield an acceptable paste. The order of adding the ingredients is completely different. First, the wettest ingredients go in (shallots and garlic) and any oil that the paste may be fried in. The oil addition is more common in the spice pastes *(rempah)* of Malaysia and Singapore. Thai curry pastes do not contain oil. Purée these wet ingredients, only adding water if needed. It is best to make large batches (double those in this book) as it give the blender something to work with. Next the drier ingredients go in, items like rehydrated chilies, lemongrass, galangal, and such. Spices like peppercorns, cumin, and coriander must be roasted and ground separately before adding to the blender.

Stop the blender often to scrape down the sides. I know I sound paranoid about introducing water, but there is reason for this. If you intend to store the paste for any length of time (one week or longer), it will spoil and change flavor more rapidly (not for the better). Also, the first stage of cooking the paste in oil or cooked-down coconut milk will take longer as the fry does not really began until the moisture has evaporated; hence the suggestion of adding oil (that you would be adding anyway) to the spice paste.

Chef Ari Slatkin uses a blender to make spice paste

Technique: Steamed Jasmine Rice

Well sort of…What we generally mean when we refer to "steamed rice" is actually boiled. The raw grains are submerged in water and simmered until the water is absorbed. Mistakenly, most restaurants refer to this as steamed rice; the water and rice are combined and boiled. There are times that rice is actually steamed over boiling water. In Thailand long grain sticky rice is soaked and steamed over water in a conical basket. There is also literally boiled rice; some Indian cooks boil large vats of water, scatter in long grain rice, cook it until tender, and then drain it (similar to how Italians cook pasta)!

Here, I have included my foolproof method for cooking perfect rice. The method works regardless of whether the rice is cooked in a rice cooker or a standard pot with a cover. Once you get comfortable cooking rice, do as most chefs in Asia do and use no measurements—just look and feel for the right ratio of water. If you need

a certain amount of rice, count on it tripling in volume from its dry state. For complete instructions on this method, visit the Web site **www.southeastasianflavors.com.**

Foolproof Method for Cooking Rice

Makes 6 cups (enough for 6–8 people or for 2–4 and leftovers for fried rice)

2   cups (14 oz/400 gm) Jasmine rice
2¹/₂ cups Water

USING A RICE COOKER

1. Rinse rice in a mesh strainer or colander under cool running water for 30 seconds, massaging it gently to remove any talc or dust. Drain well.
2. Transfer to a rice cooker and add water. Even out rice surface with your hands. Turn the cooker on (or Follow manufacturers directions).
3. When rice is done, fluff gently with a fork or wooden spoon.

USING A POT ON THE STOVETOP

1. Rinse rice in a mesh strainer or colander under cool running water for 30 seconds, massaging it gently to remove any talc or dust. Drain well..
2. Transfer to a saucepan with tight fitting lid. Even out rice surface with your hands. Add the water, plus two tablespoons of additional water to compensate for evaporation.
3. Bring rice to a boil, uncovered. Give it one quick stir, and then cover it tightly. Lower flame to lowest setting, and simmer rice for 20 minutes.
4. Remove pan from heat (do not uncover!). Allow rice to rest, covered, for 10 minutes, before fluffing gently with a fork or wooden spoon and serving.

How and Why

RICE METHODS

1. Using a strainer to rinse the rice helps measure the water accurately. If rinsed rice is tilted to remove excess water, some water inevitably remains hidden in the pot (between rice grains or below the metal plate in the bottom of a rice cooker), so it is inconsistent. Draining in a colander ensures that all excess moisture is removed before adding the measured amount of water.

2. For more individual grains, do not uncover the rice immediately after cooking —when the rice cooker "pops" (an indicator of doneness based on moisture content), or the pot is removed from the burner, the water has been incompletely absorbed, so the starchy rice is very hot and soft. Letting it rest allows excess moisture to be absorbed into the grains. The rice firms up, allowing it to be gently fluffed to separate grains.

Technique: Preparing Pummelo

The thick, pale green skin of the pummelo is simple to peel. I like to carve the peelings into ornate leaves to decorate any dish that features this citrus fruit. (See Pummelo salad recipe on page 240 to see how they look.) Separating the large fruit segments while keeping them intact takes a slow, methodical approach. The segments can be served unadorned, with a side of chili salt, or used in a fruit salad.

HERE'S HOW TO PEEL A PUMMELO

1. Trim off the ends of the pummelo, cutting right up to the edge of the flesh without cutting through it (you may have to shave off a few slices of the thick skin to find out how deep to cut).

2. Without cutting into the flesh, score four to six lines around the perimeter of the fruit from top to bottom using a knife.

3. Use your thumb to pry back the skin piece by piece, starting at the top or bottom.

4. Break the fruit apart into individual sections. Then peel away the membrane of each segment to reveal the glistening fruit segment inside.

Serve as is, or if it is dry enough, pull apart the individual pulp pods and use for the Pummelo Salad (pg. 240).

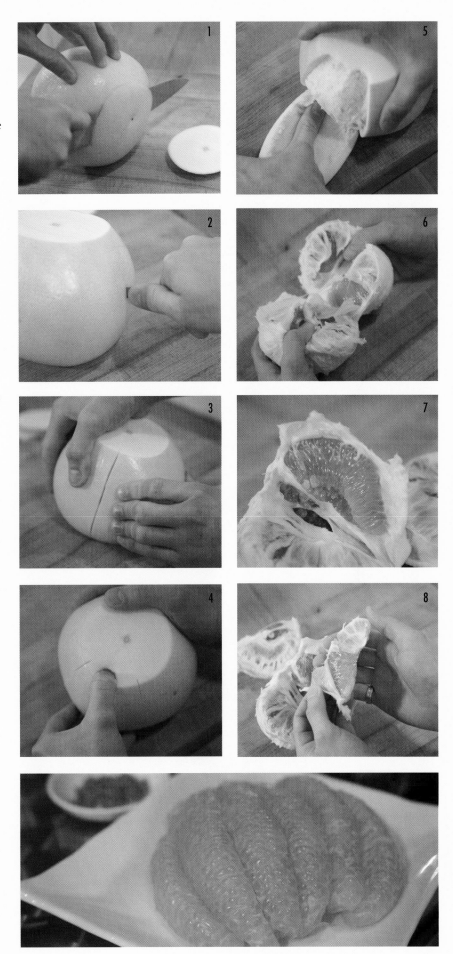

Technique: Cutting Lime Wedges—Southeast Asian Style

1. Wash limes in hot water for ten seconds. This removes dirt and excessive wax.

2. Stand the lime on a board with the stem end facing upward.

3. Make a cut from top to bottom, just off center, producing a seedless circular slice.

4. Turn lime 90 degrees (a quarter turn) and repeat the cut, this time yielding a seedless circle with one side cut off.

5. Place cut side down on a cutting board. Cut at a 45-degree angle to remove the tough center (often filled with seeds).

6. Cut the two largest pieces into halves.

7. You should now have five "wedges."

Technique: Banana Leaves

Fresh or frozen, banana leaves are not only wonderful functional plates in Indian and Malay cultures, they are also used for wrapping fish with chili sambal and grilling (pg. 326). Most of us will buy them frozen.

1. Defrost them at room temperature.

2. Wipe with a damp cloth or paper towels to remove any white dust they may have.

3. Passing them over an open flame not only makes them pliable but brings out their naturally deep green color. (You can also quick-rinse under hot water, and then rinse under cool water to make them much more pliable).

Technique: Julienne Carrots—Asian Style

1. Rinse carrots and peel thoroughly. Trim off ends and discard.

2. Cutting at an angle, slice thin, 1/16- to 1/8-inch-thick slices. Keep them organized as each slice falls from the knife.

3. Shingle the slices. (Edges overlapping toward the knife edge) in a somewhat straight line.

4. Slice into thin, julienne strips.

5. Lift and toss, removing any grossly abnormal-size pieces.

Banana Leaves

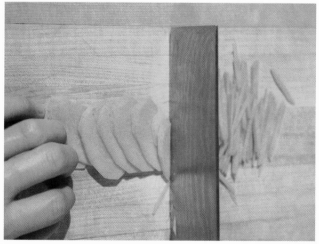

Technique: Preparing Banana Blossoms
(pg. 89)

1. Prepare acidulated water to prevent the cut blossoms from browning. Combine 2 cups of water with 1 tablespoon of vinegar or lime juice.

2. Peel back and discard any tired-looking or discolored leaves. (usually the first two or three)

3. Trim off the bottom of the blossoms (fat end).

4. Peel off the leaves one by one until the center is reached. Discard the immature bananas. You may need to grip the bottom a few times so the leaves will release easily.

5. Stack the leaves and shave them very thin.

6. Store in acidulated water until ready to serve.

Technique: Preparing Tamarind for Recipes

Using tamarind paste is the way to go—easy to prepare, bright flavored, and you can make some ahead of time. Although the package may say it is seedless, it's a half-truth. The seed casings are there, but it is strained after soaking with some warm water. For each tablespoon of paste you use, you will get double that amount of tamarind pulp called for in all of the recipes in this book.

1. Oil your knife and cut off how much you need. (It will double in volume after water is added.)

2. Transfer to a bowl and cover with triple the amount of water (by volume).

3. Let it soak for thirty minutes to soften.

4. Massage it with your hands to loosen all pulp from seed casings.

5. Strain through a sieve, pushing all the pulp through if possible.

Technique: Roasted/ Fried Peanuts

Peanuts, often called groundnuts in Asia, are an essential ingredient in the Southeast Asian Pantry! (pg. 62)

You may find peanuts tossed into a Chinese stir-fry, crushed into a Thai Papaya Salad (pg. 148), sprinkled on top of Malaysian Coconut Rice (pg. 332), or even pounded into and sprinkled on top of a Vietnamsese Peanut Sauce (pg. 201). Most traditional kitchens that would be preparing these dishes do not have ovens. They would use a wok to bring out that deep nut flavor.

Southeast Asian cooks often roast peanuts over low heat, pushing them around the wok as they develop a rich brown color. Chinese cooks have a penchant for deep-frying nuts. Western cooks usually dry-roast nuts on a pan in the oven. Each technique produces different results. Some cooks (not me) buy preroasted nuts. At least make sure they are not coated with a seasoning mixture.

- Most common: Pan-roasted—Uneven brown color yields rich, sweet, raw nut flavor. Constant attention necessary.

- Also used: Deep-fried—Even, deep flavor, very rich and crunchy. Constant attention necessary.

- Not recommended: Oven-roasted—Even color, no additional fat, and easy cleanup. Hands-off approach.

Technique: Working with Chilies
(Genus Capsicum)

GENERAL TIPS

Warning: Capsaicin, the active compound in chilies, is a severe irritant that can cause burns on any part of the body it touches. Though your hands may not sense it when you've just touched a chili, a slight rub of the eye may lead to excruciating pain. Think of some other personal activities that may cause similar irritation, and you'll quickly see the need for precautions when handling these deliciously incendiary comestibles. Disposable gloves are an excellent tool for avoiding incidents.

Technique: Preparing Fresh Chilies
General guidelines unless otherwise specified:
- Remove the crown
- Do not remove the seeds

SOMETIMES LEAVE THE CROWN INTACT

Chilies are the fruit of the plant. They begin as flower buds and hence have a floral aroma that is cherished by cooks across Southeast Asia. The freshest chilies have tender crowns that can be left on and incorporated into your recipes. Do, however, be careful as some larger chilies (fresnos and jalapenos) can possess very tough crowns that should be well trimmed.

Dried Chilies

Use a wire strainer to sift out spicy seeds.

LOWERING THE HEAT

To reduce the spiciness in a chili, remove the internal membranes and seeds. Most of the capsaicin is in these less-watery parts of the chili. Trim and scrape them with a knife to reduce the heat while retaining the flavor. This is true for both fresh and dried chilies.

- Fresh chilies—Trim off the stem end (but sometimes leave the crown for its floral flavor). If the chilies are small, halve them lengthwise and then use a small knife or spoon to cut or scoop out internal ribs and seeds. If the chilies are large, it's easier to quarter them lengthwise to remove the hot parts.

- Dried chilies—Some cooks break dried chilies and shake out the seeds. I've discovered that snipping them with scissors into 1/4- to 1/2-inch lengths is easier. Toss the cut chilies a few times, and the seeds readily separate. Lift out the chilies or transfer them to a large-holed colander. Small seeds drop through while the chilies stay behind.

Technique: Rehydrating Dried Chilies

Reconstitute chilies by soaking them in room temperature water. This rehydrates them without extracting too much flavor and color. Hot water leaches these elements out. Regardless of whether or not they're seeded, thirty minutes seems to be the ideal time to adequately soften chilies. After soaking them, drain the chilies in a sieve and then squeeze out excess moisture. Removing the moisture is especially important when making spice pastes for later use, since excess water encourages more microbial growth.

Technique: Rehydrating Dried Fungi

The slower soaking of mushrooms in room temperature water yields a much better texture than a rushed soak in warm or hot water. In addition, the use of hot water leaches out more flavor from inside the mushrooms. The ideal method for rehydration of dried fungi is to place them in a narrow container as opposed to a wide bowl. This will enable you to use less water and still cover the fungi. Use a container that has a "buddy," another container that fits inside that can be used to hold down the mushrooms under water (they tend to float when dry).

STEP-BY-STEP:

1. In narrow container (have a matching container or something to hold them down), combine the mushrooms with just enough water to barely cover.
2. Weigh them down with a heavy item or make sure the container is filled with water and mushrooms up to the top before covering.
3. Soak overnight.
4. Rub the gills under water to remove any grit. Let the dirt settle to the bottom and then decant (pour off) the clear liquid, leaving the grit behind (use a filter, if desired).

Technique: Toasting Thai and Malaysian Shrimp Paste

It's no mystery to me why many Southeast Asian homes have open kitchens. At least one part of the roof is usually open to the environment, allowing strong odors to escape the confines of the home. The aroma of fermented shrimp paste is much more powerful than its heavenly flavor. That flavor is an essential foundation of Malaysian, Singaporean, and Thai cuisines. Vietnamese shrimp paste is much wetter, and hence is not roasted before it's used.

1. Place measured shrimp paste in the center of a small piece of foil, about 6 inches in diameter.

2. Fold over the edges of the foil to enclose the paste well.

3. Push gently to flatten the paste to 1/8-inch thickness.

4. Roast the paste:

- Option 1: Hold the packet with metal tongs directly over a low flame, or place on top of an electric burner and cook for about 30 seconds on each side.
- Option 2: Heat a small sauté pan over medium heat. Once hot (about 1 minute), add flattened packet to pan. Roast for 2 to 3 minutes on each side.

5. Cool to room temperature. Peel back foil and add shrimp paste as needed.

Technique: Satay Grilling

Satay grills of Malaysia are long and narrow. The skewers of foods being grilled extend beyond the heat range. The grills are four to six inches across and two to four inches deep, with two metal rods running lengthwise. This design enables the meat to be very close to the heat without touching a lot of metal. Over a Western charcoal grill, the skewers would quickly burn. The slender grill enables the skewers to escape the fate of being burnt. But great satay *can* be created with a Western-style grill (without incinerating the bamboo skewers)! First, preheat the grill on high. Then, place a strip of foil parallel to the hottest part of the grill. Use this foil to protect the skewers from burning, and turn the skewers occasionally.

Technique: Toasting Spices

Toasting spices revives them. When in doubt, give all your spices a light toasting before using them. Some recipes require a deeper toasting, actually roasting the spices until they darken considerably—Thai curry paste falls into that category. When several spices are used in one recipe, I recommend the spices be toasted separately. The different density, moisture content, and shape are all factors that determine the length of time it takes to roast a spice. Begin separately, then intuitively you will begin to learn that some spices can be toasted together. When toasting cassia and star anise for five-spice powder, I toast them in one pan.

Many cooks new to Southeast Asian cooking are mystified as to why Southeast Asian cooks roast the spices as dark as they do. It's not a quick roast, but a slow browning of the spice, which mellows the spices' edge so more can be used and a deeper layer of flavor developed. Since each spice has different density and oil content, each spice should be roasted separately and then combined in a mortar or spice grinder. Of course, the more experienced cook may combine spices that roast at similar rates, but since their source, age, moisture, and oil content vary from batch to batch, it is hard to yield consistent results. If I'm preparing large quantities of spices, I grind each separately and then combine them. Let the spices cool before trying to grind them, as hot oils cause the pulverized spice to stick in the spice grinder, preventing the machine from achieving the desired fine grind. Unless otherwise specified, spices called for in the recipes of this book are measured whole.

Step 1

Step 3

Satay

Step 4

Curry Powders of Southeast Asia

The convenience of using premixed curry powders quickly became apparent as we developed the recipes for this book. After questioning countless cooks around Southeast Asia, I learned that a majority of cooks bought ready-made curry powders instead of roasting, grinding, and assembling their own spice blends. I tracked down the most-respected brands, got samples, and devoted weeks to replicating their intricate flavors. I got enormous help from the research and development team at Elite Spice, Inc., led by Leslie Krause. Their chemical analysis, in-depth study, and expert sleuthing helped us decipher the fundamental spice components of the curry powders used throughout Southeast Asia. Using the results of our research, Elite made a series of samples for me.

At this point I called in my friend and colleague Brad Kent. Brad is what my fellow members of the Research Chefs Association and I call a Culinologist®. The term indicates someone who is not only an accomplished chef, but also a food scientist. Brad and my team transposed the results of our curry powder project into recipes that mirror the exact flavor profiles so beloved in the various countries of Southeast Asia, so that if you're unable to find the top brand of curry powder from Thailand, Vietnam, Malaysia, or Singapore, you can make the curry powder right in your own kitchen.

At Chef Danhi & Co., we work from whole spices (whole seeds, nuts, barks, roots, etc.). We roast them individually and briefly in a dry pan, cool them, and then grind them in a mortar (faster than you think) or electric spice grinder. I recommend you do the same, since whole spices keep their potency longer than preground spices do. For accuracy, however, the recipes give measurements for ground spices. Regardless of whether you buy preground spices or grind your own, measure the spice in its powdered form.

How and Why

1. Individually toast each spice lightly in a dry pan over medium heat, cool to room temperature, and then grind into superfine powder using a mortar or spice grinder. Each spice toasts at a different rate, so it's best to toast them separately.

2. After combining measured spices, blend them mechanically. Just whisking them together is not the same as grinding the spices together; take a few minutes more to ensure harmonious flavors and colors.

3. The finer you grind the spices, the brighter the color will be. This is especially true with turmeric, which lends vibrant yellow color to spice mixes. A smooth glass, stone, or metal mortar works best for this step.

4. Store for up to six months. During the first few days and weeks, however, flavor and aromatic nuances are at their prime.

Thai-Style Curry Powder

Although Thai cookery is widely known for curry pastes, some Thai recipes call for curry powder made from ground toasted spices. The curry powder favored by Thai cooks owes much of its flavor to fenugreek seeds. While you may never have used this spice, its flavor will seem uncannily familiar to most Americans. During some classes I taught at the Culinary Institute of America, I infused sugar syrup with fenugreek and asked my students to taste the concoction blindfolded. Most said they thought they were tasting maple syrup. That's no surprise, since fenugreek is the main element of imitation maple syrup. It lends a deep sour flavor to Thai curry powder, which is balanced by the mystical essence of cumin.

Makes about 3/4 cup

6	Tbsp. Ground Coriander
3	Tbsp. Ground fenugreek
2	Tbsp. Ground cumin
2	tsp. Ground turmeric
1/2	tsp. Ground black pepper
1/4	tsp. Ground green cardamom

1. Blend all ingredients well in mortar, blender or mini-food processor. Make sure to grind spices together for at least a minute.

Vietnamese-Style Curry Powder

Vietnamese curry powder is the only one to include powdered annatto seeds, which lend a reddish hue to foods cooked with it. Sweet hints of cinnamon, nutmeg, and cloves harmonize with a dominant presence of coriander. Vietnamese curry powder is much higher in this lemony, floral spice than Indian style curry powders. Note the absence of cumin, a spice that the Vietnamese have not embraced fully.

Makes about 1/2 cup

5	Tbsp. Ground coriander
1	Tbsp. Ground paprika
1	tsp. Ground dried hot red chilies
3	Tbsp. Ground turmeric
1	tsp. Ground anise seed
1 1/2	tsp. Ground cinnamon
1 1/2	tsp. Ground nutmeg
3/4	tsp. Ground cloves
1/4	tsp. Ground annatto

1. Blend all ingredients well in mortar, blender or mini-food processor. Make sure to grind spices together for at least a minute.

Malaysian-Style Curry Powder for Seafood

Compared to Thai and Vietnamese curry powders, the Malay version has a higher percentage of turmeric. This imparts a vivid yellow color to any innocent bystander that the powder touches (pg. 35). In ancient Malay and Indian cooking, folk medicine dictated that fish should be rubbed with pulverized turmeric to rid it of bacteria and smooth the fish flavors. Today, their folk wisdom has been proven. Chefs recognize the softening of flavors brought on by turmeric, and scientists acknowledge the proven antiseptic characteristics of this colorful rhizome.

Makes about 1/2 cup

6	Tbsp. Ground coriander
1 1/2	Tbsp. Ground paprika
2	tsp. Ground long dried red chilies or other dried hot red chili
2 1/2	tsp. Ground cumin
2	tsp. Ground turmeric
1/2	tsp. Ground fenugreek
1/8	tsp. Ground anise seed

1. Blend all ingredients well in mortar, blender or mini-food processor. Make sure to grind spices together for at least a minute.

Malaysian-Style Curry Powder for Meat

Paprika, made from a dried chili pepper, stands in for a hard-to-find Malaysian mild chili in this recipe. Red chilies play a dominant role in this curry, marrying with coriander to elevate rich meat flavors. Cinnamon, anise, cardamom, and other sweet spices are indigenous to the Malay peninsula, which has been one of the world's most important spice growing areas for centuries.

Makes about 3/4 cup

1/4	cup Ground coriander
3	Tbsp. Ground paprika
4	tsp. Ground cumin
1	Tbsp. Ground anise seed
2	tsp. Ground turmeric
2	tsp. Ground long red chilies or other hot red chili
1	tsp. Ground cinnamon
1/2	tsp. Ground star anise
1/2	tsp. Ground cardamom

1. Blend all ingredients well in mortar, blender or mini-food processor. Make sure to grind spices together for at least a minute.

Rice Noodles in Curried Chicken Broth with Roasted Peanuts and Crispy Sesame Crackers

Coconut Milk

Thai: *Hua Gati;* Vietnamese: *Nuoc Cot-Dua;* Malay: *Santan*

Technique: Coconut Milk

I do not recommend what most books do: scooping off the top of the can's contents, considering that "thick milk," and then using the remaining amount as "thin." I find that method too inconsistent, as the thicker milk does not always settle the same way. I have developed a foolproof method. Some cans have thick portions, while other cans do not (even when refrigerated, as some recommend). Sometimes the entire can contains thick milk—much thicker than homemade. Without further ado, here is my method:

Shake the can very well before opening it (and, incidentally, always rinse the can first to remove any dust or other foreign matter from the outside). Open the can and stir until evenly mixed. You now have a can of thick coconut milk. For thin coconut milk that emulates the second pressing, combine one part water to one part coconut milk by volume. Yes, it's very thin. But if you make fresh coconut milk, you'll see that thin coconut milk is quite watery, too. Oh yes, do not ever use Coco Lopez or any other sweetened coconut milk designed for the bar as a replacement for genuine coconut milk in cooking.

Coconut milk is not the liquid in the center of the coconut (that's coconut water). It is the creamy white liquid made from the flesh of a mature coconut—those old dark brown coconuts with the hard shell, not the younger coconuts with the pared-down light brown husk still attached or the still round and green coconuts that are used as a beverage and cooking medium. Most cooks distinguish the difference between thick and thin coconut milks. Thick, sometimes called coconut cream, is from the first extraction with the addition of little or no water, or the thicker part that rises to the surface from a thinner milk. See (pg. 60) for more details regarding coconut milk.

HOW DO THEY MAKE COCONUT MILK?

In Thailand, just as in Malaysia, freshly prepared coconut milk is sold at most markets, so most Thais don't use canned. A mechanical coconut milk press that I saw on a recent trip to Thailand mesmerized me. It was able to extract huge amounts of coconut milk using only a small amount of added water. Since water dilutes the creamy, slightly sweet milk, less is better. Simply, the grated coconut milk is placed in a large cloth bag and then placed in a hydraulic press, which extracts the thick coconut milk. Water is added to the spent pulp and pressed again to yield a thinner second pressing of coconut milk.

Technique: Using Canned Coconut Milk

I *do not* recommend what most books do: scooping off the top of the can's contents, considering that "thick milk," and then using the remaining amount as "thin." I find that method too inconsistent as the thicker milk does not always

The coconut milk press

How and Why

Recipes in this book call for canned coconut milk, which is what I usually use at home. But if you've got the desire and the nuts to do it, the method below will enable you to make your own thick and thin coconut milks. Thick coconut milk is used for the first stage of making many Thai curries, see pages 164, 165, 166, 167, 168, or to finish rich curries of Malaysia, such as the Nonya vegetable curry (pg. 344). Thin coconut milk is great for simmering curries, adding to broth for a slow simmer, and for Thai Chicken Soup (pg. 142).

settle the same way. When the canned milk is colder it solidifies. Some cans have thick portions, while other cans do not (even when refrigerated, as some recommend).

Technique: Making Fresh Coconut Milk

Traditionally, Southeast Asian home cooks used a handheld or stool-mounted piece of metal with sharp "teeth" to shred the meat from a cracked coconut, the first step in making coconut milk. Now, they mostly buy the coconut meat already shredded from sellers at the market.

Each vendor has his or her technique for separating the firm white flesh from the dark brown shell. In Vietnam I have witnessed a seemingly fragile woman deftly swing a machete to break the shell off piece by piece. The flesh was then mechanically ground and pressed to extract the coconut milk. In Malaysia they usually split the coconut into halves and then shred the meat by pressing the nut onto a rotating spindle armed with shredding spikes. At Chatuchuk market in Bangkok, I saw a rotating gear that

114

caught the edge of the coconut and jammed it downward into a metal wedge to separate the flesh from the shell. The meat was then ground by machine. I was astounded to see the purity achieved by simply pressing out the milk; the ground flesh was transferred to a muslin sack and then placed in a hydraulic press to expel the thick coconut cream. I even brought back one of these spiked heads from Asia and had the maintenance crew at the Culinary Institute of America mount it onto a rotary motor so we could make fresh coconut milk on campus. The students really got a lot of pleasure from tasting the fresh milk, even though we used canned milk for all of our cooking.

Assuming you don't have a device like those in Asia, there are two methods for extracting the meat from a hard coconut. You can bake it first, to loosen the nut, or you can pry it out by brute force. In any recipe where you'll be cooking the coconut milk anyway, it's much easier to remove the meat by poking holes in the shell, draining the coconut water from the center, and baking it in an oven at 400°F for 15 minutes. The shell will be easy to crack, and the meat will come out freely.

For recipes where the milk will be used raw, I crack the nut open and pry out the meat with a butter knife. I love to strain and drink the water from the center of the coconut while I make the milk, sometimes in a cocktail with gin, Asian basil, lime, and mango.

Makes about 2 cups of milk

1   lg. Mature coconut (dark brown hard shelled), about 2 lbs. (1 kilo.)
2   cups Warm water

1. Extracting the Meat: Rinse coconut milk to remove excessive dirt and husk materials. Get a large thick and heavy cleaver (you will use BACK of cleaver) or hammer. Position a large container/bowl on your work surface to catch the liquid that will flow out when you crack it. Cup the coconut in one hand, and hold the cleaver/hammer in the other. Administer a forceful blow to the center (with back of cleaver, the dull side not the knives cutting edge. Juice will run into pan. Strain into a cup to drink. Continuing hitting the coconut, rotating it as you do, creating large cracks and breaking it into a few pieces. Rinse all of these pieces to get rid of all debris. Using a thick "butter/dinner knife" to carefully pry off pieces of the white meat, it will come off with a brown skin. Some people peel the skin when making coconut milk, others leave it. For curries, I don't worry about it. But for recipes where a creamy color is preferable like Mangos with Sticky Rice (pg. 180), or for the shredded coconut meat needed for the Molten Palm Sugar Pandan Balls (pg. 350), I take the time to peel off this brown part with a vegetable peeler.

2. Grate the Meat: The finer the better. Use a rasp-like grater or a box grater to transform the chunks into fine shreds. I suggest using the shredding attachment of a food processor, or just processing it with the blade for a minute to get a fluffy powder. Either way, you should yield about 2 cups of shredded coconut.

3. Extracting the Milk: Line a bowl with a fine cloth (lint-free) or several layers of cheesecloth.
- Thick Milk: In a small bowl, combine the shredded meat with 1/2 cup of boiling, then transfer to the cloth-lined bowl, gather up sides, twist to encase coconut pulp, and wring as much thick milk out as possible. Re-line bowl with cloth. About 1/2 cup.
- Thin Milk: Combine the squeezed milk with 1 1/2 cups of warm water (at least 90°F or 32°C). Pour this mixture back in with the shredded coconut in the cloth, gather up sides, twist to encase coconut pulp and squeeze again to extract as much milk out as possible. About 1 1/2 cups.

Using Your Noodles

Fresh Rice Noodles

If noodles are actually fresh, soft, and have never been refrigerated, use your finger to pull them apart. If they are still in whole sheets, cut them into the desired shapes and lengths. I suggest that even if you don't plan to use the entire package, you separate the contents into individual strands, use what you want, and then place the remaining noodles in small bags. A simple dunk in boiling water later will bring them back to life.

- If chilled: Once refrigerated, fresh rice noodles get very firm and are tough to peel apart. This can be rectified with some lukewarm water and a lot of patience. Break or cut off however many noodles you need, and cover them with lukewarm water for 10 minutes. Then peel back the individual layers of noodles.
- If fresh: If they have never been chilled, they will soften within a few seconds of entering boiling water. Really, no more than 10 seconds is needed. Longer cooking actually ruins their texture.

center; there should not be any raw dough left in the center, yet it should still have a resilient bite. Undercooking is best, as with all of the recipes the noodles are reheated in boiling water, and you can complete the cooking process then.

Regardless of the thickness, lots of water is one tip for success. I have always used the ratio of one gallon of water to one pound of noodles. Do note that if you are cooking three pounds of noodles you can probably get away with less than three gallons of water—it does not scale up in direct relation. This is where the art of cooking comes into play, and you need to experiment as you try things out. When you have a lot of noodles I suggest you bring two pots of water to a boil and cook smaller amounts. It is not recommended to cook a second batch of noodles in water a second time, as lots of starch is released into the water when it cooks. It is best to use fresh water (no salt added) for every batch of noodles.

Drain the noodles well, rinse with hot water first to remove excess starch, then rinse with cool water until they are the water's temperature. Drain well and store at room temperature for a while (less than two hours) or refrigerate until ready to use. I do not add oil to prevent sticking—a splash of water later will release them quickly.

Dried Rice Noodles

I've found that soaking these noodles in cool water for thirty minutes to one hour before cooking yields the best texture and flavor. For some dishes, such as the street food noodle *Pad Thai* (pg. 172), they are soaked for thirty minutes and never boiled; they're added to the pan in a partially soaked, raw state. These are seasoned with a fish sauce, tamarind, palm sugar, and chili mixture and stir-fried until the noodles are tender, adding only small additions of water as necessary to soften the noodles, leaving a desirably chewy-textured noodle.

Fresh Wheat and Egg Noodles

Cooking wheat and egg noodles is no different than cooking fresh Italian pasta. These noodles cook very quickly—sometimes as fast as two minutes. Of course, the cooking time depends on the thickness of the noodles. Look at the package—most manufacturers recommend cooking times for each type of noodle. The ultimate judge of doneness can be easily ascertained by plucking one noodle from the boiling water and biting into it. Look at the

Fresh Rice Noodle Sheets

Thai: *Sen Kuaytiaw* or *Sen Lek*;
Vietnamese: *Banh Uot*; Cantonese:
Kway Teow; Hokkien: *Hor Fun*

I usually buy fresh rice noodles at my local Asian store (often so fresh they're still warm), but not everyone has that luxury. Still, no one should be cheated out of the silky smooth pleasures of fresh rice noodles. Though the recipe takes over an hour, most of that is inactive time. You'll just have to switch plates at ten-minute intervals.

These noodles float effortlessly in broths, such as the Ipoh Style Rice Noodles in Chicken Broth (pg. 306). And they're perfect for a brisk stir-fry, such as "char kway teow" (pg. 336).

Makes about 1¹/2 lbs of noodles (1.7 kg.)

2   cups Rice flour
1   Tbsp. Tapioca starch
¹/4   tsp. Kosher salt
2   cups Water
1   tsp. Vegetable oil
as needed Vegetable oil for coating (cooking spray, without flour added, works well)

1. Prepare batter: In a large bowl, whisk together the rice flour, tapioca starch, and salt. Add water and oil; whisk into a smooth batter (it will be thin, like milk). Strain out any lumps through a fine wire mesh sieve. Set batter aside to rest for at least 30 minutes.
2. Set up steamer equipment: Oil a baking sheet and two 8-inch plates. Set a steamer over a pot of rapidly boiling water (pg. 101).
3. Make the sheets: Adjust an oiled plate as level as possible in the steamer; allow it to get hot, covered for 3 minutes. Stir batter to re-distribute settled flour, and then ladle ¹/4 cup of batter onto the hot plate. Use the back of a spoon to spread out into a thin, even layer, about ¹/16 to ¹/8 inch (0.1 to 0.3 cm.) thick. Cover; cook about 8 minutes until sheet is firmly set (press with tip of finger: it should bounce back). Noodle should have an opaque appearance throughout. Carefully remove hot plate; cool to room temperature. Oil the top of noodle sheet lightly, and then use a rubber spatula to assist in peeling the noodle from the plate. Reserve the finished noodles, covered, on oiled baking sheet (they can be stacked, they will not stick). Repeat with remaining batter (you should get about 12 sheets)

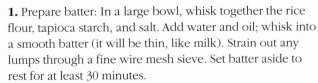

TAPIOCA STARCH

Tapioca starch, also called cassava flour, is derived from the cassava plant, which is known as *yucca* or *yuca* in the Caribbean and the American Southwest. This starch is available as a superfine powder and also as small round balls called *pearl tapioca* or *sago*. Almost as prevalent as cornstarch in Southeast Asia, tapioca is used similarly as a thickening agent. Tapioca pearls are used to enhance the texture in sweet and savory soups, puddings, and steamed dishes. Tapioca yields a viscous, almost mucous like texture. Believe it or not, it is a desirable trait.

How and Why

1. Resting the batter for at least 30 minutes yields the most resilient texture. Resting allows the starch to hydrate before it is cooked.

2. Maintain enough water in steamer. The batter needs adequate moisture to properly hydrate during steaming.

Crispy Fried Garlic

Tidbits of deep-roasted garlic flavor noodles, soups, and even fried rice throughout Southeast Asia. To the uninitiated they may seem burnt, but their brown color belies a pleasantly bittersweet nuance.

It's important to chop or slice the garlic evenly to ensure even cooking. The finished garlic stays fresh for a few days at room temperature. For longer storage, keep it in the freezer or refrigerator (bring back to room temperature before using). Save the frying oil for cooking other dishes. It lends great garlic flavor.

Makes 1/2 cup

1/2   cup Garlic cloves, peeled whole, either halved and sliced, or coarsely chopped
1/4   cup Vegetable oil

1. Air-dry sliced or chopped garlic on towel-lined baking sheet 1 hour. Set up a metal sieve over a heatproof container or bowl.
2. Heat oil in a small skillet or wok over medium-low flame for 30 seconds. Add garlic; cook, stirring often, until light golden brown (about 15 minutes). Watch closely.
3. When garlic reaches golden brown, strain, and spread evenly on a plate lined with three paper towels. Cool for 1 hour.

How and Why

1. Remove excess moisture by drying for a minimum of one hour. This helps promote even cooking.

2. Stirring constantly helps to cook the garlic evenly. Heat is higher near the sides and bottom of the pot. Stirring circulates the garlic, ensuring that no piece gets much more heat than the others.

3. The garlic will continue to darken from residual heat even after it's been strained. Drain while it's still light golden brown.

4. The garlic will not feel crisp until after it's cooled.

Curry Devil — Same technique can be used for a golden ginger garnish (pg. 328).

Crispy Fried Shallots

These caramelized shallots have the crunch factor, and their flavor is addictive. Fried shallots are essential textural components to Southeast Asian cooking. They're sold everywhere in the region. They're harder, but possible, to find in stores here, but making them is easy. The key is to cut the shallots very, very evenly. This ensures that some don't burn before others become crispy. Once you're done cooking the shallots, save their flavorful cooking oil for use in other dishes. Fried shallots freeze well. Bring them to room temperature before using them.

Makes ¹/₂ cup

8   large Shallots, halved through the root end,
           sliced ¹/₈-inch (0.3-cm.) lengthwise
¹/₂   cup Vegetable oil

1. Air-dry sliced shallots on a towel-lined baking sheet 1 to 2 hours.

2. In a small skillet or wok over medium-low flame, heat oil for 30 seconds. Add shallots; cook, stirring often until golden brown (about 15 to 20 minutes). Be careful, shallots will continue to darken after they're removed from the oil.

3. Scoop or strain shallots from of oil. Spread evenly on a paper towel-lined plate. Cool 1 hour.

How and Why

1. Dry the shallots at room temperature for a crisp texture. Air-dry for at least an hour; otherwise the edges will be brown and the centers still soft and chewy.

2. Stir often. This ensures the shallots are evenly coated with oil as they fry.

3. Stop cooking one shade before the desired color is reached. Even after removing from the oil, residual heat will continue to cook the shallots.

4. The shallots will become crisp after they've cooled. While still hot the shallots remain flimsy. Give them ten minutes to crisp up.

Pickled Green Chilies

Astaple on tables across Southeast Asia, these piquant chilies add a cutting bite to rich dishes such as Yin Yang noodles (pg. 340). Each country in the region pickles a different type of chili, but the recipe is generally the same. So addictive you should make a batch when you have extra chilies or time on hand and store them in your refrigerator. You will soon find that you reach for their tangy bite often.

Makes 2 cups (with brine)

1 1/2 cups Distilled white vinegar
1   tsp. Granulated sugar
1   tsp. Kosher salt
1/2   lb. Fresh green hot chilies,
          such as long green chilies,
          jalapenos or serranos,
          stemmed and sliced into
          1/8-inch (0.3 cm.) rings

1. Whisk together the vinegar, sugar and salt until they dissolve.
2. Add chilies to glass or plastic jar that is just large enough to hold them.
3. Pour vinegar mixture over chilies. Transfer to refrigerator to marinate for at least 3 days. Chilies will have the best flavor and texture for 3 to 4 weeks, but can still be served for up to two months.

Pork Cracklings and Rendered Pork Fat (Lard)

These golden morsels of flavor are denser than the "chicharrones" of Latin America. Starting with neutral-flavored vegetable oil ensures a significant yield of fat, which can be used for stir-frying noodles for dishes like Hokkien Mee (pg. 338). Cherish any extra that you have: Store it in the refrigerator for some stir-fried vegetables or rice later on. It's made from the cut sold in the U.S. as "pork butt," which is actually the shoulder of the pork despite its name. The recipe provides more crispy pork cracklings than needed for one recipe...but you'll see that snacking on them is addictive.

Makes about 2 cups

3/4 lb. (340 g.) Pork shoulder (butt) or belly (skin, fat and meat), cut into 1/2-inch (5 cm.) (1.3 cm) cubes
1 cup (237 milliliters) Vegetable oil

Timing Note: This recipe needs to rest overnight.

1. Combine pork and oil in a saucepan over medium-low heat. Bring to a "boil," and then lower to simmer for about 25 to 45 minutes, until pork becomes light golden brown.

How and Why

1. Two-stage cooking makes the cracklings more tender. Cooking the first day, cooling, and letting the pork pieces sit in fat overnight ensures that when these are reheated, any trapped moisture expands and puffs the cracklings, making them tender and crunchy.

2. Cooking slowly yields the most fat and makes them crisp. During Step 1, cooking over medium-low heat renders the greatest amount of fat. If the temperature is too high, the fat congeals and will not produce the desired crispness.

Remove from heat, cool to room temperature. Refrigerate overnight, still in the saucepan.
2. The next day, return the saucepan to the stove over medium heat, and cook the cracklings again, until the meat expands and turns deep brown. Using a slotted spoon or skimmer, transfer solid bits to a plate; pat with paper towels to remove excess oil.
3. Use the strained pork fat (lard) for stir-frying dishes such as Malaysian Hokkien Mee noodles (pg. 338) or the cracklings for the Vietnamese Bánh Bèo, petite rice cakes (pg. 214) and the Thai savory bites (pg. 138).

Thailand

HISTORY

Never Colonized

Rice Cultivated 4000 BCE

Portuguese Introduce Chilies in 1500's

ETHNIC DIVERSITY

Theravada Buddhism

Muslim South

Hill Tribes in North

GEOGRAPHY

Plains, Lowlands & Mountainous

Extensive River Network

Largest Country in Area

Authentic Recipes

CULINARY ETIQUETTE

Table Condiments

Sticky Rice Scoops Food with Hands

Soup as Beverage

PREVAILING FLAVORS

Lime-chili Dressed Salads

Galangal, Lemongrass & Kaffir Lime Infused Soups

Spice Paste Based Coconut Curries

Thailand has enchanted my soul since the first time I set foot there almost twenty years ago. It's an extraordinary country where my arrival is always greeted with welcoming smiles, beautiful people, and enticing food aromas. The excitement builds as I gaze from the airplane window upon the approaching capital metropolis of Bangkok. Fertile agricultural land surrounds the hectic city: rich, green, flooded rice paddies and small farms with neat rows of vegetables still thrive in these developed central plains. The newly built Suvarnabhumi airport funnels me effortlessly onto the streets for yet another culinary journey.

An elevated highway zooms directly from the airport to the city center, a spectacle of ancient city turned wild. My taxi driver lays on the horn as he weaves through the congested streets, dodging mini-trucks called *tuk tuks,* millions of scooters, and throngs of cars. Don't fret—the Thai government has created an excellent public transportation system to combat this assault on the senses. Serene parks, hundreds of opulent temples, the flowing Chao Praya River, and a network of very active canals juxtapose this chaos.

An underlying feeling of happiness—the Thai approach to life exudes a spirit of fun that they call *sanuk,* not just in their social life, but woven into the fabric of who they are. It warms my heart to see Thais greeting each other with such respect, as they bring both palms together to *wai.* This warm salutation is accompanied by a smile and a modest bow of the head. The younger person or person of lower social or business status initiates the *wai,* and it is politely returned. Simultaneously they say, *"sawasdee kop"* (*"sawasdee ka" for women*), a greeting equivalent to "hello." Another popular expression is *"mai pen rai,"* loosely translated as "it is not a problem." They will politely say this to downplay any awkward situation. At a minimum, you can *wai* and smile and be forgiven for most minor offenses.

I'm always mesmerized by Thailand's vibrant flavors. They're uniquely Thai, yet influence from neighboring cultures is unmistakable. Thailand is the only Southeast Asian country that has never been colonized. The country has absorbed characteristics of visiting cultures while retaining its identity. The Thai word for "delicious" is

"aroy," and it accurately describes the country's fragrant foods like spicy cool salads, hot-and-sour soups, rich coconut curries, and sweet fruit with steamed sticky rice.

Geography

Thailand's shape resembles an elephant head, with a broad, central land mass at the center. The two "ears" are bordered by Myanmar (Burma) to the west and Laos to the east. Cambodia is a shoulder at the southeast border. The long trunk extends down along the Gulf of Thailand and the Indian Ocean to touch the northern border of Malaysia. There, these culinary cultures collide in a fusion of flavors.

The year-round tropical climate enables the Thais to take advantage of their lowlands, plains, and mountainous regions to grow a bounty of produce, raise livestock, and harvest fresh and saltwater fish. Regional cuisines have evolved into four distinct Thai areas: North, Northeast, Central, and South. The North is less tropical, so curries are often clear broths like the Jungle duck curry on (pg. 167), not creamy like the more coconut-laden Thai curry most Westerners would recognize. Some famous dishes from the North, such as the iconic crunchy green papaya salad *som tum* (pg. 148) and the brothy coconut curry noodles called *kao soi* (pronounced like "cow soy") (pg. 178) from the city of Chang Mai, exhibit influences from bordering Burma. Northerners prefer long grain sticky rice over the fragrant jasmine rice of the central plains and southern tropical areas.

Extensive river networks provide irrigation and support the richest aquaculture industry in the world. The Gulf of Thailand provides the industrialized capital with a major port. Seafood flows into the city through the port and from the southern peninsula. June through October is the rainy season.

Tik, my friend and guide Wai's to Mrs. Vorarittinapa

The southern coastline allows open access to the gulf and the Indian Ocean, bringing a bounty of fresh seafood, including small fish that are transformed into the salty, pungent fish sauce called *nahm pla*, which is essential to a majority of dishes in the country's vast cuisine (pg. 48, pg. 98). Thailand produces most of the world's supply of this flavorful elixir. Even in big cities like Bangkok, the rivers are still heavily used for the transport of people, foods, and other goods. Communities come together daily at "floating markets" to exchange goods as they do in Vietnam.

Business as usual during rainy day on the river

Pounding papaya salad in Northern Thailand

Shrimp farming supplies some of the world demand

Produce and prepared meals at the Ampawa floating market.

History

Anthropologists agree that some of the earliest civilizations evolved in what is now Thailand, known as Siam until 1939. There is evidence of rice having been cultivated in the area as early as 4000 B.C.

Although the dishes of this region do not show noticeable European influence, the ingredients that Thai cooks rely upon do. Chilies, which many consider a hallmark of Thai cuisine, were introduced by the Portuguese during the fifteenth century, the Age of Discovery. Without them, Thailand's Culinary Identity™ would be unrecognizable.

Ethnic Diversity

It is said that the Thais are responsible for introducing Buddhism from India to the rest of Asia. Almost 95 percent of Thais are Buddhist. Monks are highly visible in all aspects of daily life—there are even seats reserved for such spiritual sages on ferries across Bangkok's Chao Praya River. Most males spend some time as young adults as monks, reinforcing a spiritual outlook that is felt throughout the Thai culture.

Culinary Etiquette

Thais snack throughout the day, selecting packets of steamed sticky rice from boats along the canals or devouring noodles while chatting with street vendors. Eating is a time to socialize with family, friends, and workmates. Family-style dining is common at large meals, but street food is made in individual portions for people on the move (pg. 22).

Like Malaysians, Thais eat with a combination of fork and spoon more often than they eat with chopsticks. Chopsticks aren't customary in Thailand except with noodle dishes. The fork is used to push rice to the spoon, which brings the food to your

Monks meander the streets for food donations of sustenance.

The Grand palace in Bangkok is a must-see.

WHERE ARE THOSE NAPKINS?

Visitors to Southeast Asia quickly realize that napkins are not provided in basic eating establishments. They're more shocked when they see the cylindrical dispenser on the table holding a very familiar type of tissue: toilet paper (yeah, you got that right). Most people carry around small pouches with tissues for this sort of situation and many restaurants offer wet-napkins, for a charge (only ten Thai baht, about thirty U.S. cents), but I strongly recommend you stay clear of them as they are most likely perfumed and would ruin your eating experience by releasing some overwhelming floral aroma into your eating arena.

mouth. Eating directly from the fork would be akin to eating from the blade of a knife at a Western-style dinner. The ease of using the fork to fill a spoon is so logical, it still amazes me that more of the world doesn't eat this way. It's how we eat in my home, even for much of our non-Asian food. Many Thais eat certain dishes with their hands, especially in the North where sticky rice is most common. Only the right hand is used for food. Two or three fingers are employed in tandem with the thumb to scoop food and push it gently into the mouth.

Thai dinners consist of numerous dishes served all at once, family style. Restaurant meals, except in fine-dining restaurants, are not served in any special order. Dishes are brought out as they are ready. Be patient and resist the urge to dive right into the food. The most-honored guest, eldest, most senior in business, or most affluent is served first. Plates, platters, or bowls are left on the table and not passed around as in most Western cultures (pg. 18). Don't be startled when someone across the table, next to a dish that is hard for you to reach, spoons some food onto your plate—it's simply a sign of hospitality. Simply say "kop kum kop (ka)" (use "ka" instead of the second "kop" if the person speaking is female, a common grammatical rule). It means "thanks."

Discussions about the food are sure to be part of the table conversation. If you feel the food is delicious, tell them so by saying it's *aroy*. If it really rocks, say *aroy maak*, meaning "very delicious." Each dish is savored on its own first, a custom that makes culinary sense. For example, if you have a meal with rice and three dishes: first take a single spoon of rice, symbolizing the respect for this staff of life. Next add a spoon of curry and taste these, then maybe

some salad and eat that, slowly making your way through the foods and enjoying the nuances that each offers.

Soup is often sipped during the meal in lieu of a cold beverage. Serving spoons are sometimes present—otherwise a communal pot is customary. Don't be surprised when your tablemate takes her own spoon and dips into the common pot to serve herself or to spoon some soup atop a small bowl of rice for flavor. Beer, water, and fruit juices are traditionally served after the meal, yet the newer generations are now adopting the Western style of drinking while eating.

Prevailing Dishes

Salads (*yam*) are a strong player on the menus of Thai restaurants (much more than in Malaysia or Singapore). Although ratios vary, many of the salads are based on dressings that contain fresh lime juice, pungent fish sauce, golden blond palm sugar, chilies, and garlic. Iconic examples include hand-pounded payaya salad (*som tum*) (pg. 148), fried kaffir ground pork salad adorned with fried kaffir lime leaves and chilies (*laarb*) (pg. 152), and mixed poached seafood salad (*yam talay*) (pg. 150).

Papaya salad with its sweet/sour/salty flavor profile

Crisp-fried leaves and chilies are nibbled along with Thai Laarb salad.

Grilling skewered bananas on the street for a daytime snack

Soups (*tom*)

Soups sometimes serve as a vehicle for noodles, making them a one-dish meal. Other times, broth fills the "moat" of a steel hot pot as fire erupts from the center. That broth is spooned into small bowls to be sipped along with the rest of the meal. Soups are categorized by intensity of flavor—*tom yam*'s powerful hot-and-sour flavor profile is at one end of the scale, and subtle *kaeng jeut*, a lighter style broth soup, is at the other. Three iconic recipes included in this book include crimson hot and sour soup (*tom tum gung*) (pg. 144), the creamy coconut milk-enriched chicken and galangal soup (*tom kah kai*) (pg. 142), and the cinnamon and star anise–spiked beef broth called "Thai boat noodles."

This red ant larvae curry lacks coconut milk.

Shells left on the shrimp yield a tender meat and a flavorful broth.

Curries (*kaeng*)

Curry is an often-misunderstood term. The term "curry" is derived from the Indian word *kari,* which simply means a sauce or a dish simmered in sauce. It's more of a *class* of dishes than a specific flavor. In Thailand people use the term *kaeng* (rhymes with "gang") to designate a spicy seasoning paste. Chefs and scholars debate the number of different Thai curries, but most agree that there are dozens. In the U.S., red, green, yellow, and Mussamun curry pastes (all recipes in this chapter) are the most popular. Although Thai curries contain some dry ingredients, they should not be confused with the dry spice blends (*masalas*) of India. Thai curries are complexly flavored pastes that rely mostly on fresh aromatics like lemongrass, galangal, shallots, garlic, coriander (cilantro) root, and kaffir lime zest.

Sweets snacks (*khanom*)

Khanom are not considered a dessert in the Western sense, since they're not served at the end of a meal. Instead, they are eaten throughout the day. Many Thai cooks specialize in these treats, as Western pastry chefs specialize in desserts. The Thais use eggs often and creatively. Egg yolks are streamed into simmering syrup to form golden threads, which are then served in bundles or are used as parts of other treats. The Thais learned much of their artistry with eggs from the Portuguese traders.

Probably my favorite khanom is Khanom Krok. These crusty, sweet-and-salty coconut custards are cooked in a special pan with mutiple divots. One batter (salted) is added and begins to cook to form the shell, then a second, sweeter batter is added and covered to cook slowly. Sometimes pieces of taro, corn, pumpkin, or scallions are used to top them. This is cooked with the cover off to get a crisp shell with an ever-so-creamy coconut custard filling.

Sticky rice steamers at the market

The first stage of Khanom Krok is to create a crisp layer.

Go to the Chatuchuck food market for the best Khanom Krok "aroy maak."

Dominant Ingredients

Rice (*khâo*) is of utmost importance in Thai cookery (pg. 72). Long grain sticky rice is essential to Thai tables, especially in the northern areas. The stark white, slender, polished grains are soaked before cooking, usually overnight. They are then steamed in specially designed conical baskets (pg. 180) to produce translucent spears of chewy rice that are used to scoop up food. The rice is eaten with your hands. It is pinched into balls and then gathered with salads, stews, and other dishes.

Fragrant jasmine rice (*khâo hom mali*) is also native to Thailand. The floral aroma is released into the kitchen as the rice simmers in water, until its pearly white grains reside steaming in the pot. The chemical compound 2-Acetyl-1-pyrroline is responsible for the "popcorn-like" flavor; it is also present in pandan leaves (pg. 37) and baked bread. Jasmine's individualistic grains are incorporated effortlessly with saucy dishes and accent their flavor without being overbearing. Thailand is the world's leading exporter of this naturally aromatic rice.

Fermented Condiments

Fermentation is one of the most important forces in flavor creation known to man and plays a role in more foods than most people are aware (chocolate, coffee, tea, most spices, wine, beer, and bread, among other things). The importance of Thai fish sauce (*nam pla*), a product of fermented fish, cannot be overstated (pg. 48). Do not be scared by the scent. Not all dishes employ the golden brown, slightly viscous aromatic liquid—just most of them.

Other fermented umami bombs that add salty, complex flavors include shrimp paste, oyster sauce, light soy sauce, and yellow bean sauce. Dried shrimp, fish, and some fermented vegetables also add fermented flavors and textures.

Presentation

Presentations of food in Thailand are more intricate and ornate than those in Singapore, Malaysia, and Vietnam. Broad leaves of the banana plant are often used as a natural serving plate. This tradition has evolved into an art form, too. Leaves are folded to create decorative displays, often representing the king's emblem or palace. Although such elaborate decorations were once held inside the walls of the king's palace, these traditional techniques are now taught in schools, homes, and restaurants across Thailand.

Tea and Coffee

Green and black teas are drunk throughout the day. But unique to Thailand is a bright orange tea that is usually served over crushed ice. It's more accurately called a "tea mix," as its black tea leaves are combined with other flavorings like roasted corn, vanilla, star anise, and even cinnamon, plus red and yellow food coloring. Possibly, the original color was garnered from ground tamarind seeds, an ingredient now absent from commercial mixes. The cloyingly sweet base is brewed with sugar in a sock-shaped cloth tea bag, cooled, poured over crushed ice, and then topped with dairy to create a floating cloud of milk. Half-and-half has become the favorite dairy used in U.S. Thai restaurants, but I find that the traditional evaporated milk makes a more balanced drink (pg. 182).

Thai coffee is usually heavily sweetened with sugar or condensed milk (taking care of the "light" and "sweet" in one flavorful addition). For the special-tasting iced coffee found in Thai restaurants, look in Asian markets for coffee labeled as "Oliang Powder." It has the addition of flavorful enhancers such as corn, soy beans, and sesame seeds (pg. 362)

Alcoholic Beverages

Thai people today drink more than in the past. Alcohol consumption goes against once-strict Buddhist teachings. Beer, rice whisky, and imported spirits are preferred. Grape wines, which are highly sensitive to temperature, require sophisticated storage in Thailand's hot climate. They are relegated to fine restaurants. Beer goes particularly well with Thai food, and several local brands are excellent, including Singha and Beer Chang.

DECORATIVE FRUIT CARVING

Seven hundred years ago, when the city of Sukhothai was the capital of the kingdom of Thailand, the art of *kae sa luk* (Thai fruit carving) was developed there. Legend has it that a servant preparing for the king's celebration of the *loi kratong* (floating lantern festival) took some creative license to carve a flower and a bird from vegetables. Thus begun the custom of decorative carving in the king's palace. The art form evolved to become an essential part of the royal era. Women were trained in the art, and competitions were held periodically. Decorative fruits and vegetables carved with ornate flowers and wildlife became identified with the culinary culture and were often used as serving vessels .

In the 1930s Thai fruit carving became part of a home economics program that helped bring this royal art to all classes of society. At that time, some practitioners of the craft began carving soap as well. Now carvers work in tourist areas, creating a bounty of colorful flowers that are sold in small decorative boxes as souvenirs. Also in Thailand today, cucumbers are carved into "leaves" to be dunked in dips or used to garnish food. Elaborate displays of kae sa luk vegetables and fruits still decorate tables for banquets, holidays, and auspicious occasions.

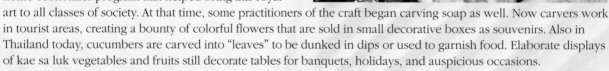

Roasted Red Chili Paste

Nahm Prik Pow

This is a common store-bought condiment, usually labeled "Chili Paste in Soya Bean Oil or Roasted Red Chili Paste in Oil." I consider it a sort of chili jam with its deep roasted flavor, sweet and salty taste, and slightly pungent dried shrimp aroma. With it, you can create deeply flavored stir-fries in a snap. It's often used a foundation for hot and sour soup, and lends its deep red color to Thai salads. Young people can be caught spreading on white bread as part of a sandwich. I am partial to it with sliced cucumbers!

Makes 1 cup

1/2 cup Vegetable oil
1 Tbsp. Dried shrimp (pg. 93)
1 cup Sliced shallots, about 1/8 inch (0.3 cm.) thick
1/2 cup Sliced garlic, about 1/8 inch (0.3 cm.) thick
1/4 cup (1/4 oz. / 7 g.) Dried red chilies, stems and seeds removed
2 Tbsp. Fish sauce (*nahm pla*)
2 Tbsp. Tamarind pulp (pg. 109)
3 Tbsp. Light brown palm sugar (pg. 58)

How and Why

Use a medium heat to achieve the proper doneness with each fried item. Medium heat gives the center time to fully develop flavors without burning.

1. Soak shrimp in warm water for 5 minutes, drain and dry with paper towels

2. Brown aromatics: Heat oil in a large skillet or wok over medium heat; add shrimp. Cook until they darken, about 2 minutes. Strain; return oil to wok. Reserve shrimp. Fry shallots while stirring often until a majority of edges are deep golden brown, about 2 minutes. Strain; return oil to wok. Fry garlic while stirring often until light golden brown, about 1 minute. Strain; return oil to wok. Fry the chilies until lightened in color, about 5 seconds. Strain; combine with shrimp, shallots, and garlic. Cool.

3. Use a mortar to pound ingredients to a smooth paste or use a mini-food processor or transfer shrimp mixture and cooking oil into a mini-food processor, and puree until very fine.

4. Give it a final cook: In a wok, combine shrimp puree with fish sauce, tamarind pulp, and sugar; and boil for 1 minute while stirring constantly. Cool to room temperature before transferring to container to store in refrigerator for up to two months.

Sriracha Chili Sauce
Nahm Prik Sriracha

While browsing my indispensable Lonely Planet guide one day in Bangkok, I noticed the small Southern seaport village of Sriracha on a map. It was only a few hours away. The next day we hopped a bus headed south to the gulf of Thailand. Upon arrival, I proceeded to ask anyone who would listen how the town's namesake chili sauce was made. Everyone, from restaurateurs and housewives to "average Joes" on the street gave me the same puzzled look, and insisted that everyone buys the stuff, and only the factories know how to make it. I never found the source on that trip, this recipe was developed by talking with Thai cooks, tasting the bottled sauces in Thailand and the USA and figuring it out.

With this recipe, it will only take you moments to transform red chilies, garlic, salt, fish sauce, sugar, and vinegar into this smooth brilliant red sauce. If you want to plan ahead and invest more time a few days of fermenting the chilies really develops a more complex flavor. From its humble beginnings in this small seaside town, Sriracha chili sauce has become one of the most used sauces in fusion foods. It's added to mayonnaise for spicy sushi rolls, squeezed on French fries with ketchup, and bottles of this Thai sauce can curiously be found in nearly every Vietnamese restaurant to accompany the classic beef noodle soup (pg. 218).

Makes 1 1/2 cups

16   (about 3/4 lb.) Long red chilies or other hot
         red chilies, roughly chopped (pg. 44)
4   cloves Garlic, roughly chopped
3/4   tsp. Kosher salt
1   Tbsp. Fish sauce (*nahm pla*)
1   Tbsp. Granulated sugar
1   cup Water
1/4   cup Distilled white vinegar

QUICK COOKED VERSION

1. In small saucepan, combine chilies, garlic, salt, fish sauce and water. Bring to a boil, lower to a simmer, and cook gently for 5 minutes. Remove from heat; cool to room temperature.
2. Transfer to blender; add vinegar, and puree until very smooth (about 5 minutes). Strain through fine wire mesh sieve, pushing as much as possible through the sieve. Add water as needed to adjust consistency.
3. Store in refrigerator for up to one month, but tastes best within first week.

FERMENTED COOKED VERSION

1. Combine chilies, garlic, salt, fish sauce, sugar in food processor and chop finely, transfer to small container, cover well and keep at room temperature for 3 to 4 days until it begins to bubble slightly.
2. In small saucepan, bring fermented chili mixture to a boil, lower to a simmer, and cook gently for 5 minutes. Remove from heat; cool to room temperature.
3. Transfer to blender; add vinegar, and puree until very smooth (about 5 minutes). Strain through fine wire mesh sieve, pushing as much as possible through the sieve. Add water as needed to adjust consistency.
4. Store in refrigerator for up to one month, but it tastes best within first week.

How and Why

1. Ferment the chilies for the most flavor. Fermenting the ingredients allows for the development of flavor as natural yeast grow.

2. With long red chilies or Thai bird chilies leave the "crown" on the chilies to maximize their inherent the floral flavor. Snip off the stem but leave the "crown" (the base of the flower bud) that connects the stem to the fruit (pg. 44).

Thai Sweet Chili Sauce

Nahm Jim Gai

Sweet, spicy, sour, and salty all at once, this syrupy dipping sauce is the essential companion to certain dishes, such as Thai fish cakes (pg. 140). Over the years some of my students have helped me as much as I have taught them. Fah Vorarittinapap is one of them. Not only has she provided me a place to cook at her Lemongrass Café Restaurant in Houston, but she also introduced me to her family in Thailand. They taught me that this fundamental condiment is referred to as "grilled chicken sauce," underscoring the association of this sauce with the grilled chicken of Northeast Thailand (pg. 154). Gai is the transliteration of the Thai word for chicken, it is pronounced as "guy," the name "Nahm Jim Gai" roughly translates as "chili sauce for chicken."

Makes 1 cup

2   Tbsp. Roughly chopped long red chilies or other hot red chilies (pg. 44) seeds are optional, leave them in if you want it spicy.

1   medium Thai bird chili, red, roughly chopped

1   Tbsp. Roughly chopped garlic

1 1/2 tsp. Kosher salt

1 1/4 cups Granulated sugar

2   Tbsp. Fish sauce (*nahm pla*)

3/4 cup Distilled white vinegar

1/2 cup Water

1. In a mortar, pound both chilies, garlic, and salt into a rough paste (if not using a mortar, finely mince chilies and garlic).

2. Combine chili mixture with sugar, fish sauce, vinegar and water in a 2 qt. (2 L.) saucepan; bring to a boil. Boil over medium heat for about 10 minutes, until reduced to 1 cup.

3. Cool to room temperature. Sauce will thicken when cooled. Store in refrigerator. Bring to room temperature before serving. For the best flavor, use within the first few weeks (though sauce can be stored in the refrigerator for up to three months).

How and Why

1. Pound the aromatics in a mortar for the most authentic texture and appearance. Pounding the ingredients will yield a more rustic appearance, with jagged edges that are characteristic to this sauce.

2. Measure the yield to ensure the right thickness/viscosity. To attain the right consistency, enough water must be cooked out to create a dense sugar syrup when cool.

Cucumber Relish

Achat

Sweet, sour and vibrant, this relish is classically served with red curry spiced fried fish cakes (pg. 140) or golden chicken satay (pg. 156). Some Thais like to add chopped cilantro. Others prefer a sprinkling of chopped roasted peanuts. This cooling dish is a great stand-alone snack, but is an especially refreshing accompaniment to grilled fish or shrimp. Add carrots, tomatoes, or cabbage to make it a more substantial side salad.

Makes 1 1/2 cups

1/4 cup Granulated sugar

1/2 tsp. Kosher salt

1/4 cup Water

1/4 cup Rice vinegar (unseasoned)

1 medium Cucumber, Kirby variety preferred, semi-peeled, quartered lengthwise, cut into 1/4-inch (0.6 cm.) thick slices

1 medium Shallot, halved and thinly sliced, about 1/8 inch (0.3 cm.) thick

1 Tbsp. Minced ginger

1 small Thai bird chilies, thinly sliced into rings, 1/8 inch (0.3 cm.) thick

1. Combine sugar, salt and water in a saucepan. Bring to a gentle boil, whisking until salt and sugar dissolve. Transfer to mixing bowl, add vinegar and whisk well.

2. Immediately before serving: toss this dressing with the cucumbers, shallots, ginger, and chilies.

How and Why

1. Dissolving sugar and salt in water before adding the vinegar preserves the dressing's natural taste and acidity. If the vinegar was heated, it would lose some fragrance and tartness.

2. To avoid watery relish, dress within 30 minutes of serving, or reduce water to 2 Tbsp. Dressing the cucumbers too early extracts their moisture, depleting their crunch and creating a washed-out relish.

Fried Peanut Snack with Kaffir Lime, Lemongrass, and Chilies

Tom Yum Krob

Only a few years ago, you could only find these spiced nuts in Thailand. The familiar name Tom Yum infers that the flavor is hot and sour with an edge of sweet, similar to the Hot and Sour Shrimp soup (pg. 144). Keeping with that theme mini shrimp with their thin shell still in tact are fried and added or small fish like the ones used in the Malaysian Coconut rice (pg. 332).

Now a version is even sold at non-Asian markets in the U.S., but homemade are much better. Don't be shy about personalizing recipe, especially during the last stage of stir-frying. I sometimes customize them with minced ginger or ground coriander. Save the leftover cooking oil for use in other dishes. Oh yeah: go get a beer and go at it!

Makes 2¹/2 cups

1   cup Vegetable oil for frying
¹/4 cup Dried Long red chilies or other hot red chilies
        (pg. 44)
¹/2 cup Kaffir lime leaves, fold back and pull out veins,
        ripped into 1-inch (2.5 cm.) pieces
2   cups Raw peanuts, skinned
2   stalks Lemongrass, trimmed and minced
2   Tbsp. Tamarind pulp (pg. 109)
¹/2 tsp. Kosher salt, ground extra fine
        (in mortar or spice grinder)
1¹/2 tsp. Granulated sugar

1. In a small sauté pan or wok, heat oil over medium heat to about 350°F (a piece of lemongrass should sizzle immediately when added).

2. Add chilies; cook briefly, 5 to 10 seconds, stirring to ensure even cooking. The chilies should lighten in color, and may puff slightly. Drain on towels. Blanch the lime leaves in the frying oil the same way, cooking until they stop sizzling (15 seconds at most, uneven lighter appearance is normal); drain on towels. Add the peanuts to the oil. These will take considerably longer to cook, up to 5 minutes until they are golden brown. Scoop or strain out peanuts.

3. Drain oil from pan, leaving just one tablespoon. Set the pan over high heat. Stir-fry lemongrass for 10 seconds, it should not brown. Add the fried peanuts and stir-fry 10 seconds. Add sugar, salt and tamarind and mix rapidly coating the peanuts evening. Continue to stir-fry until the excess moisture has evaporated and mixture has coated peanuts. (the audible sizzle will subside)

4. Add whole fried chilies and lime leaves; toss well. Transfer to towel-lined pan, sprinkle evenly with salt and sugar. Cool to room temperature before serving.

How and Why

1. Remove veins from the lime leave before frying. The veins become tough when fried.

2. Test the oil temperature with a lemongrass stalk before frying. This ensures the oil is hot enough, preventing too much oil absorption.

A plethora of dried chilies are on display at the Chatuchuk Food Center in Bangkok.

Explosively Flavored Savory Bites in Wild Pepper Leaves

Miang Khum

Sweet, salty, crunchy, sour, savory and spicy. This one-bite wonder exemplifies what Thai flavors are all about: as you slowly chew on these packets, flavors explode on your palate like fireworks' grand finale. Khum translates as mouthful and miang refers to multi-component snacks. Great for casual parties, these little morsels can be set up for guests to assemble to their own tastes. If the pepper leaves ("bai cha-ploo") are not available, use large spinach leaves, yu choy or other bitter greens leaves that are about 2 inches (5 cm.) in diameter.

Makes 30 pieces

1/4 tsp. Thai shrimp paste (*gkapi*), toasted (pg. 111)

3/4 cup Light brown palm sugar (pg. 58)

2 Tbsp. Fish sauce (*nahm pla*)

1/2 tsp. Finely grated galangal

1/2 cup Tamarind pulp (pg. 109)

30 leaves Betel (wild pepper) leaves, choy sum or large spinach leaves, large stems removed

60 pieces (about 1/4 cup) Halved, Peanuts, roasted in dry pan (pg. 108)

60 (about 1/4 cup) Dried small shrimp, about 1/2 inch (1.2 cm.)

4 Thai green or red bird chilies, sliced into thin rings, about 1/8 inch (0.3 cm.) thick

60 pieces (about 1/4 cup) Lime, cut into pieces the size of a kernel of corn (skin, rind and flesh)

60 pieces (about 1/4 cup) Diced ginger (young ginger if possible), 1/4-inch (0.6 cm.) dice

60 pieces (about 3 Tbsp.) Diced shallots, 1/4-inch (0.6 cm.) dice

1/2 cup Shredded coconut (pg. 115), or store bought, toasted in a dry pan until browned in spots

1. Combine palm sugar, shrimp paste, fish sauce, galangal, and tamarind juice in a small saucepan over medium heat; cook until sugar dissolves and the mixture thickens into a syrup, about 5 minutes (it is important that temperature should be 235°F or 113°C). Transfer to metal or glass bowl. Note: it will thicken as it cools. This is the palm sugar sauce.

2. Assemble the snack: Hold a leaf in the cupped palm of one hand. Spread about 1/2 teaspoon of palm sugar sauce on leaf. Add one or two pieces each of peanut, shrimp, chili, lime, ginger, and shallot. Finally, add a large pinch of toasted coconut.

3. Fold into a tight bundle, pop into your mouth, and chew to start the flavor party in your mouth.

This recipe uses the whole lime—zest, pith and flesh.

Mobile vendors set-up shop on busy streets in Bangkok.

To-go packages have everything you need to assemble your own.

138

How and Why

1. Cooking the palm sugar sauce to the right temperature yields the proper viscosity. Use an accurate thermometer to ensure that the sauce attains the right flavor and texture.

2. When assembling the bites, use only one ot two pieces of each main item for a balanced bite. Each ingredient plays a role in the overall flavor.

3. Toasting the coconut in a dry pan yields a deeper flavor. Instead of an even oven-roast, pan-toasting creates unevenly dark coconut with a more dynamic flavor.

Spicy Fish Cakes
Tod Man Plah Grai

Small curry spiked fish cakes are a common appetizer and street-food in Thailand. The small misshapen bouncy fish cakes are addictively good as they get dipped in Thai sweet chili sauce (pg. 134) and the cucumber relish (pg. 135). I remember sitting by the Udompasat Dam along the river, watching catfish the size of my suitcase being reeled in one after the other. That day, my host "Noi" and his wife, "Saa" at Gayson Restaurant, crafted fish cakes from that local catch, served with glasses of Jonnie Walker Black Label and soda. It seemed like an unlikely beverage pairing, yet they went together nicely.

Yield: 24 pieces

1/2 lb. (227 g.) Fresh catfish, snapper, monkfish, or
       yellowtail, cut into 1-inch (2.5 cm.) pieces
3   Tbsp. Red curry paste (pg. 159)
       [4 Tbsp. if made in blender) or store bought
1   lg. Egg
1   Tbsp. Fish sauce (*nahm pla*)
1   Tbsp. Granulated sugar
1   large Ice cube
6   medium Kaffir lime leaves, vein removed, sliced into
       very thin strips, 1/16 inch (.1 cm.) thick
1/2 cup Thinly sliced long beans,
       about 1/8 inch (0.3 cm.) thick
1/2 cup Holy basil or other Asian basil leaves
       Oil for frying
1   recipe Thai sweet chili sauce (*nahm jim gai*)
       (pg. 134)
1   recipe Cucumber relish (*achaat*) (pg. 135)

1. Prepare equipment for fish paste: Place food processor work bowl and blade in freezer. Also chill (not freeze) fish very well, about 20 minutes.

2. Make fish paste: Add the ice cube to food processor and grind until it become fine crushed ice, almost a powder. Add curry paste, egg, fish sauce, sugar, and chilled fish to processor. Run on high speed, scraping occasionally, until mixture becomes a thick paste. Keep going until the food processor begins to work really hard (you will hear it slow down, mixture pulls to center and gathers on blades.

3. Test the seasoning: Sauté a tablespoon of mixture, taste and adjust seasoning with fish sauce, sugar, and/or curry paste. Transfer mixture to mixing bowl. Gather with hands and throw down into bowl to "slap" mixture; repeat 10 times until it is slightly sticky.

4. Fold in lime leaves and sliced long beans until thoroughly incorporated. Finally, fold in basil leaves until evenly distributed. However, basil leaves should poke out from the cakes in an irregular way. The exposed parts will get crispy while the internal leaves stay succulent.

5. Fry the cakes in batches of 6 pieces: Heat oil in a small pot to 350°F (177°C). Lightly moisten hands to prevent sticking, then hand-form small cakes, 1 to 2 tablespoon each, and drop directly into hot oil. Keeping your hands damp will make sure the paste does not stick at all. Fry until fish paste browns and protruding basil leaves are crispy. About 2 to 3 minutes, cut one in half to check that they are cooked in the center, before serving. Repeat with remaining paste.

6. Serve with Thai sweet chili sauce and cucumber relish in small bowls.

Herbs that jut out from paste are desirable as they get crisp.

How and Why

1. Patiently pulse processor until fish and aromatic spices create a semi-smooth paste. It will begin as a chunky mess, and then progress into a smooth paste with wet appearance.

2. Slapping meat results in a resilient texture. Traditionally this is made in mortar and pestle where it is pounded until sticky to attain a bouncy texture, either way they form an emulsion with the meat, water and other ingredients.

Galangal and Coconut Chicken Soup
Tom Kah Gai

Rich yet light, this Thai classic uses decorative stalks of lemongrass, lime leaves and galangal to infuse the soup. So warn uninitiated guests that these pungent aromatics are not very palatable. You may choose to remove them prior to serving. Straw mushrooms are only available canned in the U.S. While these are fine, feel free to substitute fresh oyster mushrooms.

Makes 4 to 6 servings as part of a multi-dish meal

2	cans (about 14 fl. oz. or 414 ml. each) Coconut milk (divided use)
2	cups Light chicken stock or broth
3	stalks Lemongrass, trimmed, sliced on diagonal into 3-inch (7.5 cm.) lengths, lightly bruised with blunt object
5	large Kaffir lime leaves, bruised lightly
8	slices Galangal (*kah*), about 1/8 inch (0.3 cm.) thick
6	Thai bird chilies, split lengthwise
1/2	lb. (227 g.) Chicken thigh meat, cut into bite-size slices, about 1/4 inch (0.6 cm.) thick
1/2	can (15 oz. or 425 g. can) Straw mushrooms, drained (liquid discarded), halved
1/4	cup Fish sauce (*nahm pla*)
1/4	tsp. Kosher salt
1/4	cup Lime juice
1/4	cup Cilantro leaves

1. In large saucepan, combine only one can of coconut milk, chicken stock, lemongrass, lime leaves, galangal, and chilies. Bring to boil; lower heat and simmer 15 minutes.
2. Add chicken; simmer until chicken is cooked (about 2 minutes). Add straw mushrooms, tomatoes, second can of coconut milk, fish sauce, and salt.
3. Bring back up to hot (but not boiling), add lime juice, and adjust seasoning with additional fish sauce and lime juice.
4. Place cilantro leaves into bowls then ladle in soup. Serve immediately.

Kah is the Thai word for galangal, see page 34 for more information on this powerful rhizome.

How and Why

1. Only use half of the coconut milk at first to ensure a fresh coconut flavor. Simmering dulls the coconut flavor, even though it infuses coconut flavor into the other ingredients; reserving half to be added at the end gives the soup a fresh coconut flavor.

2. Lime juice added at the last moment keeps the flavors bright. Just like coconut milk (and even more so), lime juice's lively flavor dulls when cooked. Adding it at the end preserves its delicate aromas and bright, tart taste.

Thai Hot and Sour Soup
Tom Yum Goong

Aromas of lemongrass, kaffir lime leaves and galangal waft through the dining arena where this lightly sweet, spicy, brothy treasure is served. On my last journey to the small city of Lumnaria in the Lopburi province of Thailand, the family of one of my former students, Fah Vorarittinapap, showed me how rural Thais add a natural layer of sourness with chopped young tamarind leaves. Alas, we don't grow tamarind in the West, so we use fresh lime juice.

If you can't find head-on shrimp, use stock (seafood or chicken) instead of water for this broth. Whenever you cook shrimp, collect the shells in your freezer. They can be used to enrich stock for soups like this. Just simmer them with the stock for thirty minutes, and then strain. The nuance of flavor they add can make all the difference.

Makes 4 to 6 servings as part of a multi-dish meal

2	lb. (.9 kg.)Medium shrimp, head-on
1	Tbsp. Vegetable oil
2	Tbsp. Thai Chili Jam (*nahm prik pow*) (pg. 132) or store-bought Chili Paste in Soybean Oil (pg. 56)
1	tsp. Minced cilantro roots or 1 Tbsp. minced stems
4 to 6	Thai bird chilies stems removed split in half lengthwise
8	cups (2 L.) Water or broth (seafood or chicken)
6	stalks Lemongrass, trimmed, sliced on diagonal into 3-inch (7.5 cm.) lengths and lightly bruised with blunt object
3	slices Galangal, sliced 1/8 inch (0.3 cm.) thick
10	Kaffir lime leaves, bruised
2	Plum/Roma tomatoes, cut into 1-inch (2.5 cm.) chunks
1/2	can (15 oz. or 425 g. can) Straw mushrooms, drained (liquid discarded), halved
1/4	cup Fish sauce (*nahm pla)*
1/2	cup Lime juice
1/4	cup Cilantro leaves

1. Peel shrimp, reserving and quickly rinsing the heads and shells, leaving tail attached; de-vein the shrimp and refrigerate.

2. Heat oil in 4 qt. (4 L.) saucepan or wok over high heat; add shrimp heads and shells. Cook, stirring constantly, 1 minute. Add chili paste, chilies, cilantro stems and water; bring to a boil, and then lower to simmer for 10 minutes. Strain into a new pot.

3. Add lemongrass, galangal and lime leaves; simmer 5 minutes. Add shrimp, tomatoes, mushrooms, and fish sauce. Bring back to a simmer; cook 30 seconds, until shrimp are just cooked. Remove from heat.

4. Taste and adjust seasoning with fish sauce and lime juice. Place cilantro leaves into bowls, and then ladle soup over them; serve immediately.

This humble hut doubles as an outdoor cooking facility and dining area.

1. Using shrimp heads creates richest flavor and color. The head contains much of the orange pigments in shrimp, known as carotenoids. Also some shrimp heads contain an orange dot, which is actually a droplet of delicious shrimp fat, which adds greatly to the essence of the broth.

2. By adding lime juice at the last moment, you keep the flavors bright. Once lime juice has been boiled much of its delicate aroma and bright flavor dissipate.

In Thailand the shrimp shells are often left on, resulting in a more resilient texture. Here you see a hot pot where the center chimney is filled with a gelled fuel to keep the soup fiery hot.

THAILAND

Cool Lemongrass Cellophane Noodles
Yam Woon Sen

Transparent noodles glisten in this quick herbaceous salad. Buy small bundles, about 2 oz. each. The larger bundles are unwieldy, scattering small bits of noodles all over the kitchen as you cut them down to size. My dear friend, Joyce Jue Kay, author of the fabulous book, Savoring Southeast Asia, taught me to add Thai Roasted Red Chili Paste (*nahm prik pow*) (pg. 132), which gives the dish a beautiful red hue and deeper flavor (use about 1 tablespoon). The easy to cook cellophane noodles are made from the mung bean starch and are steeped in boiling hot water for eight minutes then cooled for the salad. No further cooking is needed.

Makes 6 to 8 servings as part of a multi-dish meal

3	pkg. (about 2 oz. / 57 g. each) Bean thread noodles (*woon sen*) (pg. 68)
1/2	cup Sliced red onion, about 1/8 inch (0.3 cm.) thick, 2-inch (5 cm.) lengths
1/4	cup Lime juice
1/4	cup Fish sauce, (*nahm pla*)
1	Tbsp. Granulated sugar
1	clove Garlic, minced
2	stalks Lemongrass, trimmed and sliced very thin, about 1/16 inch (.1 cm.)
1	ea. Thai bird chili, minced
1	cup Julienne cucumber, Kirby variety preferred, bite size strips, about 1/8 inch (0.3 cm.) thick (pg. 81)
1/4	cup Mint leaves, roughly chopped
1/4	cup Chinese celery leaves (or Western celery leaves), roughly chopped

1. In a bowl, cover noodles with boiling water; soak 8 minutes. Rinse them with cool water, and drain very well. Transfer to a cutting board, and cut a few times into shorter lengths with a knife or scissors. This makes them easier to mix and eat. Rinse red onion slices under cool running water for 15 seconds to remove their pungent bite.

2. In a large bowl, whisk together lime juice, fish sauce, sugar, garlic, lemongrass and chilies. Add noodles, onions, cucumber, mint and celery leaves. If desired, fold in chili paste (*nahm prik pow*). Toss very well.

3. Chill for at least 30 minutes. Taste and adjust seasonings as needed.

Bean thread noodles made from mung bean starch are quick to prepare,
a brief soak in boiling water hydrates them in a matter of minutes.

1. Slice the lemongrass into paper-thin slices for a tender bite. This fibrous plant is eaten in this recipe, not just infused, so slice it very thinly across the grain.

2. Rinse red onions to tone down their pungent bite. Excess sulfuric compounds make them harsh, so if they are unusually powerful, soak them in ice water for 15 minutes.

THAILAND

Green Papaya Salad with Long Bean, Limes, Roasted Peanuts and Sticky Rice
Som Tum

When I land in Thailand this is the first dish I seek out. On the streets of Thailand, a tall clay mortar with a large wooden pestle signals the rhythmic pounding that characterizes this dish. Vendors make salads to order. Don't be surprised if they offer you a taste to see if you like how they seasoned it, speak up, this is your chance to tweak the flavors to suite your palate. This Northeast Thai favorite is served sticky rice, to cool its fiery bite. Though it's traditional to add fermented crabs, this is one time I throw tradition to the wind. The rank flavor and aroma of that condiment is too much for even my seasoned palate. One version I did especially like had slivers of thin-skinned limes pounded right in with the papaya. Their essential oils perfumed the simultaneously chewy and crunchy salad.

Makes 4 to 6 servings as part of a multi-dish meal

4   cloves Garlic
2 to 4 Thai bird chilies stems removed
1   Tbsp. Dried shrimp (pg. 93)
2   Tbsp. Tamarind pulp (pg. 109)
1/4   cup Lime juice
4   Tbsp. Fish sauce (*nahm pla*)
3   Tbsp. Light brown palm sugar (pg. 58)
1   cup Long beans, cut in 1½ to 2-inch (5 cm.) lengths or other green beans
4   cup Green papaya, hand-cut into rough slivers, about ⅛ inch (0.3 cm.) thick
1/4   cup Peanuts, roasted in dry pan, roughly chopped (pg. 109)
8   Cherry tomatoes, halved
1/4   Head Green cabbage, cut into 4 wedges
2   cups Steamed Sticky Rice (see Web site)

Note: *Method is adjusted from the traditional single-portion version made in the specialized mortar and pestle. With a food processor, you can make a large batch for a group.*

1. Prepare the Dressing: In mini-food processor, combine garlic and chilies together; pulse to roughly chop. Add the dried shrimp, tamarind, lime juice, fish sauce and palm sugar; pulse until shrimp are broken up a bit (still large pieces).

2. Make Salad: Combine this dressing with long beans in a bowl. Using a stiff whisk, meat mallet, or potato masher pound the beans to bruise them well (about 10 strokes). Add the papaya and peanuts; continue to pound, tossing mixture with the dressing after every few stokes. Add the tomato pieces; pound a few times to bruise lightly, and then stir to incorporate.

3. Taste and adjust as needed with more fish sauce, lime juice or palm sugar. Serve with the cabbage and sticky rice.

KNIFE AND PEELER FUSION

Slivers of papaya are usually achieved with a tool that combines a peeler and knife all in one. A three-step procedure begins with peeling, then the sharp edge of the tool is used to repeatedly whack the length of the papaya. Then the wide peeler creates thin, uneven shards of papaya. This can be replicated with an ordinary vegetable peeler and a chef's knife. First, peel the skin. Second, slam the knife into the fruit to create cuts along its length. Finally, shave off slivers with the knife blade.

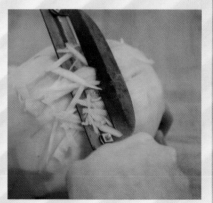

How and Why

1. Pound the vegetables for maximum flavor absorption of dressing. Bruising the vegetables tenderizes them, and allows the dressing to penetrate them quickly.

2. Resist the temptation to use a mandolin or food processor; roughly cut the papaya. This gives this salad its characteristic texture and appearance; large, sharp-edged slivers are what you're looking for.

Hot and Sour Seafood Salad
Yum Talay

Supple pieces of squid intermingle with sharp slivers of shallot in this pungent, spicy, mint- and cilantro-infused warm salad. This dish is nicely spicy, so keep a supply of cold Thai Singha beer on hand. The type of seafood you can use for this dish is very flexible. Although I call for a combination of shrimp and squid here, mussels, scallops, and lobsters are all welcome. For the most brilliant look and flavor, cook the seafood right before serving and toss it quickly with the dressing. Seafood is so tender and inviting when it's slightly warm. You can buy the Thai Roasted Chili Jam (Nahm Prik Pow) if you wish. It's sometimes labeled, "Chili Paste with Soybean Oil."

Makes 4 to 6 servings as part of multi-dish meal

1	lb. (454 g.) Small shrimp, peeled and deveined
1	tsp. Kosher salt
1	stalks Lemongrass, trimmed and sliced very thin, about $1/16$ inch (.1 cm.)
2 to 3	Fresh Thai bird chilies, sliced very thinly, about $1/8$ inch (0.3 cm.) thick
2	tsp. Minced garlic
3	Tbsp. Lime juice
2	tsp. Thai Roasted Chili Jam (*nahm prik pow*) (pg. 132) or store bought
1	Tbsp. Fish sauce (*nahm pla*)
2	Tbsp. Light brown palm sugar (pg. 58)
$1/2$	lb. (227 g.) Squid pieces, bodies cut into $1/4$-inch (0.6 cm.) rings and tentacle clusters cut into bite size pieces
2	medium Shallots, thinly sliced, about $1/8$ inch (0.3 cm.) thick
1	medium Cucumber, Kirby variety preferred, cut in half lengthwise then thinly sliced, about $1/8$ inch (0.3 cm.) thick
8	medium Cherry tomatoes, cut in halves
2	Tbsp. Roughly chopped cilantro, leaves and tender stems
2	Tbsp. Roughly chopped mint leaves

1. Massage salt into the shrimp; marinate 15 minutes. Rinse well.

2. Meanwhile, in large bowl, combine lemongrass, chilies, garlic, lime juice, roasted chili jam, fish sauce, and palm sugar to make dressing; stir until sugar is dissolved.

3. Bring 6 cups water to a boil in large saucepan. Add shrimp, stir well, and remove from heat. Stir occasionally until shrimp are almost cooked through, about 3 minutes (they should be shaped like "C"s, not like "O"s). Add squid, and allow them to cook in the let residual heat, about 10 seconds. Drain. Combine seafood with dressing in bowl. Add shallots, cucumbers, cherry tomatoes, cilantro, and mint; gently toss to coat.

4. Taste; adjust seasoning with lime juice, fish sauce, and palm sugar. Serve immediately.

How and Why

1. To get a resilient texture massage the shrimp with salt. This step is a quick "cure"; that is the salt first pulls moisture out (water migrates to higher concentrations of salt) then the shrimp pick up the salt and the water goes back inside along with the salt so when it cooks the salt retains the water inside the srimp yielding a moisture more resilient shrimp.

2. Low temperature cooking keeps the seafood moist and tender. The slower that protein coagulates, the more moisture they retain and the more tender they feel.

3. Tossing the salad immediately before serving helps ingredients retain their flavor integrity. The lime juice and sugar soften the herbs and toughen the seafood as the salad sits, so toss it at the last moment.

Spicy Pork with Roasted Rice Powder, Crispy Lime Leaves and Sticky Rice

Laarb Moo

Savory, chili-laced ground pork is served with "Table salad," an array of cold, fresh vegetables and herbs, and sticky rice in Northeastern Thailand. My sous chef, Ari, became a devotee of this recipe during our recipe testing for this book. Catfish laarb is also a popular accompaniment to table salad, and is quite "aroy" (delicious). Ground chicken or beef can be substituted for pork; I would season beef more aggressively and the chicken less so. Roasted rice powder adds a deep, toasty flavor and binds the dressing to the salad without adding oil.

Makes 4 to 6 servings as part of a multi-dish meal

FOR THE TABLE SALAD

1/4	head Green cabbage, cut into 2-inch (5 cm.) wide wedges
8	strands Long beans, cut beans into 3-inch (7.5 cm.) lengths
2	medium Cucumber, Kirby variety preferred, quarter lengthwise
6	sprigs Asian basil

FOR THE GARNISH

1/2	cup Vegetable oil for frying
1/4	cup Kaffir lime leaves, fold back and pull out veins
12	Dried red chilies

FOR THE PORK

1/2	lb. (227 g.) Ground pork (coarse), high fat content (approx. 20 %)
1	Tbsp. Ground roasted chili powder, (pg. 244)
1	Tbsp. Ground roasted sticky rice (pg. 244)
3	Tbsp. Lime juice
2	Tbsp. Fish sauce (*nahm pla*)
1	Tbsp. Granulated sugar
1 1/2	tsp. Finely minced galangal
2	small Shallots, thinly sliced, about 1/8 inch (0.3 cm.) thick
2	Tbsp. Chopped scallions
2	Tbsp. Cilantro leaves and stems, roughly chopped
1	Tbsp. Sawleaf herb, thinly sliced across narrow width (optional)
1	Tbsp. Roughly chopped mint leaves
1	recipe Cooked sticky rice (see Web site)

1. In a small sauté pan or wok, heat oil over medium heat to about 350°F (a piece of lemongrass should sizzle immediately when added). Add chilies; cook briefly, 5 to 10 seconds, stirring to ensure even cooking. The chilies should lighten in color, and may puff slightly. Drain on towels. Blanch the lime leaves in the frying oil the same way, cooking until they stop sizzling (15 seconds at most, uneven lighter appearance is normal); drain on towels.

2. Prepare Laarb: In a large skillet or wok over high heat, stir-fry pork until cooked through. Continue to cook until moisture evaporates, flavors concentrate, and the meat begins to caramelize slightly, about 6 to 8 minutes. Remove from heat. Add chili powder, roasted rice powder, lime juice, fish sauce, sugar, galangal, shallots, scallions, cilantro, sawleaf, and mint; mix well.

3. Serve warm pork laarb in a bowl, accompanied by the table salad and a small dish of fried lime leaves and chilies. The laarb is eaten with your hands, along with cabbage leaves, with other salad ingredients and garnishes.

How and Why

1. Coarsely grind the pork (grind with a 1/3-inch or 7.5 cm. die) or hand mince. Most pre-ground pork in supermarkets is too fine for this dish. Its excessive surface area makes it exude more moisture during cooking, producing a wet salad, which tastes more boiled than stir-fried.

2. Prepare the Laarb salad right before serving, for the ideal serving temperature. Although it's called a "salad," it is not served chilled; it's served room temperature, allowing the flavors to come through better.

Deep fried chilies and kaffir lime leaves are nibbled along with each bite of the pork salad, fresh vegetables and aromatic basil.

Grilled Isaan Chicken with Aromatic Lemongrass and Cilantro Roots

Kai Yaang

All over Thailand, roadsides grills roast this simple chicken dish over an open fire. It's served with steamed sticky rice and Thai sweet chili sauce (pg. 134) (nahm jim gai). The classic Thai triad, cilantro roots, garlic, and peppercorns, creates the flavor profile of the dish. For authentic appearance and flavor, use a charcoal- or wood-fired rotisserie to cook chicken. In Thailand, chicken is usually "grilled" by roasting over open flames but not actually placed on grill grates. The same marinade can be used on a whole chicken that can be roasted in the oven.

Makes 4 to 6 servings as part of a multi-dish meal

1   tsp. White peppercorns
1   stalk Lemongrass, trimmed and sliced very thin,
        about $1/16$ inch (.1 cm.)
$1^1/2$ Tbsp. Minced cilantro roots or 3 Tbsp.
        minced stems
5   cloves Garlic, roughly chopped
1   Tbsp. Light brown palm sugar (pg. 58)
$1/4$ cup Fish sauce (*nahm pla*)
1   medium Whole Chicken, 3 to 4 lbs. (1.4 to 1.8 kg.),
        or 2 lbs (1.9 kg) bone-in thighs and/or drumsticks
2   lg. Cucumber, Kirby preferred, cut into 1-inch
        (2.5 cm.) chunks
1   recipe Thai sweet chili sauce (*nahm jim gai*)
        (pg. 134)

1. Make the marinade: if using a mortar, pound the peppercorns and lemongrass into a coarse paste. Add cilantro roots and garlic; pound into a semi-smooth paste. Add palm sugar and fish sauce; stir with pestle until well combined. If not using a mortar, crack peppercorns in a spice grinder, mince lemongrass, cilantro roots, and garlic; combine with palm sugar and fish sauce and whisk until smooth.

2. Marinate chicken: Combine marinade with chicken; massage well. Marinate at least 2 hours or overnight in the refrigerator.

3. Grill or roast the chicken: Cook chicken slowly on rotisserie or grill until cooked through (165°F or 74°C), turning occasionally to prevent burning and create and even brown color. Serve with cucumber chunks and Thai sweet chili sauce on the side.

How and Why

Use a mortar and pestle for an authentic-textured marinade. When the ingredients are pounded, they split into small, short, fibrous bits. These cook differently than knife-chopped ingredients. See page 104 for more on mortar and pestle use.

At right: *Roadside stalls display the grilled chicken along side the charred chicken livers.*

Pork Satay with Peanut Sauce
Moo Satay

Mr. Bun-nom Posueng had been making satay for 30 years before he divulged his secrets to his daughter Nukchatlee Posueng. It was time for her to take over the business, with the help of her mom, Mrs. Labieng Seegao. If you're ever in Thailand's Lopburi province, stop off in the village of Lumnaria and find their stall in front of the "Nolatsaids Phettong" gold shop. You won't regret it.

For basting use an ad-hoc lemongrass basting brush. The woody tops of lemongrass stalks fray into fibrous bristles when pounded with the knife handle, creating a brush]. Use this to apply juices and marinade to the meat as it grills, just like they do in Thailand.

Makes about 30 skewers

1 1/2 lb. (680 g.) Pork leg, shoulder (butt), or loin, cut into flat strips, about 3 inches (7.5 cm.) long, 3/4 inch (2 cm.) wide and 1/4 to 1/8 inch thick (.6 to .8 cm.)

1/2 lb. (227 g.) Fatback or pork belly (skin off), cut into small slices, about 3/4 inch (2 cm.) wide and 1/4 inch (0.6 cm.) thick

7 tsp. Thai Curry Powder (pg. 112) or store bought (divided use)

1/2 tsp. Ground white pepper

1/2 tsp. Ground turmeric

1/4 cup Light brown palm sugar (pg. 58)

1 1/2 tsp. Kosher salt

2 tsp. Minced garlic

30 each Bamboo skewers, about 10 inches (25.4 cm.) long, soaked in warm water 1 hour

1 recipe Cucumber relish (*Achaat*) (pg. 135)

1 recipe Thai peanut sauce (*Nahm Raat Aahaan Thua*) (pg. 157)

1 tsp. Sesame seeds, toasted in dry pan

1/2 cup Canned coconut milk

1. Marinate the pork: Massage all but 1 tsp. of the curry powder, white pepper, palm sugar, salt and minced garlic into the pork meat and fatback (You may wish to use gloves or tongs, since the marinade will stain your skin). Marinate covered in the refrigerator overnight.

2. Prepare accompaniments: Prepare cucumber relish (pg. 135) and Thai peanut sauce (pg. 157). Whisk sesame seeds into peanut sauce.

3. Skewer the satay: Weave the marinated meat onto skewers, aiming for the center of meat so that it lays flat on skewers (see photo pg. 111). Use only one piece each of fat and meat for each skewer (fat first). Leave space at the blunt end of the skewer for handling.

4. Prepare the satay: Whisk together the coconut milk and remaining 1 tsp. of curry powder; set aside with grill brush or lemongrass brush. Before grilling, brush or dip each skewer with coconut milk-curry powder mixture.

5. Grill the satay: Grill over glowing coals or in a grill pan, turning often, until they are cooked through and the marinade has caramelized. Serve with peanut sauce and cucumber relish.

How and Why

Marinate overnight for the maximum flavor penetration and tenderness. The sugar and salt tenderize the meat and hold in the moisture when grilling it.

Mrs. Vorarittinapa helps turn the satay as it grills.

Thai Peanut Sauce
Nahm Jim Thua

Peanut sauce is a recent addition to the Thai cook's repertoire. Satay originated further south in Indonesia. However as Thai food has become popularized in the U.S., satay and peanut sauce have been associated with Thai Food. Thai Style peanut sauce uses aromatics such as lemongrass, galangal, chilies, coriander, cumin, and turmeric. Tamarind balances rich coconut milk and sweet palm sugar (tamarind pulp technique pg. 109). It cooks for only 10 minutes, very quick when compared with over an hour with Malaysian peanut sauce.

Makes 3¹/₂ cups

3	cups Canned coconut milk, stirred (divided use)
¹/₄	cup Red curry paste (pg. 159) (add 1 more tablespoon if paste was made in blender) or store bought
¹/₄	tsp. Ground turmeric
1	cup Water
¹/₂	cup Light brown palm sugar (pg. 58)
1	Tbsp. Fish sauce (*nahm pla*)
¹/₂	tsp. Kosher salt
1	cup Peanuts, roasted in dry pan (pg. 109), finely ground
¹/₄	cup Tamarind pulp (pg. 109)

1. Heat 1 cup of coconut milk in a wok or 4 qt. (4 L.) saucepan over medium heat. Cook, stirring often until it thickens substantially and oil begins to separate out of creamy milk, about 5 minutes. Stir in curry paste and turmeric well, cook, stirring constantly for 2 minutes "roasting" the paste to develop the flavors.

2. Add 2 cups of coconut milk, water, palm sugar, fish sauce, salt, and peanuts; bring to a boil while stirring constantly. Lower heat; simmer for 10 minutes. Stir in remaining coconut milk and tamarind and bring back up to a simmer.

3. Taste and adjust seasoning to taste with fish sauce, palm sugar, and tamarind.

How and Why

Adding the coconut milk in stages keeps its flavor fresh. While the coconut milk serves important cooking roles with the curry paste, the final addition later in the cooking process helps it infuse a sweet, fresh taste into the sauce.

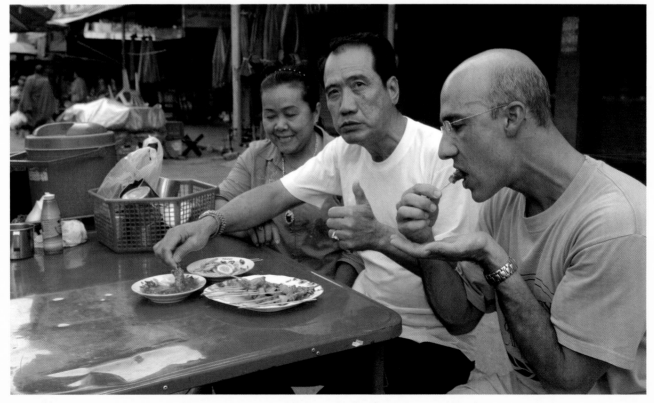

Mr. Vorarittinapa gives a generous bath of peanut sauce to the satay.

Thai Curries

Cooking with Thai Curry Pastes

The first stage of preparing an authentic Thai curry is to fry the paste in coconut milk, a step called "cracking the coconut milk." "Frying" in milk may sound odd, but the extra-rich top layer of the milk (coconut cream) separates and becomes quite oily when cooked over low heat. The paste is added and fried to intensify its fragrance, and to infuse the oil with flavor. As shown in the photo for Red Curry, the oil remains in the curry. Although the oil can be skimmed off, it contains precious flavor.

Additional coconut milk is used for simmering and often also added at the end for a creamy finish. When using canned coconut milk, I stir up the entire can to have a consistant viscosity, pour some into the hot pan and cook, stirring constantly until it separates while releasing the roasted aroma. Look to page 114 for some tips on making or buying and using coconut milk. When you prepare an authentic Thai curry from scratch, the aromas and textures of the experience will transport you as you work. Incorporating these flavorful pastes into your daily cooking can be fun, so jump in and get cooking!

The Color of Curry

Thai curries generally contain coriander, cumin, peppercorns and dried chilies. Red curry paste is one of the spiciest (though some chefs assert that green is spiciest). The deep red hue comes from its dried red chilies. Red curry dishes commonly feature chicken, beef or duck. Green curry paste abounds with fresh green chilies and cilantro root, which add an earthy quality that pairs well with pork and eggplant. Yellow curry paste (colored by ground dried turmeric) is frequently used with seafood. Tart tamarind pulp is often added to yellow Thai curry to balance the sweetness of its coconut milk and palm sugar. The sweet spices of southern Thai Mussamun curry reflect Muslim Malay and Indian influence—cinnamon, cloves and small amounts of cardamom spice up the coconut sauce.

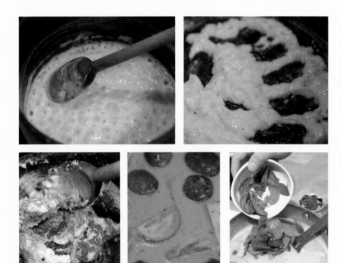

A myriad of curries fill pots at the Chatuchuk Food Center in Bangkok.

Begin by boiling down the coconut milk to evaporate the water. Continue cooking until the oil begins "cracking the coconut milk" to separate and a roasted aroma develops. Add the curry paste and roast in coconut oil to enliven spices and infuse the fat with its color and overall flavor. An additional amount of coconut milk is added along with the protein and vegetables and simmered until cooked through. Fresh herbs, often basil is added at the end.

Jungle Curry   Massamun Curry   Green Curry   Red Curry   Yellow Curry

158

Red Curry Paste
Prik Gaeng Dang

The most common curry paste in Thailand is so versatile that it flavors the best Thai fish cakes (pg. 140) the revered Kao Soi curry noodles (pg. 178) and hundreds of variations of curry meat, fish and vegetables. High quality store bought versions are available, but I like homemade, which finds its way into all sorts of unexpected places like a spoonful in a quick dip, dressing, or marinade. I suggest using a mortar when making this recipe, to create an authentic texture.

Makes: 1½ cups, slightly more if blended

1 cup (1 oz. / 28 g.) Dried red hot chilies, remove stems and seeds
1 tsp. Thai shrimp paste (*gkapi*), toasted (pg. 111)
2 tsp. Coriander seeds
1 tsp. Cumin seeds
1 tsp. White peppercorns
4 Shallots, roughly chopped
8 to 12 Thai bird, red chilies or other hot red chilies (the more you add the hotter the curry)
10 cloves Garlic, roughly chopped
1 tsp. Kosher salt
6 stalks Lemongrass, trimmed and sliced very thin, about 1/16 inch (.1 cm.)
2 Tbsp. Finely grated galangal
2 tsp. Minced cilantro root or 2 Tbsp. of minced stems
1 tsp. Grated kaffir lime zest or 2 tsp. shredded kaffir lime leaves

1. Soak chilies in 2 cups room temperature water for 30 minutes; drain, reserving rehydration water. Squeeze out excess moisture from the chilies; set aside.
2. Individually toast cumin (dark brown), coriander seeds (medium brown) and peppercorns (just until fragrant) in a dry sauté pan, cool. Pulverize spices together in spice grinder, blender or mortar.
3. If using a mortar: Begin by pounding spices until fine. Add chilies and salt; pound until smooth without any large pieces of chilies. Add lemongrass, galangal, cilantro root, and kaffir lime zest; pound until lemongrass disintegrates. Add garlic, shallots, and fresh chilies; pound until deep red smooth curry paste is achieved. Pound in toasted shrimp paste.

If using a blender or mini food processor: Grind spices in grinder or blender. Place following ingredients into the blender vessel this order: shallots, salt, fresh chilies, and garlic; Add 1/4 cup chili rehydration water. Puree until smooth, scraping sides down often to stir in stray bits. BE PATIENT—resist adding more water than needed to make it puree faster. Once semi-smooth, add soaked dried chilies, lemongrass, galangal, spices, kaffir lime zest, and cilantro root. Grind until very smooth. Add shrimp paste, and mix in well.
4. Transfer to container to store in refrigerator for up to two months.

How and Why

1. If using a blender, add ingredients from wettest to driest to avoid adding unnecessary water. The wet ingredients liquefy as they pulverize, creating a liquid base that draws in the drier ingredients.

2. If using a mortar make sure to grind the chilies finely during the first step. After the other ingredients are added the chilies only get slightly finer.

The palette of Red curry paste's ingredients. Prepared paste in center (left to right) pounded in mortar; puréed in blender; and store-bought.

THAILAND

159

Yellow Curry Paste
Prik Kaeng Leuang

This is the simplest Thai curry paste to make. In southern Thailand, the bright yellow rhizome turmeric (pg. 35) shows its color in many dishes. When cooked with the shrimp curry recipe on page 165, it may impart the look of an Indian curry, but the lemongrass fragrance gives away the fact that this is Thai all the way.

Some Thai families like to use this curry paste with thin strips of chicken. Freshwater fish and seafood also work well, and these curries benefit from the addition of bite size slices of pineapple. This makes enough paste for a couple of batches of curry.

Makes 3/4 cup paste pounded, slightly more if blended (easier in blender if doubled)

1/4 cup (1/4 oz. / 7 g.) Dried Long red chilies, remove stems and seeds
1/2 tsp. Kosher salt
2 stalks Lemongrass, trimmed and sliced very thin, about 1/16 inch (.1 cm.)
1 tsp. Ground turmeric (pg. 35)
1 tsp. Cilantro root, minced or 1 Tbsp. minced cilantro stems
1 tsp. Kaffir lime zest or 2 tsp. shredded kaffir lime leaves
4 Shallots, roughly chopped
5 cloves Garlic, roughly chopped
2 tsp. Thai shrimp paste (*gkapi*), toasted (pg. 111)

1. Soak chilies in 1/2 cup room temperature water for 30 minutes; drain, reserving soaking liquid. Squeeze out excess moisture from the chilies; set aside.

MAKE THE CURRY PASTE

2. Using a Mortar: Begin by pounding chilies and salt until semi-smooth. Add lemongrass, turmeric, cilantro root, and lime zest; pound until lemongrass disintegrates. Add garlic and shallots; pound until a smooth even yellow curry paste

is achieved. Pound in toasted shrimp paste. (See page 104 for more on using a mortar and pestle.)

Using a blender (Much easier with double batch): Chop chilies roughly. Place all ingredients into the blender vessel this order: shallots, garlic, salt, lime zest, chilies add 1/2 cup chili soaking liquid. Puree until semi-smooth, scraping sides down often to stir in stray bits. BE PATIENT: resist adding more water than needed to make it puree faster. Once semi-smooth, add lemongrass, turmeric, cilantro root, lime zest, and shrimp paste. Grind until very smooth (at least 3 minutes to achieve a bright color).

3. Transfer to smallest possible container, press small swatch of plastic wrap on surface; store in refrigerator. The fresher it's used the better, but it is fine for cooking up to one month.

How and Why

Toasting the shrimp paste rounds out its flavor. The heat accentuates it flavors while driving off some of its pungent aromas.

The palette of Yellow curry paste's ingredients. Prepared paste in center (left to right) pounded in mortar; puréed in blender; and store-bought.

Green Curry Paste

Prik Kaeng Khiew Wan

This spice paste, verdant from fresh green chilies, is one of the fundamental building blocks of Thai cookery. Kobkaew Naipinij, of the Suan Dusit University in Bangkok, is one of the most respected Thai culinary experts in the world. She took me and my former student Adam Newman (now chef) under her wing during an intensive Thai curries class there, and intimated to us that one traditional way she attains a deeper green color was to add leaves from the chili plant to the paste. Double the amount of coriander to cumin is also another tip she shared with us.

Makes 3/4 cup pounded, slightly more if blended

1	tsp. Cumin seeds
2	tsp. Coriander seeds
1/2	tsp. White peppercorns
6	small Thai bird chilies, green
1/2	tsp. Kosher salt
2	stalks Lemongrass, trimmed and sliced very thin, about 1/16 inch (.1 cm.)
1	Tbsp. Finely grated galangal
1/4	tsp. Ground turmeric
1	tsp. Minced cilantro root or 1 Tbsp. minced cilantro stems
2	tsp. Kaffir lime zest or 4 tsp. shredded kaffir lime leaves
3	small Shallots, roughly chopped
3	cloves Garlic, roughly chopped
3	Long green chilies, chopped (1/2 cup chopped) or other hot green chili (pg. 44)
1	tsp. Thai shrimp paste (*gkapi*), toasted (pg. 111)

1. In a small, dry sauté pan over low heat, individually toast cumin (dark brown), coriander seeds (light brown) and peppercorns (just until fragrant). Transfer to heatproof bowl and cool.

MAKE THE CURRY PASTE

2. If using a blender: pulverize spices together in a spice grinder or blender, making them into a fine powder. Place into the blender this order: shallots, garlic, bird chilies, long chilies, salt, and 1/4 cup water. Puree until smooth, scraping sides down often to stir in stray bits. BE PATIENT: resist the urge to add more water than needed to make it puree faster. Once mixture is semi-smooth, add lemongrass, galangal, spices, kaffir lime zest, cilantro root, and shrimp paste. Grind until very smooth.

If using a mortar: Begin by pounding spices until fine. Add chilies and salt; pound until semi-smooth. Add lemongrass, galangal, turmeric, cilantro root, and kaffir lime zest; pound until lemongrass disintegrates. Add garlic, shallots, and fresh chilies; pound until a smooth even green curry paste is achieved. Pound in toasted shrimp paste. (See page 104 for more on using a mortar and pestle.)

3. Transfer to container, press small swatch of plastic wrap on surface to store in refrigerator. The fresher the better, but it can be used for up to one month.

How and Why

If using a mortar, add the fresh chilies at the last stage. The wettest ingredients should be added after the spices are ground, otherwise it will be difficult to get the paste fine enough.

THAILAND

The palette of Green curry paste's ingredients. Prepared paste in center (begin in front counterclockwise) pounded in mortar; pureed in blender; and store-bought.

Jungle Curry Paste

Prik Kaeng Bpa

Krachai, a rhizome with oddly attractive appendages (pg. 35) lends this curry paste a heady aroma. Notice how simple this curry paste is: no cilantro roots or dried chilies. It is most similar to green curry paste, which could be substituted for it in a pinch.

Makes 3/4 cup pounded, slightly more if blended

6   small Thai bird, green chilies
1/2 tsp. Kosher salt
2   stalks Lemongrass, trimmed and sliced very thin, about 1/16 inch (.1 cm.)
1   Tbsp. Finely grated galangal
1   Tbsp. Chopped krachai (pg. 35)
1   medium Long green chili or other hot green chili (pg. 44)
3   small Shallots, roughly chopped
3   cloves Garlic, roughly chopped
1   tsp. Thai shrimp paste (*gkapi*), toasted (pg. 111)

How and Why

The krachai only needs a quick chop before being pounded. This rhizome is much more tender than its rhizome cousins (like ginger and galangal).

MAKE THE CURRY PASTE

1. Using a Mortar: Begin by pounding bird chilies and salt; pound until semi-smooth. Add lemongrass, galangal, krachai; pound until lemongrass disintegrates. Add garlic, shallots, and green chilies; pound until a smooth even curry paste is achieved. Pound in toasted shrimp paste. (See page 104 for more on using a mortar and pestle.)

Using a blender: Place following ingredients into the blender vessel this order: shallots, garlic, both types of fresh chilies, salt, and; add 1/4 cup water. Puree until semi-smooth, scraping sides down often to stir in stray bits. BE PATIENT, resist adding more water than needed to make it puree faster. Add lemongrass, galangal, krachai, and shrimp paste. Grind until very smooth.

2. Transfer to container; press a small swatch of plastic wrap on surface to store in refrigerator. The fresher it's used, the better, but it keeps for up to one month.

The palette of Jungle curry paste's ingredients. Prepared paste in center (left) pounded in mortar; (right) pureed in blender. Store bought is not readily available, and hence not shown here.

Massamun Curry Paste
Prik Gaeng Massamun

The Indian and Muslim influence in southern Thailand shows in this spicy curry paste. Unlike other Thai curry pastes, which are raw until they go into a dish, Massamun curry paste is cooked when it's made. This brings out a deep red color and also acts as a preservative measure.

Toasting each spice deeply is critical (pg. 111). The dark roast softens the rough edges, enabling the paste to absorb more spices without becoming overwhelming. This creates the profound spice flavor of Massamun curry. If you are making the beef curry (pg. 168), start the beef simmering in the coconut milk before you begin to prepare this curry paste. It'll save you a lot of time.

Makes 3/4 cup if pounded, slightly more if blended

1/2 cup (1/2 oz. / 14 g.) Dried red chilies, remove stems and seeds
2 tsp. Cumin seeds
1 1/2 tsp. Coriander seeds
1/2 tsp. White peppercorns
2 pods Green cardamom pods
1 2-inch (5 cm.) piece Cassia (Cinnamon), broken in a few pieces
3 Cloves
pinch Ground mace
pinch Ground nutmeg
1/2 tsp. Kosher salt
2 stalks Lemongrass, trimmed and sliced very thin, about 1/16 inch (.1 cm.)
1 tsp. Finely grated galangal
2 tsp. Minced cilantro root or 2 Tbsp. minced cilantro stems
1/2 tsp. Grated kaffir lime zest or 1 tsp. shredded kaffir lime leaves
4 cloves Garlic, roughly chopped
3 medium Shallots, roughly chopped
1 tsp. Thai shrimp paste (*gkapi*), toasted (pg. 111)
1/4 cup. Vegetable oil

1. Soak chilies in 1/2 cup room temperature water for 30 minutes; drain, reserving soaking liquid. Squeeze out excess moisture from the chilies; set aside.

2. In a dry small sauté pan over medium-low heat, individually toast cumin (dark brown), coriander seeds (light brown); transfer to a plate to cool. Combine peppercorns, cardamom, cassia, and cloves. Toast these spices until just until fragrant and beginning to smoke; add to plate with cumin and coriander to cool.

MAKE THE CURRY PASTE

3. Using a Mortar: Begin by pounding all the spices until very fine (or speed this up by grinding first in an electric spice mill); remove from mortar and reserve. Add soaked chilies and salt; pound until semi-smooth. Add lemongrass, galangal, cilantro root, kaffir lime zest; pound until lemongrass disintegrates. Add garlic, shallots and spices; pound until dark red smooth curry paste is achieved. Add and pound in toasted shrimp paste. (See page 104 for more on using a mortar and pestle.)

Using a blender: Pulverize spices together in spice grinder or blender; reserve. Place ingredients into the blender in this order: shallots, garlic, salt, and 1/2 cup chili soaking liquid. Puree until smooth, scraping down sides of blender vase often to incorporate stray bits. BE PATIENT: the urge to add more water than needed to make it puree faster (though some may be needed). Once semi-smooth, add soaked red chilies, lemongrass, galangal, spices, cilantro root, kaffir lime zest and shrimp paste. Puree until very smooth.

4. Cook the curry paste: Heat oil in a wok or 2 qt. (2 L.) saucepan over medium heat. Cook curry paste, stirring often, until it darkens substantially and oil begins to separate out of paste, about 5 minutes.

5. Transfer to the smallest possible container. Press a small swatch of plastic wrap on the surface to prevent contact with air. Store in refrigerator. The fresher it's used, the better. But it will be good to cook with for up to two months.

The palette of Massamun curry paste's ingredients. Prepared paste in center (left to right) pounded in mortar; pureed in blender; and store-bought.

Red Curry Chicken with Asian Basil and Fragrant Kaffir Lime Leaves

Gaeng Kai

Leaves of Asian basil punctuate this dish with anise-like flavor. Glistening oils float on its surface, revealing the essential technique of "frying" the curry paste in separated ("cracked") coconut milk (pg. 60), the only way to truly unlock the flavors hidden in the paste. For a one-dish (plus rice) meal, add vegetables to the simmering curry, such as bamboo shoots, peppers, or tender snow peas. The sauce can be made ahead, and served with roast duck or seared beef in place of chicken.

Makes 4 to 6 servings as part of a multi-dish meal

1	can (about 14 oz.) Coconut milk, stirred well (divided use)
1/4	cup Red curry paste (pg. 159) (add 1 more tablespoon if paste was made in blender) or store bought
1	cup Water or light stock
1	Tbsp. Fish sauce (*nahm pla*)
1	Tbsp. Light brown palm sugar (pg. 58)
1	lb. (454 g.) Boneless chicken thighs, cut into bite size strips, about 1/2 inch (1.3 cm.) thick
6	Kaffir lime leaves, bruised lightly
1/4	cup Asian basil leaves

1. Heat 1 cup of coconut milk in a wok or 4 qt. (4 L.) saucepan over medium heat. Boil, stirring often until it thickens and oil begins to separate out of the milk, about 5 minutes. Add curry paste; cook, stirring constantly for 2 minutes to develop the flavors.

2. Add remaining coconut milk, water, fish sauce, palm sugar, chicken, and kaffir lime leaves and cook; stirring often until chicken is cooked through and tender, about 3 to 5 minutes. Stir in basil and cook for 5 seconds.

3. Taste and adjust seasoning with additional palm sugar, fish sauce and/or salt.

How and Why

1. Fry the curry paste in the reduced coconut milk to avoid any raw flavor. Since this sauce does not simmer for long, it's necessary to fry the spice paste to soften the raw flavor.

2. Add the basil toward the end, but still make sure to cook it for a few seconds. The maximum flavor is released into sauce, and the leaves turn a dark green. If the basil is undercooked, it turns black.

Leaves of Asian basil punctuate this dish with anise-like flavor.

Yellow Curry Shrimp, with Tamarind and Green Papaya

Kaeng Leuang Goong

Seafood curry is most common in southern Thailand due to the extensive coastline. Catfish, mackerel or small sardines also work beautifully in place of shrimp in this recipe. Mild green papaya slices simmer in the golden gravy, soaking up all the curry's intense flavors.

Makes 4 to 6 servings as part of a multi-dish meal

1	can (about 14 oz.) Coconut milk, stirred well (divided use)
1/4	cup Yellow curry paste (pg. 160) (add 1 more tablespoon if paste was made in blender) or store-bought
1 1/2	cups Water or light stock
1	Tbsp. Fish sauce (*nahm pla*)
2	tsp. Light brown palm sugar (pg. 58)
1	cup Green papaya, peeled and seeded, bite size slices, about 1/4 inch (0.6 cm.) thick (pg. 91)
1	lb. (454 g.) Shrimp, any size, peeled and deveined
2	Tbsp. Tamarind pulp (pg. 91)
1	medium Long red chilies, sliced into thin rings (pg. 44)

1. Heat 1 cup coconut milk in a wok or saucepan over medium heat. Cook, stirring often until it thickens substantially and oil begins to separate out of creamy milk, about 5 minutes. Stir in curry paste; cook, stirring constantly for 2 minutes to develop the spices' flavors.

2. Add water, sugar, papaya, and fish sauce; simmer until papaya is almost cooked they will become translucent, but still very firm, about 3 minutes. Add shrimp; simmer, stirring often until shrimp opaque. Stir in remaining coconut milk and tamarind; bring back to a simmer.

3. Taste; adjust seasoning with additional palm sugar, fish sauce and/or salt. Transfer to serving dish and garnish with chili rings.

Turmeric begins as a fresh rhizome, becomes shriveled and hard when sun-dried, and then is ground into an easily used powder form.

How and Why

Fry the curry paste in the "cracked" coconut milk to get the most color. Turmeric's color (pg. 35) is oil soluble and hence the most amount of color will be released in the fat based milk.

Green Curry with Pork, Eggplant and Basil
Kaeng Khiew Wan Moo

This green curry is not as hot as its red cousin, but is just as complex in flavor. A handful of basil leaves gives a fresh edge to the creamy sauce that most commonly envelops chicken, I have adapted this for pork to give you a span of proteins used in this chapter. The hard-to-find small (pea-size) Thai eggplants that are customarily used in the dish may be replaced with more commonly available golf ball-size green eggplants or even Chinese or Japanese long slender eggplants can be cut into large chunks and tossed right in.

Makes 4 to 6 servings as part of a multi-dish meal

2   cans (about 14 oz. ea) Coconut milk, stirred well (divided use)

3   Tbsp. Green curry paste (pg. 161) (add 1 more tablespoon if paste was made in blender) or store-bought

1   cup Water or light stock

1   Tbsp. Fish sauce (*nahm pla*)

1   tsp. Light brown palm sugar (pg. 58)

1   lb. (454 g.) Pork butt, shoulder, or leg, cut into bite size slices, about 1/4 inch (0.6 cm.) thick

4   medium Thai green round eggplants, stem removed, cut in 1/4's. If not available, use 1/2 cup pea eggplants or 1 cup Chinese eggplant (bite size pieces).

1/2   cup Asian basil leaves

1   medium Long red chili, cut into strips, 1/8 inch (0.3 cm.) thick

1. Bring 1 cup coconut milk to a low boil in a wok or large saucepan over medium heat. Cook, stirring often until it thickens substantially, and oil begins to separate out, about 5 minutes. Stir in curry paste; cook 2 minutes to develop the flavors, stirring constantly.

2. Add remaining coconut milk, water, fish sauce, palm sugar, pork, and eggplant; simmer, stirring often, until pork and eggplant are cooked through and tender, about 10 minutes. Stir in basil; simmer 10 seconds more.

3. Taste and adjust seasoning with additional palm sugar, fish sauce and/or salt. Transfer to serving dish; serve garnished with chili strips.

How and Why

Add the basil at the end, but still make sure to cook it for a few seconds. That way, its maximum flavor is released into sauce, and the leaves turn a dark green. If they remain raw, the will turn black as the steep in the curry.

Jungle Curry with Duck, Long Beans, Oyster Mushrooms and Holy Basil

Kaeng Bpa Bpet

Northern Thailand doesn't have coconut trees like the south does, so northern curries don't feature coconut milk, much to the surprise of many Westerners. Free of the unctuous milk, these spicy curries exhibit a brilliant clarity of flavor. Thais sop up the delicious sauce with clumps of steamed sticky rice (see web site).

Krachai, an aromatic rhizome with finger-like appendages, gives this dish a unique taste. It is both pounded into the curry paste, and cut into thread-like julienne as a vegetable garnish for the sauce. Do not fret if you cannot find fresh krachai: preserved krachai sold in small glass jars is just as good in this dish. This recipe is for curry of duck, but freshwater fish (such as catfish) is also common in jungle curries of the north. To save some time, you can buy boneless duck breast and chicken stock for the curry, and skip step 1 of this recipe.

Makes 4 to 6 servings as part of a multi-dish meal

1	whole Duck (3 to 4 pounds or 1.4 to 1.8 kg)
8	cups Water (enough to barely cover duck)
1	Tbsp. Vegetable oil or rendered pork fat (lard) (pg. 121)
1	Tbsp. Minced garlic
3	Tbsp. Jungle curry paste (pg. 162) (add 1 more tablespoon if paste was made in blender) or store-bought
2	Tbsp Fish sauce (*nahm pla*)
1	tsp. Light brown palm sugar (pg. 58)
1/2	cup Pea eggplants or 4 medium round green Thai eggplants, stem removed, cut in 1/4s, or 1/2 cup or 1 cup of Chinese eggplant in bite size pieces
8	strands Long beans or green beans, cut into 2-inch (5 cm.) pieces
1/4	cup Bamboo shoots, bite size slices, about 1/8 inch (0.3 cm.) thick
8	medium Kaffir lime leaves, torn into a few pieces each
1/4	lb Oyster mushrooms, torn into bite size pieces
1	Tbsp. Fresh or brined green peppercorns (drain and rinse briefly if brined) (pg. 42)
2	Tbsp. Krachai, cut into thin threads, about 1/8 inch (0.3 cm.) thick (can be bought in jar) (pg. 35)
1/2	cup Holy basil leaves or other Asian basil
1	medium Long red chili or other hot red chili, cut into rings on angle, about 1/8 inch (0.3 cm.) thick

1. Cut the Duck and Make Stock: Remove the breast and thigh meat from the duck. Cut remaining carcass into 2- to 4-inch pieces. Slice boneless meat (should be about 3/4–1 lb. or 340 to 545 g.) into bite size slices, 1/4 inch (0.6 cm.) thick; reserve in refrigerator. In a large pot, cover duck bones with water, bring to a boil, skim foam that rises to the surface, and lower heat. Simmer 1 hour to yield a simple yet flavorful stock. Strain, and set aside.

2. Cook the Curry: Sizzle garlic with oil in a wok or 4 qt. (4 L.) saucepan over medium heat until aromatic, but not brown, 30 seconds. Stir in curry paste; cook, stirring constantly, 3 to 5 minutes, "roasting" the paste to develop the flavors. Add 2 cups duck stock, fish sauce, and palm sugar; bring to a boil. Add eggplant; cook, stirring often, until eggplant is halfway cooked, about 2 minutes.

3. Add duck meat, long beans, lime leaves, and bamboo shoots; cook until beans are almost tender, 5 minutes. Add mushrooms, cook 20 seconds until they soften (all the vegetables should be cooked by this point). Stir in peppercorns, krachai, basil, and chilies and cook for 10 seconds more.

4. Taste and adjust seasoning with additional fish sauce and/or salt. Serve immediately.

How and Why

Cooking the curry paste in the hot oil before adding other ingredients helps awaken the flavors in the paste. Some of the fat-soluble essential oils in the spices are released at this time, and would remain hidden if they were simply simmered with the liquid ingredients.

THAILAND

Massamun Beef Curry
Gaeng Massamun Neua

In this Southern Thai curry, tender cubes of beef, chunks of potatoes, and peanuts luxuriate in a thick fragrant coconut curry of spices. The curry paste is packed with what I refer to as "sweet spices": ground cassia (cinnamon), cloves, nutmeg, mace, and cardamom. Warn your guests to look out for the whole cassia stick. Whole cardamom pods are more difficult to seek out so I do not add whole ones in the curry, however add a bit extra to the curry paste recipe (pg. 163). Biting into it can be overwhelming. Beef is most commonly used but do not hesitate to prepare this dish with lamb shoulder or chicken thigh meat instead.

Makes 4 to 6 servings as part of a multi-dish meal

1¹/₂ lb. (680 g.) Stewing beef, such as shoulder or flank, large bite size pieces, about 1 inch (2.5 cm.) thick

3 cups Canned coconut milk, stirred well (divided use)

2 cups Water or light stock

¹/₄ cup Mussamun curry paste (pg. 163) (add 1 more tablespoon if paste was made in blender) or store bought

2 tsp. Grated ginger

2 inches Cassia bark (cinnamon), toasted briefly in pan

³/₄ lb. (340 g.) Gold (waxy) potatoes, 1-inch (2.5 cm.) chunks

³/₄ cup Peanuts, roasted in dry pan (pg. 109)

3 Tbsp. Tamarind pulp (pg. 109)

3 Tbsp. Fish sauce (*nahm pla*)

¹/₂ tsp. Kosher salt

2 Tbsp. Light brown palm sugar (pg. 58)

1. In a saucepan, bring beef, 1 cup of water and 2 cups of the coconut milk to a boil. Lower to simmer; cook 1 hour or until just tender, adding water as needed to keep beef mostly covered. Drain simmering liquid into one container and beef into another; cover the beef tightly.

2. Heat 1 cup of coconut milk in a wok or 4 qt. (4 L.) saucepan over medium heat. Cook, stirring often, until it thickens substantially and oil begins to separate out, about 5 minutes. Stir in curry paste; cook, stirring constantly for 2 minutes to allow flavors to develop.

3. Add 1 cup water, ginger, cassia, potatoes, peanuts, and all of the simmering liquid from beef. Simmer until potatoes are almost cooked, about 15 minutes, adding water if necessary to keep potatoes submerged. Add back the beef; simmer for 10 minutes more. Add tamarind, fish sauce, salt, and sugar; bring to a boil. Adjust consistency with water until it is the consistency of cold cream, rich and creamy.

4. Taste and adjust seasoning with additional palm sugar, fish sauce, and salt. Serve immediately, or chill overnight (remove cassia otherwise it will be overpowering the next day) and reheat to serve.

1. Simmering beef first in part of the coconut milk ensures that spice flavor will be vibrant in the finished dish. Once the beef is tender from slow cooking, the spices can be added and their flavor won't fade from excessive simmering. Alternately, thin slices of tender raw beef, such as loin, can be used in place of the stewed beef. In that case, they are added after potatoes are cooked.

2. Tamarind, sugar, fish sauce, and sugar balance the flavor. The sour tamarind balances the sweet sugar, while fish sauce rounds out the savory profile of the dish.

Pan roasted peanuts develop a profound depth of flavor.

Cassia (Cinnamomum aromaticum or Cinnamomum cassia) thicker bark possesses a flavor aroma that punctuates this curry (pg. 43).

THAILAND

Pumpkin and Pork with Scallions
Pak Fak Tong

I spent an evening with Tik, my guide in Kanchanaburi province, and his wife, Gla Porn Ongad, cooking countless dishes. This one was so simple and good that I felt it had to be included in the book. The pumpkin is most commonly known as "Kobocha," which is actually the Japanese name for this very firm, sweet, green-skinned squash with orange flesh. Some cooks peel only the outer green coating, leaving a small sections of the dark skinned under-layer remaining. It looks quite attractive and the flavor is a bit more earthy.

Makes 4 to 6 servings as part of a multi-dish meal

1/4   lb. (113 g.) Pork shoulder, leg or loin, bite size slices, about 1/8 inch (0.3 cm.) thick
2   Tbsp. Oyster sauce
1   Tbsp. Vegetable oil
1   clove Garlic, minced
1   lb. (454 g.) (usable) Kabocha squash (pumpkin), bite size pieces, about 1/4 inch (0.6 cm.) thick (See Web techniques.)
1 1/2 cups Water
1   Tbsp. Granulated sugar
1/2 tsp. Kosher salt
1   cup Scallions, green only, 1 to 1/2-inch (5 cm.) (1.3 cm.) pieces

1. Combine pork with oyster sauce and marinate 30 minutes (or overnight).

2. Heat oil over a high flame in hot wok; stir-fry pork and garlic until pork loses raw appearance (about 3 minutes). Add pumpkin, water, sugar, and salt; mix well. Lower heat and cook gently, stirring often, until pumpkin is tender (about 10 minutes).

3. Gently mix, taste, and adjust seasoning as needed. Try to achieve a slightly salty sauce with a touch of natural sweetness from pumpkin. Add scallions; cook momentarily (about 10 seconds) until they turn bright green. Serve with steamed rice.

1. Stir gently and cook just before serving to keep the pumpkin intact. This type of squash stays firm for a while, and then rapidly softens and breaks apart, so cook it less than you think is necessary; it will continue to cook even after the heat is off.

2. Add scallions at the last moment for a bright green color. If you cook the scallions too long, they lose their desirable pungent flavor and bright color.

THAILAND

171

Stir Fried Rice Noodles, Bean Sprouts, Peanuts and Tamarind

Pad Thai

Stalls dot the streets in major cities like Bangkok but the best version of this famous Thai street food I found was in Lumnaria, in Lopburi province. At that stall, the jovial used a large wok to make giant batches for her clamoring fans. She started by combining small strips of chicken, shrimp or other meat with the garlic in the first stage of the stir-fry. This was counter-intuitive, since many cooks fry aromatics alone first. Add chicken, shrimp or other meat to this dish if you wish.

Something that may surprise you is that Pad Thai stalls don't always use a wok many often employ large flat griddles for cooking Pad Thai, pre-seasoned noodles of various shapes are at the ready, kept warm. Place your order, a portion slides into the hot spot, and the stir-frying commences. Like much of Thai cooking: no wok, no problem. Use a sauté pan for equally authentic results. Additional crunchy raw bean sprouts, dry-roasted peanuts, lime wedges, and ground chilies are served on the side, allowing the guest to customize the texture and flavor to taste.

Makes 4 to 6 servings as part of a multi-dish meal

1/2 lb. (227 g.) Dried flat rice noodles,
        1/4 inch (0.6 cm.) wide
1/4 cup Fish sauce (*nahm pla*)
2   tbsp. Tamarind pulp (pg. 109)
1/4 cup Light brown palm sugar (pg. 58)
2 to 3 tsp. Ground roasted dried red chilies (pg. 244)
2   Tbsp. Vegetable oil
1   Tbsp. Minced, shallots
2   Tbsp. Chopped, garlic
2   large Eggs, lightly beaten
1   Tbsp. Chopped dried shrimp (pg. 93)

3/4 cup Pressed bean curd, small strips, about 1/4 × 1/4 ×
        2-inch (.6 × .6 × 5 cm) strips (pg. 75)
1   Tbsp. Shredded salted radish, rinsed briefly (pg. 81)
1   cup Chinese chives, cut into 1-inch (2.5 cm.) lengths
        (or substitute scallion greens)
2   cup Bean sprouts, trimmed (divided use)
1/2 cup Peanuts, roasted in dry pan (pg. 109),
        chopped (divided use)
2   medium Limes, cut into wedges (pg. 108)
2   Tbsp. Ground roasted dried chilies (pg. 244)

1. Set up ingredients: Soak the noodles in room temperature water for 30 minutes; drain well. Whisk together the fish sauce, tamarind, palm sugar, and chilies. Get everything else lined up in the order they are needed (since this stir-frying goes very quickly).

2. Stir-fry the noodles: Heat wok over high heat, add oil (it should barely smoke); add the shallots; cook until they begin to brown. Add garlic; cook until golden brown. Add drizzle more oil if necessary, and then add the eggs, spreading them with a spatula to create flat omelet. Break the egg up into bite size pieces, then stir in the dried shrimp, bean curd, radish, and soaked noodles. Coat these ingredients with the oil, and stir-fry 30 seconds.

3. Add the seasonings: Add fish sauce mixture and stir-fry until the noodles are tender, adding small additions of water as necessary to soften the noodles (this can take from $1/2$–1 cup water). Fold in the Chinese chives, $1^1/2$ cups of bean sprouts, and $1/4$ cup of peanuts. Cook for 10 seconds to soften bean sprouts. Taste and adjust seasoning with fish sauce, tamarind and/or sugar.

4. Transfer to platter: Garnish with remaining bean sprouts, peanuts, ground dried chilies and lime wedges

Don't hesitate to prepare an entire plate of crunchy condiments for your guest to customize the crunch factor.

Stir Fried Rice Noodles, Bean Sprouts, Peanuts and Tamarind
Pad Thai

PAD THAI OMELET
Discover you are at the Chatuchuk Food Center, right across the street from the massive weekend market in Bangkok and you will see one deft cook envelop her Pad Thai in a thin sheath of omelet. She makes the noodles, pushes them aside, and then pours eggs to create thin sheet. Once cooked, the noodles go on top, and it gets wrapped up and served.